Class in English History 1680–1850

R. S. Neale

BASIL BLACKWELL
OXFORD

© R. S. Neale 1981

First published in 1981 by
Basil Blackwell Publisher
5 Alfred Street
Oxford OX1 4HB
England

British Library Cataloguing in Publication Data
Neale, Ronald Stanley
 Class in English history, 1680–1850.
 1. Social classes – England – History
 I. Title
 301.44′0942   HN400.S6   c.2
  ISBN 0-631-12851-4

Typeset in 11/13 Baskerville by
Pintail Studios Limited, Ringwood, Hampshire
Reproduced from copy supplied
printed and bound in Great Britain
by Billing and Sons Limited
Guildford, London, Oxford, Worcester

Contents

		Page
Preface		v
Introduction – Social History		1
Chapter 1	Marx, *Class* and *Class* Consciousness	17
Chapter 2	Mannheim, the Sociology of Knowledge and Social History	47
Chapter 3	'The World we have Lost' and how Class and Class Consciousness can help to Find it	68
Chapter 4	Historians, Class and the Early Nineteenth Century	100
Chapter 5	The Five-class Model	120
Chapter 6	Class and Class Consciousness, or The Right to the Whole Product of Labour	154
Chapter 7	Women and Class Consciousness	193
Chapter 8	Theory and the Poverty of Theory	216
Index		246

Preface

This book owes much to many people who probably do not recognize that I am indebted to them; students, colleagues, fellow historians, and participants in seminars and conferences who, over years, have either read or heard bits of it and through their reactions prompted a new thought, an expanded explanation, a specific sentence, a turn of phrase, and, sometimes, a rewriting of major parts of the argument. And this is because this book is very much a teacher's book; its purpose is both to instruct and to educate by encouraging critical discussion. Therefore it has to be clear at the same time as it raises with students serious issues of method as well as of interpretation. If the book succeeds in provoking educationally fruitful discussion as well as have the 'bits' when given in the form of lectures and seminars I will be well pleased. That I have not raised other issues or commented upon the work of more than a handful of historians is because I have written only about those things in which I have been engrossed as I have learned what it is to be a social historian and because the book as it stands is already one third as long again as the one I intended to write.

Some of the people to whom I am indebted may even recall those occasions which prompted me to further explanation or revision even though they may not do so as vividly as I do; seminars on the social history of eighteenth-century England, on Marx and social theory, on theory and method in social science, as well as other lectures and seminars in the departments of History and Economic History at the University of New England since 1972. The ANZAAS conference at Perth and the David Nichol Smith Seminar in Canberra in 1973, seminars in the History of Ideas Unit at the Australian National University early in 1974, lectures and seminars at the universities of Melbourne and Tasmania in 1974 and 1975, the Australian Historical Association's conference on social history at Sydney University in 1976. And then there were many other occasions, too, when, as member of an audience or participant in a seminar, I was provoked to enthusiasm or outrage and to further writing and rewriting.

But there are personal debts, too. To J. P. Belshaw, until recently Professor of Economics at the University of New England, who first gave me the opportunity to teach and research in economic and social history in my own way. To the council of the University of New England for two periods of study leave spent in England in 1971 and 1978 and for a further period in August and September 1977 spent at the Huntington Library in California. To Eugene Kamenka and the Australian National University who gave me four months in the History of Ideas Unit at the Australian National University and time to work on the collection of eighteenth-century books and pamphlets held in the Australian National Library. To an exceptional class of honours students who, throughout 1975, suffered my obsessions about the eighteenth century without too much damage to their understanding. To Linley Lloyd who, untutored in the ways of history and historians, lent herself as a guinea pig to read three of the chapters to test the sense they would make to a novice. To Jenny Weissel who patiently and intelligently typed many versions of the 'final' typescript. And to Margaret Neale who went without vacation in three Australian summers while this book was written and rewritten although I suspect that consequently she is a better potter than she was and better off than otherwise she would have been. To her I owe most of all.

Introduction – Social History

The study of intellectual history can and must be pursued in a manner which will see in the sequence and co-existence of phenomena more than mere accidental relationships, and will seek to discover in the totality of the historical compex the role, significance, and meaning of each component element. It is with this type of sociological approach to history that we identify ourselves.

Karl Mannheim, *Ideology and Utopia*,
1936 (London, 1972), p. 83

There are many histories; political, constitutional, military, international, diplomatic, scientific, intellectual, economic. The mitosis seems endless. The most recent manifestation of this trend, a mutant form of economic history called economist's history,[1] takes me back to a world I thought I had left behind many years ago – a technical college world in which was taught English, GCE English, builder's English, and, most refined of all, plumber's English. Today, in my present world, there is economist's history. Tomorrow there will be statistician's history and the day after, mathematician's history; histories defined not by sets of problems or areas or subjects of study but by techniques and specialisms borrowed from the natural sciences and by paradigms from positive economics. Furthermore, those who use these techniques and paradigms frequently assume and assert their superiority over all other ways of knowing. Indeed, it may be that we are being led to anticipate the second coming of Auguste Comte. Fortunately we still live in a pluralist world and there is also social history.

[1] A term used in the mid-1970s by some economists in Australia to refer to those forms of econometric history of which they approved.

Social history, however, is in a parlous state. What has been said about it before is still true. Some historians are happy to believe that social history is economic history with the hard bits left out. Some might even go as far as to say that it is what remains after the economist's economic historians have had their specialist bite, in which case they might agree with A. L. Rowse that social history is about how society consumes what it has produced.[2] Other definitions accepted by historians include G. M. Trevelyan's notion that social history is 'the history of a people with the politics left out',[3] and Harold Perkin's 1962 formulation. This claims that social history is close to total history – a sort of pre-economist's economic history with the politics put back – and that the task of a social historian is to 'present the natural history of the body politic, exposing and explaining its ecology, anatomy, physiology, pathology, and, since the body politic may be presumed to exist on more than the physical plane its psychology too; its awareness of itself, its conscious aims, criteria and ideals'.[4] Certainly if one is to judge according to the evaluation of what constitutes social history by the review editor of *New Society*,[5] the social history of modern Britain can be treated as well as defined in a myriad ways. This editor's list covers the following topics; the local history of Lancashire and Cheshire miners, the prevention and punishment of nineteenth-century crime, Marie Lloyd and the music hall, a history of the pin-up, a work on the Owenite communities in Britain, several books on the courts and the law, a history of the London taxicab, an economic history of working hours in British industry, and a study of knitting and crochet patterns in the 1920s, 1930s and 1940s.

What seems clear is that while there is a great variety of published social history there are few social historians, and even those few suffer from a continuing uncertainty about the nature and status of the subject. E. J. Hobsbawm, in his role as editor of the World University series on the history of British society, seems to reflect this uncertainty. 'Since', he says, 'social history is itself in

[2] A. L. Rowse, *The Use of History* (London, 1946), p. 69.
[3] G. M. Trevelyan, *English Social History* (London, 1944), p. vii.
[4] Harold Perkin, Social history, in H. P. R. Finberg (ed.), *Approaches to History* (London, 1962), p. 61.
[5] *New Society*, **22** (531), 7th December 1972.

the process of development, the individual authors have been left free to define their field, though they have all agreed to treat certain common questions and subjects.'[6] Most obvious among these common subjects Hobsbawm sees class and social structure, but also demography, urban studies and mentalities. Harold Perkin, using a rather different organic analogy in 1969 than in 1962, appears more certain about the nature of social history. It is 'a vertebrate discipline built around a central organizing theme, the history of society *qua* society, of social structure in all its manifold and constantly changing ramifications'.[7] What Perkin means by this is demonstrated in the rest of his book. In essence it is as Hobsbawm sees it – the emergence of a class society, but in the form in which Perkin sees it, as a *viable* class society. Thereby hangs a tale of definition and concept formation which indicates another aspect of recent social history, its conceptual cloudiness. This book looks at some aspects of this problem.

Another book, *Essays in Social History*, edited by M. W. Flinn and T. C. Smout, raises other issues in connection with social history which also arise in the course of the argument in this book. Since *Essays in Social History* seems to put the imprimatur of the Economic History Society on these editors' version of social history it is worth attention. The following is a list of contents:

1   From social history to the history of society – E. J. Hobsbawm
2   Sociological history: the Industrial Revolution and the British working-class family – Neil J. Smelser
3   Time, work-discipline, and industrial capitalism – E. P. Thompson
4   Changing attitudes to labour in the mid-eighteenth century – A. W. Coats
5   The first Manchester Sunday Schools – A. P. Wadsworth
6   The myth of the old Poor Law and the making of the new – M. Blaug
7   The language of 'class' in early nineteenth-century England – Asa Briggs
8   Nineteenth-century towns: a class dimension – J. Foster

[6] J. F. C. Harrison, *The Early Victorians* (London, 1971), p. xiii.
[7] Harold Perkin, *The Origins of Modern English Society 1780–1880* (London, 1969), p. ix.

 9   Nineteenth-century social reform: a Tory interpretation of history – Jenifer Hart
10   Reasons for the decline of mortality in England and Wales during the nineteenth century – T. McKeown and R. G. Record
11   Trade unions and free labour: the background to the Taff Vale decision – J. Saville
12   The position of women: some vital statistics – Richard M. Titmuss

As can be seen, the collection is as much a miscellany as that in *New Society*. Both collections indicate the catholicity of social history. Moreover, it is not immediately apparent from the collection itself what the editors consider to be the defining characteristics of social history. Indeed, their principal criterion for including an article is what they refer to as 'academic merit'. Significance for or contribution towards describing or clarifying social history, or defining the subject by reference to the writings of social historians, seems not to have been considered. Of course, if the editors believe that the nature of social history is best grasped via the writings of the social historians included in the collection then social history *is* what is included.

To compensate for their own reluctance to tackle the problem of defining or describing social history the editors substitute E. J. Hobsbawm's 1971 *Daedalus* article. It seems that we are asked to accept Hobsbawm's as the latest if not the last word on the subject. If this is so it is necessary to take more than a passing glance at what he has to say.

According to Hobsbawm social history is the history of society. Moreover, it *is* history. That is, it is concerned with revealing what actually happened in and to whole societies defined as specific units of people living together. It involves, therefore, at the outset, a judgement about the central nexus of the subject. In regard to making such a judgement Hobsbawm believes there is a consensus that the correct procedure is to work upwards and outwards from the process of social production in its specific setting. He considers that such a procedure will also lead to a concern for the relationship between theory and practice, and focus attention upon the need for social historians to be theoretically explicit. He writes:

Once again the tendency is to treat economic movements (in the broadest sense) as the backbone of such an analysis. The tensions to which the society is exposed in the process of historic change and transformation then allow the historian to expose

1. the general mechanisms by which the structures of society simultaneously tend to lose and re-establish their equilibria, and
2. the phenomena which are traditionally the subject of interest to the social historians, for example, collective consciousness, social movements, the social dimension of intellectual and cultural changes, and so on.[8]

Hobsbawm then argues that the issues and questions thrown up by such an approach to social history regarded as the history of society, appear to have clustered around six topics or complexes of questions. They are:

1 Demography and kinship
2 Urban studies
3 Classes and social groups
4 History of 'mentalities', i.e., collective consciousness or culture
5 Transformation of societies – modernization
6 Social movements and phenomena of social protest.

According to Hobsbawm, demography and urban studies are well established intellectual fields of study which need no explanation or definition whereas there are serious problems with the other clusters of questions. For example, there are problems of conceptualization in regard to classes and social groups, and problems of approach and coverage in relation to 'mentalities' and movements of protest and social transformation. Hobsbawm has something to say about each of these topics, but in this introduction I do not intend to discuss them because there is one major question to ask him, namely: What is the central thrust of the argument which makes his paper more than a catalogue of issues or topics?

My own answer is that the central thrust comes very close to arguing that social history is virtually the Marxian Materialist Conception of History. I point this out not to attack or to criticize it. Hobsbawm's position, like that more recently argued by Stedman Jones,[9] is one with which I generally concur provided,

[8]M. W. Flinn and T. C. Smout (eds.), *Essays in Social History* (Oxford, 1974), p. 11.
[9]Gareth Stedman Jones, From historical sociology to theoretical history, *British Journal of Sociology* **27** (3), 1976, pp. 294–305.

that is, we are clear about the nature and content of that Materialist Conception of History, including the concepts class and class consciousness. Thus, right at the outset there is the issue of relationships between theory and history.

No – I draw attention to Hobsbawm's Marxist interpretation of the nature of social history in order to observe that two influential non-Marxist historians, Flinn and Smout, appear to accept its validity and are prepared to waive their rights to write their own introduction in its favour. This points either to the great superiority and sophistication of the approach or to the immaturity of social history and the inadequacy of other sociological models for use by historians. As Weber once observed, it also has its dangers for the unconscious Marxist. He wrote: 'The Materialistic conception of history is not to be compared to a cab that one can enter or alight from at will, for once they enter it, even the revolutionaries themselves are not free to leave it.'[10] Social historians should take note. They might note, too, that the ghost of Marx haunts all the contributors to the *Journal of Social History*'s recent symposium on social history.[11]

The inadequacy of other sociological models is illustrated by Neil Smelser's essay, which the editors include because according to them it exemplifies 'the contribution sociology is at last making to social history'. Smelser admits at the outset that his concern is not that of the historians. Like the econometric historians he is primarily interested in model-testing rather than in using models or theories as heuristic devices to open up the past. He says:

The thing that set my research off most from what many historians do is that I approached the Industrial Revolution as a case illustration of an explicit, formal conceptual model drawn from the general tradition of sociological thought. Stated in very general terms, this model says that under conditions of social disequilibrium, the social structure will change in such a way that roles previously encompassing many different types of activities become more specialized; the social structure, that is, becomes more complex and differentiated. It was this abstract, analytic model – the details of which I shall spell out presently – that generated problems for me, not the period of the Industrial Revolution as such. I might well have

[10]Quoted in Karl Mannheim, *Ideology and Utopia* (London, 1972), p. 67.
[11]*Journal of Social History*, **10**, 1976–77, pp. 129–45. Especially Elizabeth Fox-Genovese and Eugene D. Genovese, The political crisis of social history: A Marxian perspective.

chosen industrial change in another country and another period, or even an instance of rapid social change in which industrialization did not occupy a significant place.[12]

Smelser's model is one in which under conditions of social dis-equilibrium structural differentiation will occur. In his 'history' of the Industrial Revolution the disequilibrating factor is technology in the cotton textile industry. This generated tension in the family consequent upon structural differentiation. He says, 'It was only when the industrial and urban changes began to affect the traditional relations *within* the family that really furious protest and disturbance began[13] . . . the quiescence of the factory operatives (in the 1820s) is traceable to the persistence of certain fundamental family relations in the factory setting'.[14] None of this is derived from testing the model in the Popperian or falsifying sense, it is simply what the model asserts. What Smelser means by testing involves excluding all other influences which might have induced or inhibited movements of social protest such as: differences in life experience and expectations between first and fourth generation factory operatives, changes in values and ideas over time such as one might subsume in the concept 'class consciousness', alterations in the rhythm of economic life as other sectors of the economy became integrated into a larger economic system, and influences from outside, from other groups and their values. All that Smelser considers is family relationships and technology. It is my view that the social historian who wishes to write the history of society has to do better than that.

And that is what Foster attempts to do in his paper on the cotton weavers and spinners of Oldham which is also included in the volume. In his view serious – that is, revolutionary – protest is the product not of the break up of the family consequent upon new technology but arises from the creation of community in which family is a part. But there are also problems about the testing of Foster's version of the Marxian model which will be discussed in chapters 1 and 5. What I emphasize at this point is that if social historians follow Smelser they are likely to end as econometric

[12]Flinn and Smouth, *Essays in Social History*, p. 24.
[13]*Ibid.*, p. 29.
[14]*Ibid.*, p. 31.

historians – as model-testers. If they follow Hobsbawm they will end as Marxists – of a sort.

The other articles in the collection are a mixed bag with as many contributions from authors working mainly in the fields of economics, political science, medical history and social work as in social history *per se*. In fact, apart from the contributions by Hobsbawm. Thompson and Briggs, and excluding Smelser for the reasons given, the best of the essays and certainly the essays which, in my view, make the best contribution to defining social history as a serious intellectual discipline are written by those who have come to social history from or with another discipline. Even so there is a serious gap in the collection. Let me illustrate. Several of the articles deal with relationships between institutions and attitudes, thus, Thompson, 'Time, work-discipline and industrial capitalism', Coats, 'Changing attitudes to labour in the mid-eighteenth century', Briggs, 'Language of "class" in early nineteenth-century England'. Another author, Hart, 'Nineteenth-century social re-form: a Tory interpretation of history', even refers to the connec-tions between an Idea as elaborated in books, i.e. Benthamism, and institutional development. However, none has anything to say about the social conditions of thought or the interplay of thought with attitudes and social conditions (perhaps I should partially except Coats from that stricture). I believe that thought is too good and fruitful a field to be left to the philosophers or to historians of economic thought, science, art and ideas. But more than that, I believe that what social historians have to do, indeed must do, is to understand and make explicit those perceptions that men and women had of themselves, at the highest as well as the lowest levels of society and of culture, that led them to perceive themselves and their societies in certain systematic ways and thus to want to perpetuate or change themselves and their societies, and then to relate those perceptions to the life experiences of men and women. As we shall see, self-perception and its consequences for social action are important, perhaps the most important components in the formation of class and class consciousness.

Our world, capitalist first, industrial next and technical–bureaucratic now, has developed over the last millennium, it is the central process of the recent past. Accompanying these stupendous

changes there have been changes in ideas and perceptions about
the nature and potential of men and women. And I reiterate that a
social history which does not as a matter of central concern seek to
unravel the connections between these two areas of human activity
can never warrant the name History of Society. For example, a
social history of nineteenth- and twentieth-century Europe which
does not incorporate a serious study of socialism as an
idea/ideology arising and developing in specific social and
economic contexts would deprive its students of exposure to
patterns of perception and of thought increasingly significant in the
past and of overwhelming significance today. And a social history
of eighteenth-century England which failed to incorporate a study
of the concepts of civil society and property, and the thought of
Locke, Shaftesbury, Mandeville, Adam Smith, Tom Paine, Mary
Wollstonecraft, as well as many others in that turbulent and disturbed period in which bourgeois society was established, but which
concerned itself exclusively with demography, working conditions,
real wages and urban growth, could never be a History of Society.
In short, it is my view that a social history that does not concern
itself with ideas and ideology and, therefore, with the development
of human consciousness can never be a History of Society, and it
will be a very poor social history.

I also believe that without a methodology which makes *a priori*
claims about the unity of the past and at the same time points to the
nexus or the nature of the connections between experience and
perception, social historians will be content to follow their own
private pursuits with the result that there will never be a discipline
of social history and this area of inquiry will remain as fragmented
as the review editor of *New Society* and the editors of *Essays in Social
History* have found it. I also fear that as a result it will succumb to
the positivist threat and go the merely model-building, model-
testing and quantitative way of economic history and Neil Smelser.
Therefore, I would like to see social historians recognize that the
core of their discipline is akin to the sociology of knowledge.

Karl Mannheim writing in 1936 called social history that

new type of intellectual history which is able to interpret changes in ideas
in relation to social historical changes – which can and must be pursued in
a manner which will see in the sequence and co-existence of phenomena
more than mere accidental relationships, and will seek to discover in the

totality of the historical complex the role, significance, and meaning of each component element.[15]

This is that kind of holistic history that Karl Popper was convinced he had killed and buried under a variety of names; holism, essentialism, anti-naturalism or historicism, when really all he had managed to do was make an historicist straw man out of some very malleable droppings from various stables in order the better to knock him down. Nevertheless, in spite of Karl Popper, it is still permissible to ask the general question: How does the social and economic framework of society clearly defined, including the knowledge built into it in a variety of ways, influence the further development of that society and its accumulation of knowledge, and how does that knowledge impinge upon the social and economic framework of society? And then to devise procedures with which to try to find answers to the question in general and to subsets of questions relating to physical areas and periods more manageable by those of us with smaller minds.

For example, in a paper entitled, 'Bath: Ideology and Utopia, 1700–1760'[16] I report on my attempt to look at a small 'whole' piece of the world which is not the logical and absolute whole of Popper's *Poverty of Historicism* but which can be thought of as *Gestalt*. I do so with the aid of explicit concepts drawn from the work of art historians and within a generalized Marxian framework. I believe that in looking at Bath in this way I can experience its 'wholeness' in a way which Professor Popper cannot know. All that Professor Popper can properly comment upon is the inadequacy of my concepts and conceptual framework and my lack of ability to describe that small 'whole' piece of the world which I claim I can experience. In fact I would like to see social historians strive to overcome that problem, too, and write a social history that displays the past more as Picasso has painted Kahnweiler and less as Hogarth painted Captain Thomas Coram. I am all too conscious that my own social history is still predominantly Hogarthian. But that is no

---

[15] Karl Mannheim, *Ideology and Utopia*, pp. 45 and 83.
[16] R. S. Neale, Bath: Ideology and Utopia, 1700–1760, in R. F. Brissenden and J. C. Eade (eds.), *Studies in the Eighteenth Century*, vol. III (Canberra, 1976), pp. 37–54. This paper, considerably expanded, is now the central chapter in R. S. Neale, *Bath, 1680–1850: A Social History* (London, 1981).

reason for not trying harder. To this end I will say something about devising procedures for this Kahnweilian kind of social history.

First, I draw attention to Hans Neisser, *On the Sociology of Knowledge*, 1965. Neisser believes, and I agree with him, that the sociology of knowledge, which in our case I take to be social history, will define itself by its procedures. He claims that unless historiography takes cognizance of these procedures, it 'will remain a field which a critical sociology of knowledge will have to watch most carefully'.[17] By this he means that social historians will themselves come under rigorous scrutiny by sociological practitioners of the sociology of knowledge who might demonstrate, for example, that what hitherto has passed as 'history' has merely been that which was part of the vocational training for male elites and/or that its 'truth' value is low. Or, they might come under attack from social theorists such as Althusser and Hindess and Hirst whose criticism of history will itself be criticized in chapter 8. At this point, in connection with the claim that history is probably ideology, I would like once more to quote from Mannheim, this time about the significance of the existence or absence of concepts, especially the absence of the concept 'social'. Mannheim wrote:

The absence of certain concepts indicates very often not only the absence of certain points of view, but also the absence of a definite drive to come to grips with certain life-problems. Thus, for example, the relatively late appearance in history of the concept 'social' is evidence for the fact that the questions implied in the concept 'social' had never been posited before, and likewise that a definite mode of experience signified by the concept 'social' did not exist before.[18]

The fact that 'social history' is a late-comer and still seemingly a catch-all for bits of history that do not conveniently fit into other historical 'disciplines' suggests to me that many historians still lack 'a definite drive to come to grips with certain life-problems', as well as with problems of method and procedure.

I suggest, therefore, that the basis of social history must have three procedural strands, each of which can draw upon much recent work in social history, work which itself may not have been

[17] Hans Neisser, *On the Sociology of Knowledge* (New York, 1965), p. 20.
[18] Karl Mannheim, *Ideology and Utopia*, p. 246.

produced with the object of furthering the development of social history as a sociology of knowledge.

Social history should be explicitly theoretical. My own preference is for something 'Marxisant' if not Marxist and I recommend the work of Mannheim, Dahrendorf, Lukacs, Wallterstein, Barrington Moore. But, on the whole I prefer Marx. What I mean by this should become clear in the course of this book. There may be other theorists – Weber and Durkheim spring to mind. Nevertheless, I believe that any social historian of the recent past, say of the last 300 years, must make himself familiar with Marx, his antecedents and followers, for two reasons. First, Marxism is an essential part of the past to be studied. Secondly, it is itself an aid to studying the past, including its own past. In this regard it may well be that a neo-Marxian approach can explain a greater range of phenomena than other approaches and it is to be preferred for this reason.

Social history must focus attention on social structure and changes in social structure. At one extreme it must focus on the smallest, most common and intimate group to which men and women have belonged, the family, and must do so in a more penetrating way than Smelser or the demographic historians. Since one way of understanding our own families, their structures and their norms, is to compare them with other families, I strongly recommend all historians of the white Anglo-Saxon world to Chie Nakane's *Japanese Society*. At the other extreme it should draw attention to the paramount importance of the expanding urban environments in which the individual and the family have made their homes, and the social groups to which individuals belong. Both of these sets of structures must be observed within specific and changing economic modes of production.

Social history should be a study of the ideas, knowledge and culture of the communities studied. This should not be thought of only as a study of a conventional 'best'. It should consider both ideology and utopia in Mannheim's sense, hence it should concern itself with political ideas and action; it should distinguish culture from society, and the ideal from the expected and the actual; it should include law and convention, architecture as well as art, popular art and craft as well as high art; creativity in all its varieties, and human perception as expressed in the highest branches of thought as well as in everyday attitudes and acts.

Then there is the difficult bit. This is to delineate objectively the interconnections between these procedural strands, particularly those between social structure or social classes and thought. Hence the importance of theory. As Mannheim pointed out:

Nothing is simpler than to maintain that a certain type of thinking is feudal, bourgeois or proletarian, liberal, socialistic, or conservative, as long as there is no analytical method for demonstrating it and no criteria have been adduced which will provide a control over the demonstration.[19]

Yet historical writing overflows with such claims as well as with claims even more difficult to substantiate; claims about the national character of thought and spirits of the age, and claims in which the centuries are endowed with characters and are held to cause change. How often do we read and hear these claims being made? And how often in our own work do we make them? It is my task in the rest of this book to examine the credibility of some of these claims, in particular the claims that some historians make when they use the concepts class and class consciousness in their attempts to explain the history of England in the eighteenth and nineteenth centuries. However, since almost all of the historians who use these concepts in historical explanation refer to some notion about Marx's views on class either with the purpose of confirming, refuting or adapting them, I continue in chapter 1 with my views on Marx's notions of *class* and *class* consciousness using this italicized form whenever I refer to those views in order to distinguish them from other views about class and class consciousness[20]

The discussion of Marx on class in chapter 1 also sets the style of most of the rest of the book, especially chapters 1 to 5 and chapter 8. That is to say I approach the question of class in English history out of concern for the epistemological status of the claims historians make when they use some model of class or some class terminology to explain aspects of English history in the period 1680–1850. Therefore, the main area of discourse in the book is historiographical and theoretical. Nevertheless, there is also much of the 'stuff of history' in the book, particularly in chapters 6 to 7, although

---

[19] *Ibid.*, p. 45.
[20] In a similar way Marxian is used for Marx's own thought and Marxist for that of later interpreters.

every chapter will have its share. For example, in chapter 1, although I concentrate mainly on Marx's theory I do so recognizing that Marx was an historical figure and part of the history of the period I write about. Similarly, in chapter 5, which may be thought of as mainly theoretical, I also write about one aspect of J. S. Mill who was also an historical figure and part of the history of the period. In fact throughout the book I move freely from questions of a theoretical or methodological nature, through historiography to history and back again. Thus, in chapters 6 to 7, which may be thought of as primarily about the 'stuff of history'. I also touch upon questions of method. I write in this fashion because my purpose is not to add another description or narrative of class formation, although description will emerge, but to conduct a dialogue with students of history and social theory about the ways they have used and still use the concepts class and class consciousness as central organizing themes in their accounts of England in the eighteenth and early nineteenth centuries. I write like this, too, because of the original didactic purpose of the book which has grown out of a series of lectures in a course in English Social History given at the University of New England, New South Wales, and out of papers delivered at various seminars and conferences. In the course on social history I expected my students to have some acquaintance with the main writings, particularly the historical ones, alluded to. To this end they were issued with an appropriate book of readings and a list of additional readings. Consequently I have no doubt that readers who are familiar with the books I refer to will enter more readily into the dialogue than those who are not, and will wish to interrupt and challenge me on questions of 'fact' and interpretation thus making the dialogue a three-way, or even a four-way one, if we also invite the subjects of our discourse to take part.

And that is what should happen because, like the lectures from which it sprang, this is a book that should be argued over. It should be argued over because the discussion of class and class consciousness around which it is constructed should also be part of the development of consciousness of those who enter into dialogue with it – and I have no preconceptions as to where that consciousness will lead – only hopes. This is because the issues I seek to highlight are too frequently mystified by both academic historians and

Marxist dogmatists. At the same time the problems to be resolved multiply to become almost infinite in number and complexity.

One of these problems, at least as it is likely to concern many historians, is that they will find the book insufficiently empirical and that it does not contain enough of the 'stuff of history' to satisfy them. My only answer to such historians is the book itself, and I scarcely expect that answer to convince them. What I hope to do is to appeal to those of my colleagues and their students who share my disquiet about the belief that solutions to problems in history are always and only to be found in more of the 'facts', in more description of isolated or discrete events, and that empirical history is its own court of appeal. Yet even a superficial reading will show the book to be full of 'facts', all of which are historical and have something pertinent to say about comprehending the epoch under review. Certainly it may be the case that some of them are unusual 'facts' in this present context. Yet it should also be clear that I am more concerned with the basis of the choice and interpretation of 'facts' than with the 'facts' themselves.

Another likely problem is that the book will appear to philosophers of history and social theorists to be insufficiently theoretical and inadequately philosophical and that I appeal to too many of the 'facts' of history to illustrate or test my use of theory and, perhaps, that I do not discuss the 'facts' or instances of history generally favoured by its philosophers. My answer to them is that while I believe that history must be theoretical and philosophical it is my view that it has to be so in ways meaningful and helpful to historians and their students as they address themselves to those problems which puzzle working historians. The traditional separa-tion, at least in the English-speaking world, between the theory and philosophy of history and the practice of historians should not be allowed to continue. Like Stedman Jones I want history to become theoretical history, or what I call a sociology of knowledge.

There may even be the objection that I range too widely in my selection of the 'stuff of history' in a book on class in English history; that when I include discussion on Japan and Germany and Hungary I pass from the little known to the wholly unknown and confuse my readers at the expense of describing for them the reality that was England. And the same might be said for the way I range from Picasso to Hogarth, from Marx to Mannheim, from Popper to

Althusser, from Sarah Scott to Elizabeth Sharples – all in a work about class in England in the eighteenth and early nineteenth centuries! Of course I have to admit it: I am as eclectic in my choice of themes and persons as in my selection of theorists and philosophers of history, but not, I believe arbitrary or merely subjective. For while I frequently break the linearity and specificity of English history, I do so deliberately. My choices arise from my didactic purpose – the dialogue I seek – and the Materialist Conception of History, out of which came the question of class and class consciousness in the first instance. In this respect the argument in the book is my justification – for all that other historians would have written and would have me write a different book. And the book will stand or fall as it encourages or inhibits dialogue and the development of consciousness because the book, ostensibly about class in English history, is in reality about the development of consciousness now – and that is what history is about. Therefore, as a work of history it is also a work of theory and historiography and as a work of theory and historiography it is one historian's contribution towards a comprehension of the current situation – towards consciousness. As such it is also a justification and defence of history in the face of those threats to its very existence as a worthwhile intellectual discipline which will be encountered in chapter 8. And in that chapter I mix historiography, history, theory and philosophy to argue a case in and about a real world which cannot afford the luxury of a discipline 'history' which turns up its nose at all other manifestations of human consciousness. History must become theoretical or it will become irrelevant.

1
Marx, *Class* and *Class* Consciousness

But it cannot emancipate itself without abolishing the conditions of its own life. It cannot abolish the conditions of its life without abolishing all the inhuman conditions of life of society today which are summed up in its own situation. Not in vain does it go through the stern but steeling school of labour. It is not a question of what this or that proletarian or even the whole proletariat, at the moment regards as its aim. It is a question of what the proletariat is, and what, in accordance with this being, it will historically be compelled to do. Its aim and historical action is visibly and irrevocably foreshadowed in its own life situation as well as in the whole organisation of bourgeois society today.

Karl Marx and Friedrick Engels, *The Holy Family*
(1844–45) in Marx/Engels, *Collected Works*
(London, 1975), vol. IV, p. 37

Class lay at the very heart of Marx's analysis. He believed that societies are transformed through the antagonism inherent in class and that men, through their actions as members of *classes* in capitalist societies, drive themselves towards consciousness of themselves as their own creators, as Promethean. He believed, that is, that it is through *class* as the mediating category of social relations that men as they are become what they are able to be, and that it is through *class* that men work towards the redemption not merely of some men but of the whole of mankind. One could say that it is through *class* that the pessimism of Pope's observation, 'Man Never Is, but always To be blest', is to be proved false. Since this is so and since Marx without *class* is like Hamlet without the Prince it is necessary to examine closely the meaning which Marx gave to *class* and to its related concept *class* consciousness.

Unfortunately Marx never set out his ideas about *class* in any short clear statement. Consequently we have to sense and clarify his meaning from a variety of texts and contexts. One way of doing this would be to adopt the procedure used by Ralf Dahrendorf in *Class and Class Conflict in an Industrial Society* where he links together a long series of quotations from Marx's writings to produce a reconstructed narrative of Marx's views on class. Such an approach is all right as far as it goes. Unfortunately it does not go far enough for it does not include all the important passages on class in Marx and is silent about the most important aspect of *class*, *class* consciousness. My approach in this chapter, therefore, will emphasize the importance of *class* consciousness in Marx's views of class, the central role of *class* and *class* consciousness in the Marxian model of social change and, since this book is intended for history students, it will describe that level of *class* consciousness considered by Marx as appropriate for industrial workers in the third quarter of the nineteenth century.

In the uncompleted third volume of *Capital* where Marx began to consider *class* in some detail, he asked the question 'What constitutes a class? . . . What constitutes wage-labourers, capitalists and landlords as the three great social classes?' His first attempt at an answer was similar to that given by Perkin, Foster, Kitson Clark and a host of others whose views will be considered in chapter 4. It proceeded thus, 'At first it is the identity of revenues and sources of income. They [classes] are three large social groups, whose components, i.e. the people of whom they consist, earn their living by wage, profit and rent, i.e., by utilizing their labour power, capital, and land ownership.'[1] However, according to this first attempt at a definition, the rest of which is quoted at the head of chapter 4, Marx considered that it would be possible to identify a great proliferation of classes. Thus, doctors and civil servants would form two different social groups or classes distinguished by the fact that their members' incomes have the same source; professional piecework service in the one case and salary derived from taxation in the other. Marx clearly found such an approach not very fruitful. He also rejected all attempts at definitions based on 'differences in the size of purses' because they only lead to a proliferation of social

---

[1] Karl Marx, *Das Kapital*, new edn (Berlin, 1953), vol. III, p. 421.

groupings or classes and are exercises in mere social stratification rather than in the identification of *classes*. But the crux of his rejection of these approaches to *class* was that he considered that all attempts to identify *class* according to income, even source of income, or of consumption, use for their criteria secondary characteristics which belong to the realm of distribution and consumption. This is unsatisfactory because distribution and consumption are themselves the product of production. And the key to production is property. He wrote: '*The property question*, relative to the different stages of development of industry, has *always* been the life question of any given class' [my italics].[2] There is little doubt that in Marx's view the basis of *class* is a property relationship. However, on another occasion he added, 'There is no property anterior to the relations of domination and subjection which are far more concrete relations.'[3] In this passage he indicated that, in his view, property itself derived from a power relationship prior to property itself.

But what did Marx mean by property and the relations of domination and subjection which preceded it? In this context he meant bourgeois or private property, a definition of which is impossible in any common-sense or positivistic terms since it is essentially a relationship. All that might be attempted is a description of it. For Marx this meant 'nothing else than to give an exposition of all the social conditions of bourgeois production. To try to give a definition of property as of an independent relation, a category apart, an abstract and eternal idea, can be nothing but an illusion of metaphysics or jurisprudence.'[4] The social conditions of bourgeois production and property which would have to be described and to which Marx referred lay in the past. They comprised all the factors involved in primitive accumulation. These included the military constitution of the Germanic tribes which overran Europe with the collapse of Rome, bringing with them the notion and practice of private possession and, in the early eighteenth century, the power and role of the English state. While I

[2]Quoted in Ralf Dahrendorf, *Class and Class Conflict in an Industrial Society* (London, 1959), p. 11.
[3]Karl Marx, *Critique of Political Economy* (Berlin, 1947), p. 258.
[4]Karl Marx, *Poverty of Philosophy* in Marx/Engels, *Collected Works* (London, 1975), vol. VI, p. 197.

have more to say about these events later on in this chapter this brief mention of Marx's statements about these facts makes it clear that in his view property relations, which are the determinants of *class*, are themselves the product of historically determined legal relations and of state power. Marx expressed it concisely. Writing of the English state in the early eighteenth century he said, 'Force is the midwife of every old society pregnant with a new one. It is itself an economic power.'[5] The force used to create and protect property rights was the force of state power both at home and abroad.

However, relationships between collective or state power and property were not merely unidirectional. The process was something like this; when, in the more distant past, societies through their collective or state power created or consolidated private property rights, power that was once the power of a society which it vested in its state 'became the private power of a private person'. In this way the collective or state may be thought of as having shed its power and private persons to have gained it. However, property rights, no matter how they were created, immediately they were created distinguished those with from those without property. In this way society was effectively divided into two groups: the propertied and the propertyless. The former exercised power over the latter. Subsequently the propertied sought to consolidate and protect their property rights and did so by calling upon the state for help. Thus, the state reacquired power, until, as Marx put it 'the state becomes but a committee for managing the common affairs of the whole bourgeoisie'.[6]

In Marx the paradigm of property relationships is the wage contract which embodies this new form of power. Instead of the patriarchal form of power characteristic of pre-industrial society, which was localized and personal, the wage contract represents power over strangers, that is, it is remote, legalistic and impersonal.[7] Morever, the laws which embody that power are passed and eventually enforced by the state. In short, since property flows from power and itself bestows power, *class* is a

[5] Karl Marx, *Capital*, Everyman ed (London, 1962), vol. 2, p. 833.
[6] Karl Marx, *Manifesto of the Communist Party*, in Marx/Engels, *Selected Works* (Moscow, 1950), vol. I, p. 35.
[7] Karl Renner, *The Institutions of Private Law*, ed. B. Kahn Freund (London, 1949), p. 115.

matter of power as well as property and in Marx the two are inextricably interconnected, *class* relationships *are* power relationships.[8]

According to Marx, England in the third quarter of the nineteenth century had moved further than any other nation towards producing a society polarized into two classes based on property and power. He wrote:

Even there, however, this class structure is not displayed in a pure form. Intermediate and transitional stages obliterate the border lines there as everywhere (although incomparably less in the country than in the towns). However, this does not matter for our investigation. It has been demonstrated that it is the permanent tendency and law of development of the capitalist mode of production to separate the means of production increasingly from labour, and to concentrate the separate means of production more and more in large groups – in other words, to transform labour into wage labour, and the means of production into capital. At the same time, land ownership tends to be separated from capital and labour, and to be converted into the type of land ownership corresponding to the capitalist mode of production.[9]

Clearly Marx's perception of the social structure of England in the mid-nineteenth century was complex. One characteristic of it was a movement in the industrial sector towards a two-class society based on private property. There was also a slower transformation of landed property, but, as Marx observed, the contrast, in the nineteenth century, between the propertied and the propertyless was greater in the agricultural than in the manufacturing sector. No doubt this was because capitalism in England, and therefore in the world, had its origins in an agricultural sector distinguished by feudal relations. Marx also noted the existence of intermediate and transitional classes. However, none of these classes was important for his argument which was primarily concerned with analysing the conditions for and predicting social change in the immediate as well as the distant future rather than with description of an unchanging present. What mattered for Marx was the inevitable polarization into the two major antagonistic *classes* of the capitalist mode of production, the bourgeoisie and proletariat, which would

---

[8]This view has also recently been re-stated by Gareth Stedman Jones, From historical sociology to theoretical history, *British Journal of Sociology* **27** (3), 1976.
[9]Karl Marx, *Das Kapital*, vol. III, p. 421.

be brought about by the incessant and unremitting accumulation and concentration of property as capital.

So far in this chapter I have tended to use the term class rather indiscriminately and, for the most part, the classes I have referred to are merely social groups defined objectively by position within the process of production, that is, capitalists and industrial workers, or bourgeois and proletarians. But they are not *classes* in Marx's fullest sense of the term. They are merely *classes* in themselves but not yet *classes* for themselves. This is so because those potentially antagonistic relations between capitalists and industrial workers which Marx saw implied in this merely objective classification into the two *classes* will only be realized in practice; when, in consciousness, their members acknowledge their position and act accordingly as a *class*-conscious group, that is, as a *class*. Which is to say that industrial workers or real proletarians must act like a proletariat.

But what does it mean to act as a *class* and what did real nineteenth-century proletarians or industrial workers have to do to act as a proletariat and warrant the designation 'a proletariat'? Did they have to form trade unions? Agitate for the six points of the Charter? Demand of Parliament that it introduce legislation restricting the hours of work to ten per day? Condemn British participation in the Crimean War? Form a Labour party? Organize a revolution? That is, just what did they have to do and where do we have to look for evidence of *class* consciousness in the Marxian sense?

Many historians have addressed themselves to this question and it is this question which Marx asked and answered in the extract from *The Holy Family* quoted at the beginning of this chapter. Approaching the issue from a slightly different angle he wrote: 'It is not a question of what this or that proletarian or even the whole proletariat, at the moment *regards* as its aim. It is a question of *what the proletariat is*, and what, in accordance with this *being*, it will historically be compelled to do.'[10] In posing the question in this manner Marx showed that *class* consciousness within his scheme is not the same as the psychological consciousness of individual

---

[10]Karl Marx and Friedrick Engels, *The Holy Family*, in Marx/Engels, *Collected Works* (London, 1975), vol. IV, p. 37.

proletarians nor the mass psychological consciousness of all proletarians. It is not mere individual or group or class perception. It is, on the contrary, as Lukacs said 'the sense become conscious of the historical role of the class'.[11] This sense of the historical role of the *class* requires a perception of the antagonism which inheres in class relations as defined. Along with this must go an understanding of the fact that every *class* struggle is a political struggle and that every political struggle must be aimed at the overthrow, almost certainly the revolutionary overthrow, of the existing political state. In Marx's own words *class*-conscious proletarians must comprehend that 'An oppressed class is the vital condition of existence for every society founded on the antagonism of classes. The emancipation of the oppressed class thus implies necessarily the creation of a new society.'[12] Furthermore, a member of the proletariat must grasp the idea that the new society will not merely reverse the positions of oppressor and oppressed and will not necessarily make the poor rich. Thus, real proletarians, to be members of the proletariat, must comprehend that a *class*-conscious proletariat will eschew the idea that revolution will achieve what the mass of real proletarians might regard as in the interest of the group or class to which they belong. Marx expressed this idea very early in his life and held to it throughout his political career. Thus, in *A Contribution to the Critique of Hegel's 'Philosophy of Right'* (1844) Marx asked himself where lay the possibility of German emancipation.

Our answer is in the formation of a class with radical chains, a class in civil society that is not of civil society, a class that is the dissolution of all classes, a sphere of society having a universal character because of its universal suffering and claiming no particular right because no particular wrong but unqualified wrong is perpetrated on it; a sphere that can claim no traditional title but only a human title; a sphere that does not stand partially opposed to the consequences, but totally opposed to the premises of the German political system; a sphere, finally, that cannot emancipate itself without emancipating itself from all other spheres of society, thereby emancipating them; a sphere in short, that is the complete loss of

[11]Georg Lukacs, *History and Class Consciousness* (London, 1971), p. 73. Lukacs also wrote, 'In a word, opportunism mistakes the actual, psychological state of consciousness of proletarians for the class consciousness of the proletariat', p. 74.
[12]Karl Marx, *The Poverty of Philosophy,* in Marx/Engels, *Collected Works* (London, 1975), vol. VI, p. 211.

humanity and can only redeem itself through the total redemption of humanity. This dissolution of society existing as a particular class is the proletariat.[13]

The key to this passage is the last sentence: 'This dissolution of society existing as a particular class is the proletariat.' Its implications warrant some discussion.

At this early stage in his political career Marx was very much under the influence of Hegelian terminology and concepts. His notion of 'a class that is the dissolution of all classes' has undertones of Hegel's Universal Class, that class of disinterested and impartial professional men and bureaucrats who, according to Hegel, could alone act justly in the interests of the whole community and contain by the rule of law and proper institutional practice the worst divisive effects of the incessant competition between interest groups which characterized the modern form of society which the eighteenth century, followed by Hegel, dubbed 'civil society'. However, in his *Critique of Hegel's 'Philosophy of Right'* (1842) Marx demonstrated that Hegel's Universal Class was no more impartial than any other group in civil society. He showed, instead, that the justice administered by Hegel's Universal Class was designed and administered in the interests of the ruling landowning class – interests which were based upon and flowed from property rights. Because of the partiality of Hegel's Universal Class Marx sought the redeemers of society in other social groups and attempted to locate a new Universal Class which would not act according to its own narrow class interest but which would be compelled to act according to the interest of the whole society in order to achieve 'the total redemption of mankind'.

I turn now to consider how Marx identified such a *class* and note that the dialectical form in which it is identified and through which it develops is also to be a part of the *class* consciousness of the *class* in question.

In the later 1840s and early 1850s, Marx's political and moral thought passed through the sieve of English political economy and it appeared to lose some of its Hegelian and humanistic associations and it is in the context of his revision of Hegel that the central

[13] Karl Marx, *A Contribution to the Critique of Hegel's 'Philosophy of Right',* ed. J. O'Malley (Cambridge, 1970), pp. 141–2.

proposition about the determination of consciousness and, therefore, of *class* consciousness in the Marxian system has to be understood.

My investigation led to the result that legal relations as well as forms of state are to be grasped neither from themselves nor from the so-called general development of the human mind, but rather have their roots in the material conditions of life, the sum total of which Hegel, following the example of the Englishmen and Frenchmen of the eighteenth century, combines under the name of 'civil society', that however the anatomy of civil society is to be sought in political economy ... it is not the consciousness of men that determines their being, but, on the contrary, their social being that determines their consciousness.[14]

In stating that 'it is not the consciousness of men that determines their being', Marx was clearly crossing swords with Hegel, and his statement must be understood in that context. In stating that on the contrary it is 'their social being that determines their consciousness', he was not merely standing Hegel on his feet but introducing a new concept – 'social being' – and a new meaning of consciousness. In brief, this proposition raises three questions; What is social being? What is consciousness? And, in what sense and how does the one 'determine' the other? In order to understand how Marx answered these questions it is not enough merely to confine oneself to an examination of the logic of the *Preface to the Critique of Political Economy*. It is necessary to go back to the early period of Marx's writing and trace the subsequent development of the Marxian dialectic.

In the *Paris Manuscripts* Marx considered the nature of Man as *gattungswesen*, that is as a generic or species being. According to Marx Man as *gattungswesen* has certain physical and social needs and is an innately productive and creative being whose essence it is not only to make and create things but in the process to make and create himself as a self-conscious, self-directing being, and, therefore, to live authentically as *gattungswesen*. This authentic essence is also social. Thus, when Man first produced to satisfy his merely physical needs he also and at the same time, as part of the first historical act satisfying those needs, produced new needs which were both physical and social. In satisfying these new needs

[14]Marx/Engels, *Selected Works* (London, 1950), vol. I, pp. 328–9.

and as part of the first historical act he produced such things as the family group and language, the latter the first conscious expression of his social being. Thus, the early Marxian concept of Man as *gattungswesen* connotes at least the man/woman group bound by physical needs but also linked by social needs and by language, rather than the archetype of eighteenth-century England represented by Christian in *The Pilgrim's Progress* and by Defoe's Robinson Crusoe.

For Marx Man's species being was always social being. Further, he shared with Hegel the notion that civil society was both the realization and negation of that social being. He argued that in the beginning Man was prevented from living authentically as *gattungswesen* by his dependence on a niggardly nature and by lack of self-consciousness. And it was his view that although Man was by nature Promethean he was neither conscious of that fact nor able to realize his authenticity except painfully through practice in the material world where he lived his actual life. Thus, in the course of time, in the passage from Germanic through feudal to capitalist society, Man had realized his own powers, developed his own con-sciousness, and created the material conditions for living authentically as *gattungswesen*. However, the highest product of Man's self-making was the form of civil society which characterized eighteenth-century England and much of early nineteenth-century Europe. In this society private property and private right, elevated to the status of moral as well as legal absolutes, created the condi-tions for a two-*class* society. These *class* divisions made community, based on the notional fact that Man's being was social being, impossible. Consequently, any existent state was not moral and not, as Hegel believed, 'the Divine Idea as it exists on earth' administered by a disinterested Universal Class. Thus, civil society, while historically necessary for the development of authentic social being, was also alien to it. In *On the Jewish Question* Marx expressed it thus, 'Man in his most *intimate* reality, in civil society, is a profane being. Here, where he appears both to himself and to others as a real individual he is an *illusory* phenomenon.'[15] Nevertheless, Marx belived that as Man did develop his social being through practice in

---

[15]R. C. Tucker (ed.), *The Marx-Engels Reader* (New York, 1972), p. 32.

civil society he would move closer to realizing his essence (*gattungswesen*) in consciousness. In negating his existence he would become conscious of his own becoming. In the course of time and through his burgeoning consciousness he would begin to shape his own destiny in civil society and the political state in accordance with his *gattungswesen* until he consciously destroyed both in their existent forms.

Because, in the Marxian system, Man's being was social being, change was mediated by social groups rather than by World Historical Individuals as in Hegel. These mediating groups were those *classes*, membership of which was granted by those property relationships which lay at the heart of civil society and which have already been described. In the penultimate epoch of historical development, capitalism, the mediating *class* was to be the proletariat as the Universal Class. Marx held that until Man, in the form of the proletariat, attained full consciousness in the sense and manner to be described in the rest of this chapter he would be propelled towards such consciousness by the dialectical laws of the materialist conception of history. But, once having reached full consciousness via the proletariat, Man would have total self-control and self-determination, and the negativity of the dialectic would cease to act as the engine of historical development; pre-history would end, history begin.

Let me review and emphasize some of the argument so far. This early Marxian system had many of the elements of Hegel's: first, the dualism of being, which in Marx is social being, and which incorporates the distinction between essence and existence, and reality and appearance; second, the driving force, the negation and transcendence of existence; third, the concept of the development of human self-consciousness as the realization of essence. Therefore, at this stage in Marx's thought the concept of Man as *gattungswesen* was similar to Hegel's notion of rational self-consciousness except that Marx's system began with assumptions about human needs and innate capacities and not with an abstract self-consciousness which is easily thought of as mind or even as some occult entity struggling to occupy human consciousness. Indeed, the imagery of *Spirit* in Hegel's writing shows that there can be little doubt that in his system Spirit is an occult entity which in the historical process alienated itself whereas, in the early Marx, it is Man who is held to be alienated *from* himself. These points of departure of Hegel and Marx, the one in heaven the other on earth, were quite different.

It was Marx's departure point which enabled him to move even further away from Hegel's system until in his final model of the capitalist stage of development there is no demiurgos striving to realize itself in the world, not even Man considered as an alienated *gattungswesen.* Instead, in the capitalist epoch of Marx's mature system, the dynamic of historical change is the fact that Man simply is alienated. That is to say that Man, rather than being alienated from his essence as *gattungswesen,* is alienated from the product of that essence. The meaning and significance of this state-ment as a necessary component in *class* consciousness cannot be grasped without a brief excursion into the political economy of history and the history of political economy.

In Marx the key to the political economy of history is labour power in a system of private property. But in the history of political economy, according to Marx, bourgeois economists brought up in the English empiricist tradition of the eighteenth century identified labour merely as they did land and capital, that is, as a universal, discrete, objective factor of production. Thus land, capital and labour were perceived as three separate entities or things known as such through experience. Further, given that private property had the status of a moral absolute, the owners of each of the separate factors or 'facts' of production, who constituted the three great classes of classical economic thought, were held to be morally as well as legally entitled to receive the whole of the value which each class contributed to the production of wealth. Not so, said Marx. Marx, like Hegel, considered that the facts of existence, in this case the factors of production, derived no authority or status merely from the fact of their existence. Rather their reality was only to be understood as part of the social relations which gave them existence. Marx expressed it thus:

Capital consists of raw materials, instruments of labour and means of sub-sistence of all kinds, which are utilized in order to produce new raw materials, new instruments of labour and new means of subsistence. All these component parts of capital are creations of labour, products of labour, *accumulated labour.* Accumulated labour which serves as a means of new production is capital.

So say the economists.

What is a Negro slave? a man of black race. The one explanation is as good as the other.

A Negro is a Negro. A cotton spinning jenny is a machine for spinning cotton. It becomes capital only in certain relations. Torn from these relationships it is no more capital than gold in itself is *money* or sugar the price of sugar. . . .[16]

Or, one might add, a Negro a slave.

Therefore, Marx argued, capital, perceived in bourgeois political economy only as a thing used to produce more things, is more than the thing perceived. It is a form of labour power in certain social relations; labour power which through time has become divided between labour (proletarians) and capital (bourgeois) as owners. As owners, labour and capital cannot exist without each other and they are locked together in an unavoidably destructive symbiotic relationship. Their joint parent, labour power, is the reason for the existence, the perishing and the transcendence of both. This follows from the negativity of private property. The argument is as follows.

The triggering device for capitalist development was private property. This, as already mentioned, was part of the cultural luggage the Germanic peoples brought with them in the form of private possession in their conquest of Europe. With time private possession became private property and the propellant released by private property was a particular social form of labour power. This came about because, in a system with private property, some men – indeed, most men – finish up with no property, hence, private property is also the negation of private property, that is, labour power. According to Marx this process which creates labour power as the only marketable commodity possessed by those without property or connection with the land was a necessary condition for the emergence of capitalism. It took some six or seven hundred years before it became the characteristic form of work in England by the mid-eighteenth century. A parallel movement also occurred in the generation of a stock of money and the institutions of credit which could be used to set labour to work to produce for purposes of exchange. Marx called this stage in the development of capitalism the 'so-called' primitive accumulation; it cannot easily

---

[16] *Selected Works*, vol. I, p. 83.

be interpreted dialectically. Therefore, it is probably only in relation to the mature form of civil society, capitalism, that the
dynamic of the dialectic can be properly grasped.

In capitalism those without property are compelled to sell their
labour in order to live. Further, the owners of private property
cannot produce wealth; this capacity is the prerogative of labour
power. But the owner and seller of labour power, the labourer, sells
his labour power to the capitalist in return for value (a real wage)
equivalent only to the cost of producing and reproducing that
labour power. The amount of labour effort so recompensed Marx
called necessary labour: it is paid for out of variable capital. The
main part of labour power, called surplus labour, is appropriated
by the owner of capital (private property) who uses it to produce
surplus value (profit) which he turns into fixed or constant capital.
The accumulation of fixed or constant capital alters the organic
composition of capital by raising the ratio of constant to variable
capital. Since, in the act of production, only variable capital, that
part of capital which buys surplus labour, contributes to surplus
value, the rate of profit on *total* capital, variable plus fixed or constant capital, will tend to fall. Since real wages, the payment for
necessary labour, are constantly squeezed by capitalists as they
endeavour to raise the rate of profit by extracting more surplus
labour, there is also an inbuilt tendency towards underconsumption. Therefore, the owners of capital find themselves in an inescapable bind, a product of the symbiotic relationship referred to
earlier. In order to frustrate the tendency of the rate of profit to fall
they have to seek new markets, innovate and invest in cost-reducing
technology. In doing so they add to the stock of fixed or constant
capital and generate recurrent economic booms which, however
much they might increase employment and real wages in the short
term, cannot raise aggregate demand at the same rate as investment and innovation can increase output. Moreover, every incre-
ment of investment which adds to the stock of fixed or constant
capital also adds pressure to the downward drift of the rate of
profit. Since the system depends on an elaborate circulation of
money and commodities, at the peak of an economic boom almost
anything can interrupt the flow of economic activity. The most
likely interruption would be a tightening of bank credit when it is
most needed, which is another contradiction inherent in the

system. Such a tightening of credit turns the economic boom into a crisis. Once the crisis has broken, the long-term tendency to underconsumption reasserts itself, capital is concentrated, the reserve army grows, and the two classes are further polarized. Therefore, according to Marx:

Capital does not consist in accumulated labour serving living labour as a means for new production. It consists in living labour serving accumulated labour as a means for maintaining and multiplying the exchange of the latter.[17]

This is the first aspect of the fact of Man's alienation. It means that Man's labour power has been appropriated by the owners of capital for their private use and turned into more capital which then dominates the lives of labourers and determines the whole of economic activity and the social and cultural milieu.

However, as already pointed out, labour power is more than an economic category. Labour power as a factor of production is merely appearance. Even to think of it as the product of social relations is to miss its essence. For, in spite of what has been said earlier, the fact is that labour power is the essence of Man as *gattungswesen*. And, in so far as capital accumulates by appropriating the product of labour power, the labourer, whose individual labour power is finite, is diminished. Therefore, capital as private property in labour is property in the alienated product of the essence of Man. Marx expressed this notion on several occasions:

In exchange for his labour capacity as a fixed available magnitude, he [the worker] surrenders its *creative power*, like Esau his birthright for a mess of pottage.[18]

But the exercise of labour power, labour, is the worker's own life activity, the manifestation of his own life. And this *life activity* he sells to another person in order to secure the necessary *means of subsistence* . . . He does not even reckon labour as part of his life, it is rather a sacrifice of his life.[19]

In short, labour power has two sides: considered economically through its ability to generate surplus value it creates capital as private property; but surplus value is produced by surplus labour

[17] *Ibid.*, p. 85.
[18] Marx, *Grundrisse*, Pelican Marx Library (Harmondsworth, 1973), p. 307.
[19] *Selected Works*, vol. I, p. 77.

which, considered humanistically by Marx, also appears as the alienated product of the essence of Man. Therefore, in Marx, capital is more than mere private property in physical things, or in things disguised in money, or in things disguised in credit. It is private property in labour – property in the essence of Man which enables some men to appropriate the product of the essence of all other men. The principal legal manifestation of this relationship was the development of law relating to wage contracts. Capital, therefore, is alienated labour, labour power which has been objectified, privately appropriated and reified until it appears as a non-human force outside Man whose notional owners, capitalists, have economic and legal powers of appropriating more surplus (alienated) labour from proletarians. In this sense capital is a force as hostile as it is necessary to Man.

Therefore, capital, considered within the Marxian dialectic, is derived from private property which in its very nature is also the negation of private property. In civil society the negative aspect of private property is manifested in the *class* of real proletarians in process of becoming the proletariat. But according to Marx, through the power of appropriation of surplus value inherent in private property, the proletariat is also the negation of Man's essence as a social being, as *gattungswesen*. However, real, living proletarians, who suffer from false consciousness, do not perceive this in consciousness, although they will eventually do so through experience and practice in an ever-changing economic and social milieu which subjects them to increasing economic pressures and makes ever increasing demands on them. This can only take place over time. Consequently, the Marxian like the Hegelian dialectic is necessarily historical. Thus, in the capitalist epoch, capital (private property) accumulates and the economic system changes and grows because of the tendency of the rate of profit to fall. But, as we have seen, the drive to maintain the rate of profit also increases the size of the *class* of proletarians, which as a *class* is the negation of private property, and, via its effects on underconsumption and immiseration of social position (alienation), generates *class* consciousness within the ranks of the workers and creates conditions for the ultimate negative aspect, revolution. The outcome of revolution is not to destroy but to transcend capitalism. Thus, private property as capital which is the negation of the essence of

Man, is its own negation; it has been so from the very first moment of capital and as a necessary condition of capital, and it propels itself forward to its own destruction and transcendence by its own inherent negativity until it achieves the negation of negation. It is in this sense that social being determines consciousness. When it does accomplish this, Man (the proletariat) as inheritor of social knowledge and technology, will be able to live authentically as *gattungswesen*, that is, Man will self-determine his own entire becoming. When this comes about, the dialectical laws of historical development will no longer hold true.

What I have briefly outlined is the dialectical base of what Marx called the Materialist Conception of History. Marx believed it was true. He also considered that real living proletarians would arrive at a growing consciousness of its truth and, therefore, of their own role as the proletariat, through praxis, that is, in their struggle to comprehend the economic system which holds capital and labour, bourgeois and proletarians in the vice-like bind already outlined. As real proletarians arrive at a fuller consciousness of the truth of the theory, its members will be able to identify the objective conditions for their self-redemption, and act. Thus, they will become a proletariat, that is, the dissolution of society existing as a particular class. The final cleansing act which would raise the mass of real proletarians to full consciousness of their own becoming would be revolution.

In Marx, therefore, social being is to be taken to mean the condition of man's unwilled living in his presently historically conditioned milieu in which the willed actions of any single man have played an infinitesimally small part. In the capitalist period, and in the period and place covered in this book, these unwilled conditions include all those relations of capital and labour in the circumstances of private property just described. The consciousness to which Marx referred includes ideology and false consciousness as well as that true *class* consciousness which is the end of it all. The statement that social being determines consciousness has to be understood as only occurring through praxis, that is, the dialectically linked processes of living and thinking in certain unwilled circumstances which generate and release a will to change or perpetuate those circumstances. It is the will to change circumstances in certain ways that Marx calls *class* consciousness. When that has taken place, consciousness will determine all.

To find out how Marx translated the concept, the proletariat as the dissolution of society existing as a particular class and the *class* consciousness which it represents, into practical political language comprehensible to real proletarians, and to find out what degree of *class* consciousness Marx thought appropriate for real proletarians in the third quarter of the nineteenth century, it is necessary to comment in detail upon his *Critique of the Gotha Programme.* Although in this critique Marx described the degree of *class* consciousness he thought appropriate for German workers after a mere forty years of industrialization and concentration of capital it can also serve as a yardstick for the degree of *class* consciousness of English workers compared with which all other levels of consciousness must be regarded as false consciousness. Consequently, this critique has particular importance for all Marxist historians who seek to demonstrate the existence of *class* consciousness among workers in England in the nineteenth century.

The *Critique of the Gotha Programme* was written as a series of comments upon the draft programme put before the Gotha Unity Congress in 1875. This Congress aimed to unite the two existing German workers' organizations, the Social–Democratic Workers' Party led by Liebknecht and Bebel, and the Lassallean General Association of German Workers. Marx considered that the Unity programme smacked of opportunism of the worst kind. To show how it did so he dissected its clauses one by one and subjected them to scathing and sometimes vitriolic comment. He tore clause three to shreds. It read: 'The emancipation of labour demands the promotion of the instruments of labour to the common property of society and the co-operative regulation of the total labour with a fair distribution of the proceeds of labour.'[20] Marx began his attack by asking 'What are the proceeds of labour, and what is a fair distribution?' In his answer to the question of a fair distribution he set about those socialists (and there were many of them in the mid-nineteenth century) who believed that the worker had a right to the whole product of labour, who believed, indeed, that each individual worker had the right to the product of his own personal labour contribution. According to Marx this was a mere bourgeois notion and

---

[20] Karl Marx, *Critique of the Gotha Programme,* in Marx/Engels, *Selected Works,* vol. II, p. 19.

one characteristic of the early co-operative phase of European socialism. He argued that no individual worker could really expect to receive the value of the whole product of his labour because there must be deductions from the total social product to defray the costs of maintaining the economy as a functioning whole. These deductions included a fund for the replacement of obsolescent or worn-out equipment, the provision of new equipment to sustain growth, the allocation of an insurance fund to meet emergencies and unforeseen developments, payment for non-productive administrative and public services such as education, and the creation of a fund for the benefit of those unable to work; the young, the sick and the old. His point was that before any distribution could occur the proceeds of labour must be substantially diminished, but that the Unity programme was silent on such matters. Moreover, the important question of whether distribution should be made according to each individual's contribution to input or whether, because of innate inequalities of strength and ability, rights 'instead of being equal would have to be unequal', which would result in some receiving more and some less relative to their contributions, was also not mentioned.

Because the Unity programme was deficient in these matters, Marx argued that the socialist vision it embodied was perverse and narrow, dominated by mere bourgeois notions of equal right. He wrote

What we have to deal with here is a communist society, not as it has *developed* on its own foundations, but, on the contrary, just as it *emerges* from capitalist society; which is thus in every respect, economically, morally and intellectually, still stamped with the birthmarks of the old society from whose womb it emerges. Accordingly, the individual producer receives back from society – after the deductions have been made – exactly what he gives to it.[21]

Understood in this light the Unity programme aimed to foist on the party 'as dogmas, ideas which in a certain period had some meaning but have now become obsolete verbal rubbish'.[22] Thus the programme obscured the economic and political realities of the *class*

[21] *Ibid.*, p. 21.
[22] *Ibid.*, p. 23.

struggle and ignored the moral objective of socialism. Consequently, Marx elaborated what was necessary to be done and when
it could be done:

In a higher phase of communist society, after enslaving subordination of
the individual to the division of labour, and therewith also the antithesis
between mental and physical labour, has vanished; after labour has
become not only a means of life but life's prime want; after the productive
forces have also increased with the all-round development of the
individual, and all the springs of co-operative wealth flow more
abundantly – only then can the narrow horizon of bourgeois right be
crossed in its entirety and society inscribe on its banners: from each
according to his ability, to each according to his needs![23]

This, according to Marx, is what real proletarians have both to
understand and to aspire to if they are to become 'the dissolution of
society as a particular class' – the proletariat.

But, said Marx, why all the fuss about distribution? According to
him,

Any distribution whatever of the means of consumption is only a consequence of the distribution of the conditions of production themselves . . .
Vulgar Socialism (and from it in turn a section of the democracy) has
taken over from the bourgeois economists the consideration and treatment
of distribution as independent of the mode of production and hence the
presentation of Socialism as turning principally on distribution. After the
real relation has long been made clear, why retrogress again?[24]

As we have seen Marx claimed that the real relation is a *class*
relation derived from power relationships contingent upon
property. The Unity programme had nothing to say about this
either.

Further on in his *Critique* Marx referred again to the power
aspects of *class* relationships in the attack he made on the
Lassallean version of the *iron law of wages* which he thought
underpinned much of the argument in the Unity programme. The
essence of Marx's critical comment was that the real evil of the
capitalist system lies in the unequal power relationship involved in
the wage contract. In this relationship the worker parts with his
labour power but receives in exchange just enough to subsist, or

[23] *Ibid.*, p. 23.
[24] *Ibid.*, pp. 23–4.

what Marx referred to as mere permission to live. It is a system of slavery and as such it is a power relationship. Indeed, capitalism is a system of 'slavery which becomes more severe in proportion as the social productive forces of labour develop, whether the worker receives better or worse payment'.[25] Marx emphasized that it is this slavery of the system that is at fault, not the fact that the slaves are poor. He concluded his critique of the Lassallean notion of the iron law of wages with the following words: 'It is as if, among slaves who have at last got behind the secret of slavery and broken out in rebellion, a slave still in thrall to obsolete notions were to inscribe on the programme of the rebellion: slavery must be abolished because the feeding of slaves in the system of slavery cannot exceed a certain low maximum!'[26] This statement alone should have convinced the German Social Democrats at Gotha and all those who adopt an economist position that Marx's critique of capitalism did not hang upon the fact that most were poor and likely to get poorer. As Marx made plain it is essentially the authoritarian and alienating relations inherent in capitalism, relations subsumed and brought to their highest degree of antagonism in *class* relations, which he attacked and which he believed would be removed through the mediation of the proletariat. Thus, while the Unity programme concluded by calling weakly for 'the elimination of all social and political inequality', Marx said it ought to have asserted the need for the abolition of all *class* distinctions, that is, property relations, for then 'all social and political inequality arising from them would disappear of itself'.[27]

There are other criticisms which Marx levelled at the Unity programme. The programme claimed that it was possible to achieve a 'free state' by negotiation with the government. Marx believed this most unlikely since once again it ignored the reality of power. The fact was that the Prusso–German Empire was 'nothing but a police guarded military despotism, embellished with parliamentary forms, alloyed with a feudal admixture, already influenced by the bourgeoisie and bureaucratically carpentered'.[28] To expect that the rulers of such a state would peacefully resign their powers

[25] *Ibid.*, p. 27.
[26] *Ibid.*, pp. 27–8.
[27] *Ibid.*, p. 28.
[28] *Ibid.*, p. 31.

to some form of social democracy was political naïveté of the highest degree.

Another example of political blindness was the failure to recognize the fact that compared with the feudal landlords and the lower middle class, the bourgeoisie was then a revolutionary class. Instead the Unity programme persisted in regarding all the ruling classes opposed to the proletariat as 'only one reactionary mass'. According to Marx this simplistic political reasoning was contrary to his own analysis and was a deliberate act of confusion on Lassalle's part designed to put a good complexion on Lassalle's alliance with the absolutist and feudal opponents of the bourgeoisie in Germany. Rather, it should be an axiom of classical Marxism that: no bourgeoisie, no real proletarians; no real proletarians, no proletariat; no proletariat, no redemption for mankind. Therefore, no bourgeoisie, no redemption. A point which Marx was to make again in his argument for England's involvement in the Crimean War.

In short, the thrust of all Marx's criticisms of the Unity programme was that the document either obscured or ignored the question of the distribution of political and economic power and reduced socialism to bread and butter questions, that is to matters of narrow self-interest. Further, it offered no vision of a proletariat as the dissolution of society existing as a particular class able to transcend the narrow horizon of bourgeois right. Yet as we have seen, only such a *class* could inscribe on its banners the moral imperative: 'From each according to his ability, to each according to his needs!' Thus, the Unity programme failed to express all that a *class*-conscious proletarian should be encouraged to arrive at in consciousness. Such a consciousness should encompass an awareness of the importance of these arguments of Marx, and a total comprehension of the historical movement and contradictions of capitalism which, through involving the worker in active participation in the world, would bring him to such an awareness. As Marx said: 'It is not a question of what this or that proletarian or even the whole proletariat, at the moment *regards* as its aim. It is a question of *what the proletariat is*, and what, in accordance with this *being*, it will historically be compelled to do.'[29]

[29] See footnote 9.

Because of this complex nature of *class* consciousness, which had to incorporate the notion of the dissolution of society as a particular class, and because, as we have seen, Marx was aware of the fact that socialism as espoused in the nineteenth century was necessarily contaminated by the values of the society which gave it birth, he also belived that there must be a revolutionary component in *class* consciousness. Revolution was also a necessary cathartic or cleansing act as well as a necessary political one. In 1846 he wrote:

Both for the production on a mass scale of this consciousness, and for the success of the cause itself, the alteration of men on a mass scale is necessary, an alteration which can only take place in a practical movement, *a revolution*; this revolution is necessary, therefore, not only because the ruling class cannot be overthrown in any other way, but also because the class *overthrowing* it can only in a revolution succeed in ridding itself of all the muck of ages and become fitted to found society anew.[30]

It is possible to interpret this passage in such a way as to show that Marx believed that the mature kind of *class* consciousness he had written about in *The Holy Family*, and which has been emphasized in this chapter, was not a necessary precondition for the initiation of the proletarian revolution. But in this passage Marx wrote about the problem of the conversion to *class* consciousness of the mass of workers. He was not concerned with the development of *class* consciousness among the revolutionary elite or party whose role was to lead the revolution and to ensure that the revolution was the correct one. As Marx knew from experience, this preparation for and identification of the time for revolution was a more difficult task. For example, early in his political career he had lived through a period of difficult choice when, in 1848, he had attempted to steer the German workers away from the 'Cologne Revolution' which he regarded as a senseless exhaustion of the workers, '*before* the day of decision'. As Marx well knew the identification of the 'day of decision' required a sophisticated political analysis. Consequently, in the address of the Central Committee to the Communist League in 1850 Marx and Engels drew lessons from the debacle of 1848 and set out conditions for worker participation in future revolutions and 'days of decision'. Above all these conditions required 'a protracted revolutionary development',

[30] Karl Marx and Friedrick Engels, *The German Ideology* (Moscow, 1964), p. 86.

during which workers 'must contribute most to their final victory by informing themselves of their own *class* interests, by taking up their independent political position as soon as possible, by not allowing themselves to be misled by the hypocritical phrases of the democratic petty bourgeoisie into doubting for one minute the necessity of an independently organized party of the proletariat. Their battle-cry must be: 'The Permanent Revolution.'[31] It was as part of this protracted revolutionary development that twenty-five years later Marx produced his critical notes on the Unity programme to convey to socialist parties and party leaders the idea that leaders of the revolution at least must possess mature *class* consciousness and that party members in consciousness must come close to it. In short, that there must be a vanguard of a revolutionary *class* with a correct idea of revolution and *class* consciousness as a condition for revolution. The act of revolution will only convert the masses. Nevertheless, it may still be argued that mature individual *class* consciousness may only arise in a context of mature collective *class* consciousness and that this can only happen at the point of the 'dissolution of society existing as a particular class'. At which point *class* consciousness merges into consciousness perceived as autonomous and undetermined.

Thus, in Marx's conception of class, *class* consciousness incorporates a revolutionary consciousness which transcends a mere political consciousness. It surrounds political consciousness with an aura shining with ideas of emancipation and redemption, that is of the idea of the dissolution of society existing as a particular class being the proletariat. Over fifty years ago when the political turmoil which was occurring in Eastern Europe augured world Communist revolution, Georg Lukacs concluded his essay, 'Class Consciousness', with a paragraph which said just this:

Thus we must never overlook the distance that separates the consciousness of even the most revolutionary worker from the authentic class consciousness of the proletariat. But even this situation can be explained on the basis of the Marxist theory of class struggle and class consciousness. *The proletariat only perfects itself by annihilating and transcending itself by creating the classless society through the successful conclusion of its own class*

[31] Karl Marx and Friedrick Engels, *Address of the Central Committee to the Communist League* (March 1850), in *The Revolutions of 1848*, ed. D. Fernbach (Harmondsworth, 1973), p. 330.

struggle. The struggle for this society, in which the dictatorship of the proletariat is merely a phase, is not just a battle waged against an external enemy, the bourgeoisie. It is equally the struggle of the proletariat *against itself*: against the devastating and degrading effects of the capitalist system upon the class consciousness. The proletariat will only have won the real victory when it has overcome these effects within itself. The separation of the areas that should be united, the diverse stages of consciousness which the proletariat has reached in the various spheres of activity are a precise index of what has been achieved and what remains to be done. The proletariat must not shy away from self-criticism, for victory can only be gained by the truth and self-criticism must, therefore, be its natural element.[32]

What Lukacs has to say about self-criticism to the Hungarian workers in 1920 and Marx to the opportunists among the German Social Democrats in 1875 must also be said by any Marxist historian, writing about the development of an English working class, to himself and to the subjects of his study. That is he must measure his claims to have proved their *class* consciousness not against the counter-claims of non-Marxist historians but against the yardstick represented by Marx's own concept. And he should not be too greatly distressed if he should find his subjects falling short of it and guilty of one or other variant of false consciousness. They will all be contaminated by the society which produced them. Certainly Marx would have regarded some level of false consciousness as appropriate for early nineteenth-century socialist movements, especially for those in existence before his own system was made known.

However, if, like John Foster, the historian writes to claim that his subjects were *class* conscious in 1842 or by some other specified date, he must show that their *class* consciousness – or, as Foster would have it, their intellectual commitment – approximated closely to that which I have attempted to describe. Therefore, in the Oldham case, referred to by Foster, it is not enough to show that the spinners had politicized an industrial dispute in 1841 nor yet that they sought the revolutionary overthrow of the existing political order. What has to be shown is that the objectives of the revolutionaries went beyond mere bread and butter ones conceived in the interest of a particular section of society but were more

---

[32]Georg Lukacs, *History and Class Consciousness*, pp. 80–1.

touched with Marx's notion of the proletariat as the dissolution of all classes than coloured by mere bourgeois or petit bourgeois ideas of equal right. This, Foster does not do. Indeed, his own argument that a hitherto *class*-conscious proletariat was 'liberalized', that is, bought off by the Ten Hour Movement, suggests that the Oldham spinners even at the peak of their class consciousness fell substantially short of Marxian *class* consciousness and were immersed in bourgeois ideas of equal right. It also suggests that they were much less politically conscious than the Bath Chartists when in 1847 they, too, were deliberately subjected to the blandishments of a Whig/Tory alliance standing behind Lord Ashley and the Ten Hour Movement. The object of this Whig/Tory alliance was to oust J. A. Roebuck who had been Radical MP for Bath from 1832 to 1837 and again from 1841 to 1847. Thomas Bolwell, the leading local Chartist and a working man, saw the dangers of Ashleyism (or what Foster calls 'liberalization'), and called a meeting of Chartists. He told them,

The object of the present meeting was to disabuse the minds of the people as to the visits of the delegates [three men from the northern factory districts], and to form a committee of active working men for the purpose of securing Mr Roebuck's election ... Mr Roebuck had gone beyond Lord Ashley in what he had done, for he had laid the foundation of a system which would give the franchise to all mankind, and placed in comparison with Mr Roebuck, Lord Ashley sank into comparative nothingness.[33]

With the defeat of Roebuck the Ten Hour Movement won in Bath by a vote of 1278 to 1093 and did so mainly on the basis of sectarian differences: Roebuck had been too kind to the Irish Catholics!

The point of this brief foray into the intricacies of local politics is to show that the Radicals of Bath and their Philosophic Radical Member of Parliament, all of whom were thoroughly soaked in notions of bourgeois right and already 'liberalized', were yet able to resist the blandishments of the Ten Hour Movement, whereas the apparently *class*-conscious spinners of Oldham succumbed. Perhaps the latter did so because of rather than in spite of the collectivism of their class consciousness and because, like the

---

[33] *Bath Chronicle*, 8th July 1847. Quoted in R. S. Neale, *Class and Ideology in the Nineteenth Century* (London, 1972), pp. 58–9.

German Social Democrats at Gotha, they wanted the state to intervene in their particular interest but did not seem to mind whose state it was! Whatever the explanation, they clearly fell short of Marxian *class* consciousness as much before as after 1842.

In order to illustrate further the endless succession of traps which bestrew the paths of historians seeking to establish the extent to which the class consciousness of real proletarians approximated to that of a Marxian *class*-conscious proletariat, one can show that in one respect at least the 'liberalized' Oldham workers were more *class* conscious than Foster allows. It concerns the Crimean War. In the country generally support for the war by the working classes was led by the left-wing Chartist Ernest Jones. In 1855 the erstwhile radical but now 'liberalized' leaders of Oldham's working classes came out in support of British participation in the Crimean War. Foster comments: 'Here, therefore, we have an excellent example of false consciousness at work: the blocking out of a class analysis just because it posed such a devastating challenge to protective assumptions so carefully built up over the previous years.'[34] On the other hand Foster praises Bronterre O'Brien's opposition to British involvement. He interprets this opposition as a correct *class* analysis which linked the war to loan-mongering and to Empire – as it undoubtedly was. But the question is, was O'Brien correct in concluding, because it could be shown that Britain had important commercial interests in the Balkan and eastern Mediterranean regions, that the war should be opposed by the working classes on the grounds that it was an imperialist war? Who was correct? Ernest Jones and the Oldham radical leaders? Bronterre O'Brien?

Fortunately, if one regards Marx as a Marxist well versed in his own method of analysis, it is not necessary to look very far for an answer. Marx wrote extensively on the Eastern Question and on the question of Britain's involvement he noted: 'In this instance the interests of the revolutionary Democrat and of England go hand in hand. Neither can permit the Czar to make Constantinople one of his capitals, and we shall find that when driven to the wall, the one will resist him as determinedly as the other.'[35] And it was his view

---

[34] John Foster, *Class Struggle and the Industrial Revolution* (London, 1974), p. 242.
[35] Karl Marx, *The Eastern Question* (London, 1897), p. 19.

that the English working class led by Ernest Jones 'pledging the people to war' set an example to the ruling classes. He continued: 'While the English Queen is at this moment feasting Russian Princesses, while an enlightened English aristocracy and bourgeoisie lie prostrate before the barbarian Autocrat, the English proletariat alone protests against the impotency and degradation of the ruling classes.'[36]

The theoretical consistency of Marx's position on the Crimean War can only be understood within the whole world context of the Materialist Conception of History in which Western bourgeois society alone is seen as revolutionary and progressive and capable of producing a further progressive form of society. Within this world historical model, nineteenth-century Russia is characterized as an oriental despotism virtually unable to generate any new form of internal social relationships but able successfully to organize itself for war and territorial aggrandisement. Consequently, Russia was not to be regarded as reactionary merely but as fundamentally and woodenly conservative and as the despotism which in 1848 had successfully put an end to all liberal and democratic hopes in Eastern Europe. Since, twenty years later, Marx bitterly criticized the Unity programme for regarding the Prusso–German aristocracy and bourgeoisie as one undifferentiated ruling mass, it should be possible to grasp the consistency of his argument. Certainly in the mid-nineteenth century, capitalist societies were very thin on the ground. In Europe they were confined to three or four regions on its western edge. The dominant form of society was still either feudal, absolutist or despotic. The success of the proletarian revolution and a socialist future required that they be prevented from expanding their spheres of influence either separately or jointly. Thus Russia must either be contained or destroyed. Hence the English working classes should support their indigenous, progressive bourgeoisie and their own mixed ruling class against Russian despotism.

Foster's problem is that he writes within a compressed and narrowly regionalized model rather than with a world historic model of Marxism. There can be little doubt that Ernest Jones had a better understanding of Marx than Bronterre O'Brien. But

---

[36] *Ibid.,* p. 62.

whether the men of Oldham took the 'correct' stance for the same reasons as Jones is another matter. I do not argue that their position shows them to be *class* conscious.

This chapter began with a description of Marx's concept of class in which it was emphasized that *class* in Marx is basically a property relationship and that as such it is necessarily a power relationship within a two-class model. However, a definition of *class* according to objective position in the production process merely identifies the source of potentially antagonistic relationships. Before groups so defined can be regarded as *classes* in the fullest sense their members must become *class* conscious and act accordingly. Since the problem of *class* consciousness is essentially a question of the *class* consciousness of the proletariat, the discussion focused on that question. It showed that the concept of the proletariat and its *class* consciousness referred above all to the notion of the proletariat as the dissolution of all classes and therefore, that the *class* consciousness of the proletariat must transcend their merely proletarian class consciousness. Next, the relationship between the *class* consciousness of the proletariat and the consciousness which Marx held to be determined by social being, and the way in which the unfolding of consciousness is regarded as an integral part of the Marxian dialectic were also described. This, too, is part of *class* consciousness.

The Unity programme was then examined to show how Marx, in 1875, translated the concept, the proletariat as the dissolution of society existing as a particular class and the *class* consciousness which it represents, into practical political language. It was emphasized that it meant that workers' leaders had to pass in consciousness and practice beyond a mere bread and butter socialism tinged with ideas of bourgeois right and lean more towards a socialism concerned with the issue of domination and subjection and the way in which consciously creative men would inscribe on their revolutionary banners the slogan 'from each according to his ability, to each according to his need', and would do so conscious of their historic mission as laid out for them by Marx in the Materialist Conception of History. It was argued that this is the yardstick against which to measure all other class consciousness and class perceptions in order to decide whether the class consciousness of real proletarians was *class* consciousness or false consciousness. Foster's account of the development of *class* consciousness in Oldham was then mentioned. In relation to the yardstick described it was found deficient. Therefore, I argued, it was class consciousness falling well short of *class* consciousness even at its peak. In the course of the discussion it became clear that any attempt to identify *class* consciousness in nineteenth-century England is fraught with many traps for the unwary historian, particularly if he works in a narrow regional compass instead of with the world historic vision that characterizes the Marxian analysis.

I conclude the chapter by saying that any historian who wishes to come to grips with Marx's concepts of *class* and *class* consciousness in order to refute or substantiate either or both through empirical inquiry must familiarize himself with the whole corpus of Marx's writing.

2
Mannheim, the Sociology of Knowledge and Social History

This conception of history depends on our ability to expound the real process of production, starting out from the material production of life itself, and to comprehend the form of intercourse connected with this and created by this mode of production (i.e. civil society in its various stages), as the basis of all history, and to show it in its action as state, to explain all the different theoretical products and forms of consciousness, religion, philosophy, ethics, etc., etc., and trace their origins and growth from that basis; by which means, of course, the whole thing can be depicted in its totality (and, therefore, too, the reciprocal action of these various sides on one another).

Karl Marx, *The German Ideology*,
1846 (Moscow, 1964) pp. 50–1

Nothing is simpler than to maintain that a certain type of thinking is feudal, bourgeois or proletarian, liberal, socialistic, or conservative, as long as there is no analytical method for demonstrating it and no criteria have been adduced which will provide a control over the demonstration.

Karl Mannheim, *Ideology and Utopia*,
1936 (London, 1972), p. 45

In Marx's system *class* consciousness is a concept embodying the notion of true, that is, non-ideological knowledge. And it is a corollary of the argument in chapter 1 that a fully *class*-conscious proletarian, a member of the proletariat, who with the aid of the Marxian system refuses to accept social facts at their face value and becomes conscious of their historical determination, would possess true knowledge of his own alienated situation in the scheme of things as well as knowledge about the position of other groups and classes. Thus, he would possess knowledge about the ideological nature of all non-Marxist thought in capitalist societies and knowledge about the true path to non-ideological knowledge. In short, a *class*-conscious proletarian, a member of the proletariat, would know, as Marx knew, that the corpus of his thought was, like that of the natural sciences, true science. A Marxist historian would also observe these things and know them to be true.

The antithesis of *class* consciousness is ideological knowledge, or more succinctly, ideology. Thus, it is argued, positivist social sciences which do not make the Hegelian and Marxian distinctions between appearance and reality, such as classical political economy and its descendants, accept as data social 'facts' as they appear generated by the rules and norms of the ongoing socio-economic system. According to Marxian thought is is on the basis of the analysis of such 'facts', such as the money cost and immediate sources of capital, and prices or, in criminology, the criminal statistics, that positivist social scientists produce predictions and policy recommendations which simply serve to perpetuate a system which prevents men from arriving at true knowledge of themselves and their own productive and creative capacities. Such 'knowledge' merely leaves man alienated. It is ideology. Ideology is not necessarily 'false' in any sense that could be empirically demonstrated according to the rules of positivist social science. However, it is held to be 'false' in the sense that the explanatory and manipulative power of ideological knowledge is limited by the fact that it accepts the *status quo*, uses as its data facts taken at their face value, and thereby functions as an expression and legitimation of the interests of the dominant class. It is systematically distorted knowledge, therefore not knowledge. A Marxist knows this to be true and the Marxian analysis correct.

However, as will be shown in chapter 4, many non-Marxist historians claim to be able to connect patterns of thought and behaviour to objectively determined social groups or classes with the aid of varying conceptual frameworks at odds with the Marxian one. Thereby they put forward causal explanations of historical phenomena and historical change using different concepts of class and class consciousness. Consequently history textbooks and monographs, like idiomatic speech, are littered with 'class' explanations of history between which it appears impossible for the non-Marxist historian to choose. Certainly if one goes a step further than Marx and considers that all knowledge, including Marxist knowledge, is systematically distorted by the social origins, conceptual framework or mental set of the investigator and is, therefore, ideological, the outstanding problem is to know which of the many ways is the correct way to connect thought, values and action with social structure. Thus the problem of class with which the social historian has to deal has methodological and epistemological components, which is to say that the historian who wishes to offer a class explanation of historical change must be impeccably rigorous in the methods he uses to link thought, values and action with social structure, and he must endeavour to show that these methods meet clearly formulated criteria of truth if the result of his analysis is to be regarded as an addition to knowledge.

The first steps in this enterprise should involve an attempt at clarification of the concept of class and its associated terminology. And it is because all discussion of class by historians takes as its starting point Marx's views about class, that in chapter 1 I discussed Marx's notions of *class* and *class* consciousness in relation to the interests of working historians. And I began this chapter with a reminder that according to Marx the Marxian view was correct, therefore, that it was knowledge.

In the rest of this chapter I will consider the work of Karl Mannheim and explore his notion of the sociology of knowledge as an aid in exploring the problem of class and class consciousness still further.

Mannheim argued that there is a significant class or order perspective in all thought, and, therefore, that all thought, including Marxist thought, is systematically distorted knowledge. Therefore, all thought is either ideological or utopian thought. This ideological/utopian nature of thought, which will be discussed below, may well obscure historians' perceptions of those 'objective' truths contained in the works of other historians with whom they disagree. Hence, if this proposition of Mannheim is true, it appears essential to find ways of establishing the 'truths' which may yet lodge in ideological/utopian knowledge. It is as if social historians need the intellectual equivalent of a tin mining dredge. Such a mining dredge works by pouring millions of gallons of pressurized water on everything in sight in order to turn it into a sludge which, when passed through settling boxes, leaves a residue of high quality ore. At the same time the dredge stays afloat on the water it uses and re-cycles. The catch is to stay afloat, trap the ore and avoid being left only with sludge! The importance of such an intellectual, critical device for social historians cannot be emphasized too greatly. This is because tests of 'truth' available to other social scientists are not readily available to them. For example, historians cannot easily resort to such tests of 'truth' as correspondence, utility or workability. And they can have little reliance on the coherence test which seems to depend on the existing mental set or conceptual framework of the mind which investigates that coherence, whereas the validity of any existing mental set or conceptual framework so used should be part of the problem under investigation. Further, because the positivist claim that positivist empiricism is the correct way of knowing cannot itself be subjected to its own evaluative criterion, that is, empirically tested, without recourse to some subjective notion of utility, historians cannot take refuge in mere empiricism or in what I call pebble collecting or counting lamp posts. In short, there is a real problem of knowing about historical knowledge.

It appears to have been epistemological considerations of this nature which led Mannheim to construct his sociology of knowledge, that field of inquiry which he considered appropriate for social history, as 'the systematization of the doubt which is to be found in social life as a vague insecurity and uncertainty'.[1] But he also thought of his sociology of knowledge as the means to arrive at 'objective' knowledge. It is possible that the vague insecurity and uncertainty to which Mannheim referred had psychological roots in his personal experience of revolution, counter-revolution and eventual exile following the First World War and the collapse of the Austro-Hungarian Empire of which he had been a citizen. There can be no doubt however that it also had intellectual origins further in the past, in the ferment of thought which preceded the First

---

[1] Karl Mannheim, *Ideology and Utopia* (1936), (London, 1972), p. 45. Two recent works in which Mannheim's work is more fully discussed are: G. W. Remmling, *The Sociology of Karl Mannheim* (London, 1975) and P. Hamilton, *Knowledge and Social Structure* (London, 1974).

World War and which is not itself explicable in terms of war, revolution and counter-revolution. It was in the pre-war period, as a student in Budapest, that Mannheim came under the influence of Hegelian and Marxist thought in the company of such Hungarian intellectuals as Georg Lukacs, and was profoundly influenced by the work of Emil Lask, Heinrich Rickert and Edmund Husserl. All of these scholars, as well as Max Weber, Max Scheler and Wilhelm Dilthey, were deeply concerned about the issue of relativity versus objectivity in social science and were critical of the positivist position. But it was not only in science and philosophy that fundamental changes in ways of seeing and knowing were in process. The most striking change was in painting. Between 1906 and 1914, painting, in the hands of the Cubists Picasso, Braque and Gris, underwent a paradigm shift of momentous proportions. A shift, incidentally, which scarcely gets a mention in general histories of the period but which is worth further comment because it parallels and illustrates the developments in philosophy and sociology and even in history itself, and produced the sort of solution to problems in the visual arts that Mannheim sought in sociology.

Analytical cubism has frequently been related to Kantian aesthetics. For example, Hourcade, the first of many writers to relate cubist painting to Kantian aesthetics, writing about cubism in 1912 quoted Schopenhauer's observation that, 'Kant's greatest service was to distinguish between the appearance of a thing and the thing in itself, and he showed that our intelligence stands between the thing and us.'[2] This distinction between appearance and reality is, as we know, vitally important in the thought of both Hegel and Marx. The analytical cubists also used it in their attempts to penetrate beyond and within appearance to perceive, to understand and then to represent reality as a *Gestalt*. Thus, 'Cubism disregarded appearances. Unsatisfied by the fortuities of a single visual impression, it endeavoured to penetrate to the very essence of an object by representing it, not as it appeared on a given day at a given time, but as it exists ultimately composed in the memory.'[3] And, as Picasso expressed it, 'Cubism pursues self-sufficient pictorial ends. These we may define as the means of

[2] John Golding, *Cubism: A History and Analysis, 1907–1914* (London, 1971), p. 33.
[3] D. H. Kahnweiler, *Juan Gris: His Life and Work* (New York, 1946), p. 110.

expressing everything that our reason and our eyes perceive within the limits of the possibilities allowed of by line and colour. What an inexhaustible source of unexpected joys and discoveries.'[4] So it should be with written history. Unfortunately, or fortunately for those of us who enjoy words, historians use words in place of line and colour and interleaved pages instead of a single plane surface. Consequently, there can probably be no historical equivalent of Blaise Cendrar's simultaneous book *La Prose du Transsibérien et de la petite Jehanne de France*, a poem over six feet long printed in letters of different sizes and colours on an abstract coloured background designed by Sonia Delaunay, first published in 1913. And there can probably never be the historical equivalent of Picasso's *Portrait of Kahnweiler*. Nevertheless, social history can learn from art. It may even, as Mannheim thought, learn something from the methods of investigation used by historians of art as they work to identify the succession of artistic styles. And to that we will return. In the meantime back to Mannheim.

The basic proposition of Mannheim's systematized doubt, his sociology of knowledge, is 'that there are modes of thought which cannot be adequately understood as long as their social origins are obscured'.[5] This is a proposition by now well understood by social historians and probably no longer a matter of controversy, although difficult to demonstrate. For example, what I have just briefly written places Mannheim's mode of thought in its historical milieu and illustrates by analogy what he attempted to do, but it does not explain the social origins of his thought. It does not explain the social origins of his thought because what Mannheim wrote fifty years ago about the immense problems the search for the social origins of thought poses for the investigator is still relevant today. Certainly, historians have not solved these problems. What Mannheim wrote is quoted at the head of this chapter. It reads, 'nothing is simpler than to maintain that a certain type of thinking is feudal, bourgeois, or proletarian, liberal, socialistic or conservative, as long as there is no analytical method for demonstrating it and no criteria have been adduced which will provide a control over

[4]Jean Leymarie, *Picasso: The Artist of the Century* (London, 1972), p. 75.
[5]Karl Mannheim, *Ideology and Utopia*, p. 2.

the demonstration'.[6] Accordingly Mannheim believed that in our time there are two broad slogan-like concepts, 'ideology' and 'utopia', which serve as symbols of great significance for opposing groups: he believed that these symbolic concepts have immense consequences for the masking of thought and obscuring true knowledge. The significance he attached to these symbolic concepts is shown in his use of them for the title of his collection of essays on the sociology of knowledge in which he defined them thus:

> The concept 'ideology' reflects the one discovery which emerged from political conflict, namely, that ruling groups can in their thinking become so intensively interest-bound to a situation that they are simply no longer able to see certain facts which would undermine their sense of domination. There is implicit in the word 'ideology' the insight that in certain situations the collective unconscious of certain groups obscures the real condition of society both to itself and to others and thereby stabilizes it. The concept of *utopian* thinking reflects the opposite discovery of the political struggle, namely that certain oppressed groups are intellectually so strongly interested in the destruction and transformation of a given condition of society that they unwittingly see only those elements in the situation which tend to negate it. Their thinking is incapable of correctly diagnosing an existing condition of society. They are not at all concerned with what really exists; rather in their thinking they already seek to change the situation that exists. Their thought is never a diagnosis of the situation; it can be used only as a direction for action. In the utopian mentality, the collective unconscious, guided by wishful representation and the will to action, hides certain aspects of reality. It turns its back on everything which would shake its belief or paralyse its desire to change things.[7]

It was Mannheim's belief that if the social origins of ideological and utopian thought could be analytically and accurately identified then it should be possible to arrive at the residue of truth in each and so to arrive at knowledge. Consequently, Mannheim's purpose in his endeavour to establish the social origins of thought was not merely historical or expository, it was primarily epistemological. And, because he wished to devise procedures and methods of investigation with which to establish the social origins of and, thereby, the ideological and utopian components in knowledge,

[6] *Ibid.*, p. 45.
[7] *Ibid.*, p. 36.

and to arrive at 'truth', he recommended to historians the methods of philology and the history of art. He wrote,

The most important task of the sociology of knowledge at present is to demonstrate its capacity in actual research in the historical-sociological realm. In this realm it must work out criteria of exactness for establishing empirical truths and for assuring their control. It must emerge from the state where it engages in casual intuitions and gross generalities (such as the crude dichotomy involved in the assertion that here we find bourgeois thinking, there we find proletarian thinking, etc.) even though this may involve sacrificing its slogan-like clear cutness. In this it can and must learn from the methods and results of the exact procedures of the philological disciplines, and from the methods used in the history of art with particular reference to stylistic succession.[8]

In short, there were two main thrusts in Mannheim's sociology of knowledge. First, to gain knowledge of the social origins or bases of knowledge. Second, to use that knowledge in order to distinguish the ideological and utopian components in thought and so to arrive at 'truth'. These two aspects of his system, which one might refer to as the historical and the epistemological aspects, are inextricably interwoven. Thus, if using the methods advocated by Mannheim, one becomes able to distinguish ideological and utopian thought from objective knowledge then the objectivensss or truth of stated connections between thought and social groups would be in sight. On the other hand, objective knowledge about these connections is itself a condition for distinguishing ideological and utopian thought from objective knowledge. Thus, the historian of class, like Mannheim, must have a long-standing concern with both aspects of the problem: the historical and the epistemological.

Because Mannheim claimed that there *are* modes of thought which cannot be adequately understood and therefore evaluated as long as their social origins are obscured, he was open to the charge of adopting a wholly determinist and relativist position. He denied this charge on the grounds that what he intended was to clear the ground for determining the 'truths' which are overlaid by ideological and utopian modes of thought. Consequently, because he believed it possible to arrive at objective knowledge, he called his sociology of knowledge relational rather than relative. Moreover, in

[8] *Ibid.*, pp. 275–6.

his opinion knowledge, even ideological knowledge, is not 'illusory' or 'false' even though it is systematically distorted as a result of its social origins. Thus, ideology for Mannheim was not at all identical with illusion. He argued that 'knowledge arising out of our experience in actual life situations, though not absolute, is knowledge nonetheless. The norms arising out of such actual life situations do not exist in a social vacuum, but are effective as real sanctions for conduct.'[9] Clearly, Mannheim, writing about knowledge in this context, was mainly concerned with the sources of knowledge which claim to establish 'truths' as norms or guides for action; hence he was most concerned with those whole systems or modes of thought which appear as *Weltanschauung*. Moreover, in a rapidly changing world he was concerned with arriving at the 'truth' for today rather than with 'truth' as an absolute. He said, 'Hence it has become extremely questionable whether, in the flux of life, it is a genuinely worthwhile intellectual problem to seek to discover fixed and immutable ideas or absolutes. It is a more worthy intellectual task perhaps to learn to think dynamically and relationally rather than statically.'[10]

What did Mannheim mean when he referred to relational thinking? In answering this question and in understanding Mannheim it is important not to underestimate the distinction he made between relative and relational knowledge and thought. The distinction is as follows. According to the relativist position there are no 'truths'. However, it is a very simple although trivial exercise to demonstrate that the relativist position cannot logically be held since according to its own claim it must be relative, therefore not 'true'. Mannheim did not take the relativist position. On the contrary he believed that there *were* 'truths' to be unfolded and promulgated. But, as we have seen, he also held that what passed for knowledge was obscured by the social origins of that knowledge, that 'truth' was always in process and not static, and that epistemology, which itself worked within a mental set, was of little help in identifying 'truth' as distinct from ideology.

Mannheim's own truth-seeking sociology of knowledge did incorporate tests of validity or truth. According to him the principal

[9] *Ibid.*, p. 76.
[10] *Ibid.*, p. 77.

criterion of objective knowledge should be the degree to which knowledge corresponds with reality in the sense that with the aid of such knowledge men are able to live in society and adjust it to meet changing circumstances. Thus, on ethics, he said, 'An ethical attitude is invalid if it is oriented with reference to norms with which action in a given historical setting, even with the best of intentions cannot comply!'[11] And, on the validity of theory in the social sciences, he wrote, 'A theory then is wrong if in a given practical situation it uses concepts and categories which, if taken seriously, would prevent man from adjusting himself at that historical stage.'[12] However, as already pointed out in relation to truth as *Weltanschauung*, theory in this context does not refer to a merely particularist theory such as the theory of the firm or a theory of structural differentiation, it refers to grand theory as guides to action, which, incidentally, includes inaction.

In order to elaborate his criterion of truth and his own relational standpoint Mannheim once more appealed to the problems and techniques of painting. That he misunderstood the central problem of painting is of little importance for our case which claims that Mannheim was clearly moving towards a multi-perspectival view of history similar to that developed in painting by the analytical cubists although he also sought to isolate the best of all possible perspectives. He wrote:

The controversy concerning visually perceived objects (which in the nature of the case, can be viewed only in perspective) is not settled by setting up a non perspectivist view (which is impossible). It is settled rather by understanding, in the light of one's own positionally determined vision, why the object appeared differently to one in a different position. Likewise, in our field also, objectivity is brought about by the translation of one perspective into the terms of another. It is natural that here we must ask which of the various points of view is the best. And for this too there is a criterion. As in the case of visual perspective, where certain positions have the advantage of revealing the decisive features of the object, so here pre-eminence is given to that perspective which gives greatest comprehensiveness and the greatest fruitfulness in dealing with empirical materials.[13]

[11] *Ibid.*, p. 84.
[12] *Ibid.*, p. 85.
[13] *Ibid.*, p. 271.

Little needs to be said by way of interpreting Mannheim's very clear position. He believed that objectivity in the pursuit of knowledge is best achieved with the aid of that conceptual framework which is most comprehensive in its coverage, that is, in its ability to encompass a variety of perspectives and empirical data. The way in which it is to encompass those perspectives and data is fundamentally utilitarian. Objective knowledge for Mannheim is that which permits men to manipulate and adapt society for their own ends without destroying that society. Although it is not piecemeal knowledge it does seem to rely on consensus as well as comprehensiveness for its validation. One might almost say that objective knowledge in Mannheim is social democratic knowledge. However, to designate it as such would be to place Mannheim's objective knowledge back into the category of an ideological or utopian mode of thought according to the investigator's assessment of the 'reality' of the circumstances in which the thought arose.

This was Mannheim's dilemma. If, as he claimed, all knowledge has either an ideological or a utopian component or some mix of both and is, thereby, systematically distorted knowledge, how is it possible to determine the objective component in his own system, the sociology of knowledge? His own utilitarian test is itself inadequate since the test of utility is itself a subjective one. Accordingly, the question any utilitarian must always answer is, useful to whom and for what? And no one, not even Mannheim, can avoid this question by replying, 'useful to Man', since in any society there are only men organized in a variety of social groups and, thereby, at least from a Marxist standpoint, potentially antagonistic to one another, therefore with differing views about utility.[14]

[14] At a recent seminar on Ideology at the University of New England, Dr K. R. Minogue defended himself against the charge that his own views were ideological/utopian in Mannheim's sense by arguing that his paper had been purely 'academic' and had no implications for practice, that is, his thought was without social utility. Apart from the fact that it led him to act, in the sense that delivering a seminar and taking part in discussion was action designed to influence the thought of other participants, the fact remains that not to act is to act, and, that a system of thought, the message of which is not to act, is a system of thought with implications for practice. If Minogue's system of thought were to be adopted by all thinkers there would be a divorce between thought and practice and no guides to action provided by thought. In such an abdication of reason lies confusion.

Mannheim was aware of this dilemma and himself asked the question, 'How are we to conceive of the social and political bearers of whatever synthesis there is?' His own unequivocal answer was, 'If it be once granted that political thought is always bound up with a position in the social order, it is only consistent to suppose that the tendency towards a total synthesis must be embodied in the will of some group'.[15] Thus, in the Mannheimian system it is necessary not only to devise tests of objective knowledge and to peel off the ideological or utopian layers of knowledge but crucially important also to conjure up a set of testers above or outside the main social groups in society. Only these testers would be in a position to make judgements about the correctness or utility of knowledge in any historical epoch. And, in the process, only they would be able objectively to certify the connection between social groups and thought and determine what was ideological and what utopian knowledge. Only they would be able to determine what was truly the consciousness of any social group or class. This set of testers Mannheim found conveniently to hand in Alfred Weber's 'Socially Unattached Intelligentsia' (*Freischwebende Intelligenz*) differentiated from other groups, but bound to each other, by education. They are worth looking at.

According to Mannheim:

The only concern which this stratum has in common is the intellectual process: the continuing endeavour to take stock, to diagnose and prognosticate, to discover choices when they arise, and to understand and locate the various points of view rather than to reject or assimilate them. Intellectuals have often attempted to champion special ideologies with the self-abandon of persons who seek to attain an identity they do not possess. They have tried to submerge in the working class movement or to become musketeers of free enterprise, only to discover that they have thereby lost more than they hoped to win. The apparent lack of social identity is a unique opportunity for the intellectual ... A group such as the intelligentsia abdicates only when it surrenders its self-awareness and its capacity to perform in its own peculiar way. It cannot form a special group ideology of its own. It must remain as critical of itself as of all other groups.[16]

I interpret this passage to mean that the socially unattached

---

[15] Karl Mannheim, *Ideology and Utopia*, p. 136.
[16] Quoted in K. H. Wolff, *From Karl Mannheim* (New York, 1971), p. xc.

intellectual (in our case these would be social historians) must evaluate the prevailing stock of ideologies and utopias and, presumably, the prevailing stock of ideological and utopian versions of history, according to the criteria indicated above and, having determined what is to be regarded as proper objective knowledge, promulgate it as such. It seems that a member of the intelligentsia, such as a social historian, does not have to act, merely to think. This is because action implies commitment while commitment implies immersion in some ideological or utopian mode of thought. Thus, a committed intellectual or social historian is open to the charge by other members of the socially unattached intelligentsia, and by other historians, of possessing only systematically distorted knowledge, that is, ideology.

If we try to match this idea about the proper function of the intelligentsia with the social reallity of the position of the intelligentsia in the last fifty years, the utopian element in Mannheim's sociology of knowledge will become immediately apparent. However, Mannheim's utopianism may be no bad thing in his sociology since Mannheim himself considered a utopian element in thought crucial for man's ability to shape his own history. Nevertheless, the concept of the function of the socially unattached intelligentsia does carry strong undertones of the Hegelian Universal Class and smacks of the idealistic materialism of Feuerbach and those young Hegelians who were vigorously attacked by Marx in his *Theses on Feuerbach* for their failure to understand the notion of praxis – a failure of comprehension which may also be charged against Mannheim. And I wonder whether Mannheim's socially unattached intellectual, thoughtful and uncommitted, is really Weber's bureaucrat in disguise (which is what Mannheim himself became in the last years of his life).

But, as far as the social historian and his problem is concerned, Mannheim does ignore the fact that the educator, the social historian, must himself be educated within an existing educational and social system characterized by a maze of ideological and utopian positions through which he must try to steer an objective, i.e., truth-seeking, path. For, while it may be good for the ego of the social historian to read in Mannheim that as a member of the socially unattached intelligentsia, he is his own salvation, it does not solve the problem of how correctly to attach thought, attitudes

and belief to social class or to any other component of social structure. And, if one takes the socially unattached intelligentsia out of Mannheim's system *all* knowledge must remain relative, i.e., systematically distorted, and Mannheim's distinction between relative and relational must become blurred since, the intelligentsia apart, Mannheim offers no new way of determining the ideological or utopian content of knowledge.

Thus, Mannheim's epistemological claims for the sociology of knowledge appear to have no substance and little remains of Mannheim's system which might be useful to the social historian. This valuable residue includes some concepts, such as ideology and utopia, his ideas about objective, expressive and documentary meaning, some guides to procedures such as the methods of philology and the history of art and, of course, the process of inquiry itself. Because Mannheim offers no better analytical methods for demonstrating the correct connections between thought and the experience of social groups, including social classes, and no criteria for providing controls, his system in the end is disappointing. It highlights crucial problems but, without the socially unattached intelligentsia, cannot solve them. The social historian is left to his own devices and it looks as if Hume was right when he wrote 'Thus all probable reasoning is nothing but a species of sensation. 'Tis not solely in poetry and music, we must follow our taste and sentiment, but likewise in philosophy.'[17] And, I add, in social history, too.

Of course some social historians may not be unduly worried about their inability to make 'truth' claims for the results of their labours, and we should be excused from taking them seriously. However, I suspect that most social historians do claim more than a sort of poetic antiquarianism for their work. For example, many social historians have gone and still go to great lengths to 'disprove' Marx and various schools of Marxist historians and, by implication to 'prove' the truth of some other image or version of the past. Indeed, in some areas of inquiry, such as social class in history, it is almost mandatory to attack some private notion of Marx's historical writing. And the most popular versions of the past among

[17] David Hume, *A Treatise on Human Nature* (London, 1739), p. 103.

historians, including social historians, are those which flow consciously or unconsciously from a positivist position, hence the views about class of historians such as Briggs and Best, to be discussed in chapter 5. However, since the variants of the positivist position are too many to consider here and because Maurice Mandelbaum wrote to attack Mannheim's relational approach, I would like to make a few observations about positivist history in a short discussion of Mandelbaum's *The Problem of Historical Knowledge*.

The Problem of Historical Knowledge was Mandelbaum's answer to relativism. In it he reassured historians by re-asserting the claims of positivist history. He focused his attack on the historical relativism of Groce, Dilthey and, above all, of Mannheim, and on their shared view that every historical account is the result of an interpretative act, and that the interpretative principle to be found in that *act* is a product of the historian's own interests. Needless to say, such a summary of Mannheim's relational sociology of knowledge is grossly misleading. As we have seen it merely states the starting point of Mannheim's inquiry. Nevertheless, what Mandelbaum had to say about the counter-relativist arguments of Simmel, Richert, Scheler and Troeltsch does show that historical objectivity cannot be rescued by giving up the ideal of objective knowledge in its usual sense. All of these writers argued that historical knowledge need not, and indeed could not, be a copy of reality. But they did argue that what made historical knowledge objective was an *a priori* valid element, some universal essence or value which existed in men and thereby in historians and so underpinned their interpretations as to give to history a value-based objectivity. The relativist short answer to such claims is simply to ask for an objective demonstration of the existence of universal essences or values which do result in unchallengeable objective history.

Mandelbaum, however, pursued his own attack on what he identified as Mannheim's relativism by using a correspondence theory of truth in which he distinguished statements of facts from judgements of value about the facts. Thus, the statement, 'Caesar crossed the Rubicon' corresponds with a real event which is supported by contemporary verification. Consequently, it may be argued, the historian neither invents nor shapes his observation of the event according to his interests and, 'it is fallacious to hold that valuational judgements determine the content of historical knowledge'.[18] Furthermore, said Mandelbaum, the historian can put forward causal explanations of past events with the aid of knowledge about human behaviour which is not itself value based: problems of value only arise if historians, as they frequently do, pass from statements of fact to statements of value. In fact, Mandelbaum's basic assumption was 'that the order to be found in nature and history as they are known to us may really characterize the events of the world independently of the mind's activity'[19] and that 'the facts seem to have an arrangement and order of their own'.[20] Accordingly he held the view that the facts speak for themselves according to an order which inheres in the facts themselves and which can only be elicited by the study of the facts themselves. Thus, 'historical events in themselves possess a structure which the historian apprehends and does not invent'[21] and historical understanding is almost wholly concerned with statements considered as statements of facts.

But the problem for the practising social historian is that many events are not supported by contemporary verification and only a fraction of 'reality' is verified. Thus, while there is much awaiting contemporary verification, more will never be verified. Consequently, 'true' statements about the past, such as 'Caesar crossed the Rubicon' are relatively few. This would not matter if history was merely a chronicle of statements about some events chronologically ordered. It does matter if history, social history, attempts to be synthetic, interpretative, comprehensive and true – and therefore, a guide to action. Indeed, Mandelbaum himself recognized this problem and argued for the importance to the historian of 'working hypotheses' and 'historical principles', plus an understanding of 'the principles of human motivation' as well as 'the principles of economics, of politics [and] of ethnology'. With that admission Mandelbaum's wheel of knowledge turned full circle; the natural ordering of the statements of fact about events was in fact to be seen filtered through the principles of other social sciences; psychology, psychoanalysis, economics, political science,

---

[18] Maurice Mandelbaum, *The Problem of Historical Knowledge* (New York, 1967), p. 190.
[19] *Ibid.*, p. 202.
[20] *Ibid.*, pp. 203–4.
[21] *Ibid.*, p. 202.

ethnology and many others, none of which is value free. Thus, what Mandelbaum assumed – 'that the order to be found in nature and history as they are known to us may really characterize the events of the world independently of the mind's activity' – is what has to be demonstrated. This is the puzzle that Mannheim unsuccessfully endeavoured to solve with the aid of the sociology of knowledge. Mandelbaum's own failure to demonstrate the objectivity of historical knowledge places him in good company. But it still leaves the social historian to his own devices.

Nearly thirty-five years later, after a massive and stimulating exploration of the flight from reason in our own time, Mandelbaum now appears to pin his belief in the possibility of objective knowledge to the existence in Man of an autonomous curiosity or intelligence as an innate drive, like hunger and sex, which demands to be satisfied irrespective of either will or conditioning.[22] He claims that this is *a* factor which must be taken into account when analysing the nature of thought. But this autonomous curiosity has something of the character of those universal essences which Mandelbaum found unacceptable in the writings of earlier counter-relativists. Yet even if one were to concede the existence of an innate autonomous curiosity, experience still suggests it is unequally distributed or manifested throughout human society as well as differently focused and directed as between societies. Therefore, the search for objective knowledge would still require effort to distinguish, in the solutions such an 'autonomous' curiosity might offer to its questionings, those elements in thought which Mannheim labelled ideological and utopian. Presumably this would be a task for those most richly endowed with autonomous curiosity – a group such as Mannheim's socially unattached intelligentsia, perhaps? And of them I have already written. In this search for objective knowledge my sympathies are all with Mandelbaum and Mannheim, but I find both their solutions disappointing, particularly as far as the work of the social historian is concerned.

Nevertheless, various connections between thought and experience have been and will continue to be made by social historians. And properly so. For if they cease to make them, their

[22] Maurice Mandelbaum, *History, Man, and Reason* (Baltimore and London, 1971) chapter 16.

discipline will revert to that mere chronicle and antiquarianism from which it sprang, and to which theorists such as the early Mandelbaum would condemn them. This is perhaps reason enough for pursuing our inquiry thus far and insisting upon the need for explicit theorizing and the search for conceptual clarity. Many historians, however, find in this absence of certain clear procedures for establishing correct or true connections sufficient reason for rejecting both. No doubt they would take heart from the disappointing outcome of our examination of Mannheim and the sociology of knowledge. They should not be too hasty. To reject the need for explicit theorizing and conceptual clarity and to adopt a merely empirical and particularist stance in selecting and pursuing a course of inquiry is also to adopt a theoretical position which is even more obscurantist and damaging to serious historical inquiry. Where concepts, categories and explanatory systems are used, as indeed they must be used, and only implicit assumptions are made about them, then *ad hoc* changes in terminology and concepts may be introduced to glide across difficulties in interpretation and argumentation to make it difficult, if not impossible, to follow the main thrust of an argument. Such loose procedures also frequently allow contradictory positions to be upheld with equal conviction. Furthermore, the empirical and particularist social historian, if left to his own devices, may well argue that social history can best be written by having regard to the uniqueness of each person either as an individual capable of rational free choice or as the psychologically determined product of a unique set of circumstances. Should he do so he should recognize that he intends to work within a generalized view, which could be theoretically stated, of the nature of man, and that he begins his inquiry from an *a priori* position in regard to the historical process. This *a priori* position, which cannot be demonstrated merely by reference to the histories particularist historians write, may be stated as follows: each individual is in a class of his own in a system in which relationships between classes (of one) are considered unique to each set of classes (of one) under scrutiny. The corollary of such an approach to history is that history is biography and that there can be no social history until *all* biographies have been written in relation to each other. When that has been done then the *a priori* assumption might be verified. Of course in the meantime some prior sampling technique could be used. To do that, however, would require some rigorous explicit theorizing about who to include in the appropriate sample. In short, if empirical and particularist historians who reject the need for explicit theorizing and conceptual clarity really believe that history is biography they should be called upon to say so. If they do not, they should be called upon to indicate the criteria they use for selecting the persons and issues upon which they write and the bases for those causal explanations they offer.

To this challenge some other empirical historians might reply that there is little point in such an exercise since the clarification of procedures and concepts does not reveal or teach anything about history. Further, they might emphasize that a clarified concept such as class, social class, class consciousness may become reified and be placed above or imposed upon the 'real' historical process and thus obscure it. This is true. It is equally true of all historical writing. And Mannheim's and our excursion into the sociology of knowledge was prompted by such considerations. Of course concepts do not teach anything about history. No more do a saw and a hammer make a box. Concepts are intellectual tools with the help of which one learns, describes and explains and which one uses to generate, from surviving artefacts, images of the past. Of course such concepts may be reified. We have already mentioned the dangers of conceptual simplification and reification: they are exemplified in the East European story about two comrades in 1968 discussing the nature of capitalism. The story also shows that concepts should not be thought of as definitions and cannot usefully be reduced to definitions and, therefore, that the central issues discussed in this book cannot be dismissed as matters of 'mere' semantics unconnected with the real business of historians.[23] The scene, two comrades talking.

Comrade I   What is the definition of capitalism?
Comrade II That's easy, it is the exploitation of man by man.
Comrade I   Very good. Now, what is the definition of Communism?
Comrade II It is the reverse!

One major problem with history is that it is already replete with

---

[23]Cf. J. T. Ward, *Chartism* (London, 1973), p. 84 and especially Raymond Williams, *Keywords* (Glasgow, 1976), pp. 9–24 and pp. 51–9.

such simplified and reified concepts; 'capitalism' and 'Communism' are two, but there are others: 'the Renaissance', 'the Eighteenth Century', 'the Age of Reason', *'laissez faire'*, 'the Middle Class', 'the Working Class', 'the Industrial Revolution', 'Feudalism', *'ancien régime'*, 'the French Revolution', 'Liberalism', 'Nationalism', 'the First World War', 'Imperialism', 'Romanticism'; the list is endless, and in much historical writing these concepts and even the centuries themselves act to effect change. If explicit theorizing and an emphasis on conceptual clarification does nothing more than help make explicit the assumptions and generalizations buried in such concepts which are already used to describe and explain the past, it will have made a valuable contribution to the study and writing of social history. If in the process it helps to generate new insight and brings 'truth' a little closer it will have achieved much. Social history must be theoretically and conceptually as well as chronologically rigorous.

This chapter began with the observation that Marx's concept of *class* consciousness embodied the notion of true, non-ideological knowledge and that the antithesis of *class* consciousness was ideological knowledge. It was claimed that the Marxian interpretation of the connection between social class and thought is held by Marxists to be true. However, as we shall see in chapter 4 there are conflicting claims about the connection between thought and social class. The discussion then focused on Mannheim and the sociology of knowledge. Mannheim's thought was placed in its social context. It was said that his system contained a twofold thrust, one to gain knowledge of the social origins of knowledge, the other to use that knowledge as an aid in distinguishing ideological and utopian thought from objective knowledge. These two aspects of his system were interwoven and of considerable interest to historians of class. In Mannheim's system the tests of the validity of a theory were found to be comprehensiveness and utility, that is the degree to which knowledge corresponded with reality in the sense that with the aid of such knowledge men would be able to live in society and adjust it to meet changing circumstances. As well as establishing criteria for evaluating knowledge, Mannheim charged the socially unattached intelligentsia with the task of evaluation in order to ensure objectivity. It was argued, however, that the educators, the socially unattached intelligentsia, the social historians, had themselves to be educated and were therefore in no real sense unattached. Thus, there was no new way to ensure objectivity and Mannheim's system was found to be disappointing. It had highlighted the crucial nature of the problem but left it unresolved and the social historian to his own devices. Mandelbaum's defence of the correspondence test of objectivity in history was also considered and found wanting. While the result of the discussion of Mannheim may have been disappointing, it was claimed that the process of inquiry should prove fruitful and reinforce the need for historians to be theoretically and conceptually as well as chronologically rigorous. And it is with that idea in mind that in the next two chapters I turn to an examination of some of the ways in which recent historians have used the concept 'class' in their explanations of recent English history.

3

'The World we have Lost' and how Class and Class Consciousness can help to Find it

The separate individuals form a class only insofar as they have to carry on a common battle against another class.

Marx/Engels, *The German Ideology*
(Moscow, 1964), p. 68

Thus, all societies of orders are based on consensus, a tacit agreement that derives from the particular set of circumstances in which society finds itself at a given time. This consensus determines the most important social function, namely the one that establishes one social group at the top of the social hierarchy. . . . A number of factors contrive to perpetuate this principle. There is the general interest that everyone has in maintaining the social order together with fear of the dangers created by a major upheaval. Or there is force of habit which makes it difficult to conceive of another social order. Then there are the gradually evolving links between the existing social order and a whole intellectual system which lends it rational justification. And lastly, there is the tendency of the dominant group in society constantly to engineer the same circumstances which originally gave rise to a given type of social stratification like, for example, wars in the case of feudal society.

Roland Mousnier, *Social Hierarchies*
(London, 1973), pp. 23–4

Peter Laslett's *The World we have Lost* is an unusual piece of historical writing. That is to say that it has offended both conventional and Marxist historians. Laslett would like historians to study what he calls 'Social Structural History'. The chief characteristics of this form of history are to be the study of demography, particularly the size and composition of the family, and the use of the comparative method. Accordingly Laslett claims that England in the late seventeenth century will be best understood by comparing its social structure with that of similar societies and with the social structure of England at points later in time. He makes such comparisons in his book. However, when he makes these comparisons between late seventeenth-century and early twentieth-century England, he makes no attempt to bridge the gap in time by the use of the traditional narrative form of historical writing. Therefore, because Social Structural History eschews narrative as well as theoretical analysis and is almost wholly comparative it is compelled to remain at the level of descriptive history. Nevertheless, Laslett does seek to do more than describe the social structure of England and he attempts to explain certain phenomena and aspects of social change. In doing so he moves into areas of the sociology of knowledge as mapped out by Karl Mannheim.

Perhaps the main claim that Laslett makes for the product of his researches in Social Structural History is that the organizing categories of traditional and Marxist historiography are irrelevant and misleading for the period with which he is mainly concerned, which is the late seventeenth and early eighteenth centuries. He argues that the categories of Marxist historiography – ancient, feudal, capitalist or bourgeois – and the notion of class conflict which they imply, distort our explanations of social change in that period. He writes:

Capitalism, then, is an incomplete description and historians' language is marked by many other incomplete descriptions too, of which their use of the names of countries is but one example. The historical distortions which came about from the use of capitalism, the rise of the bourgeoisie, and so on, have arisen from a faulty sense of proportion which we can only now begin to correct. With 'the capitalism changed the world' way of thinking goes a division of history into the ancient, feudal and bourgeois eras or stages. But the facts of the contrast which has to be drawn between the world we have lost and the world we now inhabit tends to make all such divisions as these into subdivisions. The time has now come to divide our European past in a simpler way, with industrialization as the point of critical change.[1]

[1] Peter Laslett, *The World we have Lost* (London, 1971), p. 21.

Thus, in Laslett's social structural history there are two epochs; the pre-industrial and the industrial. The pre-industrial epoch is 'the world we have lost', and the industrial is that which we have. A corollary of his simple division into pre-industrial and industrial epochs is Laslett's categorization of societies as either one-class or multi-class societies. According to this categorization pre-industrial England, England before about 1780, was a one-class society. However, like all societies, including other pre-industrial ones, it was scarred by social conflict and internal war. In Laslett's view the recent period of social breakdown, the English Civil War and Interregnum 1642–60, is best explained as the product of a superimposition of many internal conflicts rather than as the consequence of class conflict between two antagonistic and homogeneous classes, the outcome of which is believed to have transformed the economy and society in the interests of the successful or dominant class.

Clearly, Laslett's social structural history is at odds with what Laslett and most historians take to be the central position of Marx and Marxist historians on the nature of seventeenth-century society and on the central transforming agent at work in that society. That, in the absence of both narrative and analytical explanation, Laslett does not offer an alternative explanation of change, does not alter the significance of his charge about the incorrectness of what is generally accepted as the Marxist explanation nor does it weaken his claim to describe the social structure of England more accurately than other historians. Therefore, the issue I would like to explore, in the context of this book, is the way in which Laslett arrives at the one-class concept and what he means by it and then to question whether it allows for an adequate description of late seventeenth- and early eighteenth-century English society.

Laslett claims to base his analysis of the social structure of seventeenth-century England on Weber's distinction between class, status and power as most recently discussed and clarified by W. G. Runciman.[2] Briefly the distinctions between class, status and power made in this assessment amount to the following. *Class* is determined by three things. First, the position men have in the industrial process either as possessors or non-possessors of capital.

[2] W. G. Runciman, *Relative Deprivation and Social Justice* (London, 1972), pp. 42–61.

Second, by the opportunities of economic advantage the possession of capital provides them. Third, by *work-situation*. This latter distinguishes manual workers from those with clerical or managerial skills and tasks. *Status*, however, is conferred by such things as social estimation and prestige. While these are generally closely related to class they are not synonymous with it. They are frequently deeply rooted, widespread and easily seen in speech patterns, accent, dress, housing, leisure and cultural preferences. *Power* as a separate category in Weber's writings was by no means so clearly defined as *class* and *status*. Indeed, Weber usually described the relative power of classes and strata rather than the existence of a hierarchy based on power alone. Of modern sociologists it is Ralf Dahrendorf who comes closest to defining power groupings according to positions of authority and subordination independent of either *class* or *status* as defined above.

These Weberian distinctions between *class*, *status* and *power* appear to have only analytical or theoretical value in Laslett's work for, when he uses class as a working concept he uses it in a sense which is closer to a Marxian rather than to a Weberian definition. He writes:

> When the word class is used, in conversation and by historians it does not merely refer to status or to respect. The distribution of wealth and power is also at issue. This is obvious when the phrase class-conflict appears. For it nearly always seems to imply the clash of groups of persons defending and enhancing not simply a common status but also interest and power. The emphasis is on the solidarity of classes as groups of persons which act in championship of their conflicting aims. Such classes have a further characteristic in ordinary usage: they are nation-wide.[3]

Clearly, in this attempt at a holistic definition of class Laslett uses the concept class differently from Weber but in a sense which, while it does not incorporate the whole of the Marxian notion of *class* consciousness, comes close to doing so. It is according to the test of class in this near Marxian sense of class consciousness that Laslett claims that there was only one class, the ruling landowning class, in pre-industrial England. All other groups were simply status groups, i.e., groups granted differing degrees of estimation and prestige and distinguished by a wide range of cultural

[3] Peter Laslett, *The World we have Lost*, p. 23.

differences. The significance of Laslett's one-class notion is that he uses it to deny the existence of the bourgeoisie as a separate homogeneous class antagonistic towards the landed ruling class either before, during or after the English Civil War. Moreover, it is the basis for his opinion that conflict in the seventeenth century was not class conflict and that the conflicts that marked that century were as acute as they were only because of the superimposition of a variety of conflicts between segments of the ruling class, the type of endemic conflict characteristic of all societies, pre-industrial as well as industrial. On the other hand, Laslett does appear to accept the notion that what we choose to call bourgeois values, which are the values of a fully possessive market society, had permeated the whole of the landed ruling class. Of course, if this was so and the landed ruling class was completely bourgeois one would expect to find an antagonistic class of workers already in existence, but Laslett also denies the existence of such a class. In short, Laslett finds that conflict was intra-class rather than inter-class and that, 'Social change and development in the pre-industrial world need not, therefore, be thought of in terms of classes which rise, conflict and fall.'[4]

As already noted Laslett adopts as his actual working definition of class something close to the most rigorous Marxist definition, and it is with the help of this definition that he claims to have discovered only one class. However, as the discussion in chapter 1 should have made clear, the rigorous Marxian definition of *class* implies a significant socio-economic element which contributes to, indeed, is essential for the creation of *class* consciousness. It is that the class with a developing class consciousness develops this consciousness via its perception that its interests are antagonistic to those of another hostile class. Marx expressed this idea in the quotation at the head of this chapter in which he said, 'The separate individuals form a class only insofar as they have to carry on a common battle against another class.' The simple point is that two classes are essential for the formation of one *class*. Indeed, as was argued in chapter 2 there can be no doubt that in Marx capital implies labour and labour implies capital; it is the essence of the dialectical process in Marx that there cannot be one without the other. Therefore, a one-class society would seem a contradiction in

----

[4] *Ibid.*, p. 39.

terminology, at least in a Marxian sense. Indeed, Laslett's own definition, which is almost Marxian, seems to recognize the importance of at least one other group for the formation of a *class*. And, elsewhere in his book he also appears to concede that perceptions by the landed ruling class of groups distinguished by the possession and non-possession of property was a fact of some importance in the formation of the class consciousness of that single landed ruling class he identifies. Certainly, if one concedes the importance of two groups or classes for the formation of class consciousness, which Laslett appears to do, then there is a clear contradiction in Laslett's terminology; a contradiction which could only be avoided by a clarification of Laslett's concept of class which took cognizance of the two components of class, i.e., class in itself and class for itself, or class as stratum and class as class consciousness. Then it might be shown that, while there was no bourgeoisie as described by Marx in the *Communist Manifesto*, there were groups or strata comprising manufacturing or commercial interests at various stages of development of consciousness as well as clear signs of a development of consciousness among some sections of the landowning elite that led to their class consciousness being indistinguishable from that traditionally attributed to a bourgeoisie. It could also be shown that other groups of smaller landowners and men with a variety of customary titles did not share the political and economic values of their superiors. In short Laslett's notion of a one-class society serves to conceal more than it reveals.

It is difficult, too, to understand the historical or conceptual significance in Laslett's wish to retain a vaguely Marxian class terminology to describe a society which might be better thought of as class-less rather than one-class, particularly as Laslett believes a one-class society to be devoid of the *class* conflict inherent in those class societies we usually describe in the class terminology he wishes to retain. However, since it is the nature of the society described that really matters and since the terminology used to describe it should be able to subsume that nature without distorting it, it is important to be clear about the broad outlines of its real social structure. What follows, therefore, is a short summary of the main features of the social structure of England in the late seventeenth and early eighteenth centuries based on property relationships.

In England in the second half of the seventeenth century there were three broad groups distinguished by the possession or non-possession of landed property. The first, the ruling group, was very small. It consisted of some 4,000 families, 16,000 families if the category 'gentleman' is used as the dividing line. The Crown and the Church, as members of this ruling group, held between 5 to 10 per cent of the land. Next came some 160 peers with an average landed income of about £5,000 per annum which represented an average acreage of nearly 20,000. Peers, however, may only have been about half of all great landowners who collectively occupied about 15 to 20 per cent of all land. The rest of the ruling group, the gentry, occupied 40 to 50 per cent of the land on estates ranging from 300 acres upwards. This left about one third of the land to be divided between about 160,000 freeholder families with title to small acreages ranging, perhaps, from 60 to 100 acres. There were also a few remaining copyholders holding very small acreages on leases for ninety-nine years or three lives. These freeholders and copyholders comprised the second group, some of whom might be thought of as a true peasantry. However, there were also about 150,000 tenant farmers working land which they leased from the larger landowners. These men were capitalist farmers rather than peasants. The third group consisted of the mass of the population. Its members were neither landowners, peasants nor capitalist farmers. Even when they worked on the land they worked mainly for wages or payments in kind.[5]

In the interstices of this largely rural society, in towns like Bristol, York, Norwich and in London there were urban, commercial and manufacturing worlds where property took the form of real estate and moveables rather than landed property.[6]

[5]See the discussion in F. M. L. Thompson, The social distribution of landed property in England since the sixteenth century, *English Historical Review*, Second Series, **XIX** (3), 1966, pp. 505–17 and J. P. Cooper, The social distribution of land and men in England, 1436–1700, *English Historical Review*, Second Series, **XX** (3), 1967. For the question of the peasantry see Alan Macfarlane, *The Origins of English Individualism* (Oxford, 1978).

[6]Richard Grassby, The personal wealth of the business community in seventeenth century England, *English Historical Review*, Second Series **XXIII** (2), 1970. This shows that only four of London's Alderman, after a lifetime of effort, possessed wealth estimated at over £250,000 whereas William Pulteney, Earl of Bath, is reputed to have left £1.6m and James Brydges, Duke of Chandos made £600,000 out of the office of paymaster and at the height of his career was probably a millionaire.

There was also the Crown and members of its administration. The latter possessed many of the attributes of bureaucrats in an absolutist state and had property in position and place at court and in other public offices.

However, in the early eighteenth century, there were many among the propertied who were difficult to place in terms of their claims to property; men like James Brydges, William Cadogan and William Pulteney who were government functionaries and entrepreneurs as well as landowners. In short, while land remained the predominant form of property and the basis for distinguishing those with wealth, status and power from those without, there was a differentiation of forms of property and a consequent tendency towards a fragmentation of the ruling group as well as a comparable fragmentation of the non-propertied wage-earning group. Consequently, there were a variety of strata defined by this complex of property relations, strata which might be thought of as classes in the merely descriptive sense employed by Marx and Weber. However, I prefer to use the term stratum for this initial sorting and it is this term that I will use in the rest of this chapter. These different strata were accorded different status by custom and sometimes by law.

England, therefore, possessed a social structure characterized by many strata based on different forms of property, each with a different measure of ascribed status and power. First there was the ruling land-based stratum already deeply imbued with the values of a market society; many of its members were concerned to extract from their lands the maximum revenue either in the form of agricultural rents, ground rents from real estate development, or profits from mining and commercial ventures. Consequently, many were increasingly at odds with the claims of the Crown and the absolutist state as well as with the customary claims of cottagers, copyholders and life-holders. This stratum came very close to developing in the fullest sense as a homogeneous class of agrarian capitalists. However, the rights to property which members of this ruling land-based stratum claimed for themselves also served the interests of those groups developing in the interstices of the old society. Consequently, while landowners continued to change themselves from landlords to landowners they also helped generate new interest groups or strata such as the *monied interest*.

This monied interest was basically a product of the military role of the Sovereign in the early eighteenth century. Although its members were drawn from several strata it, too, came close to developing as a class. The monied interest was encouraged and protected by the Sovereign, or what we would now call the state, much to the discomfort and dissatisfaction of other large sections of the ruling class.

The dissatisfaction of these disgruntled landowners, mostly of the lesser sort, was exploited first by Bolingbroke, then by Pulteney. There were occasions when they, too, appeared to be developing into a third class. The nature and strength of the class perception of some of the members of this group is illustrated by the outburst of the anonymous author of *A Defence of The People*, published in London in 1744. Replying to the charge that opposition to the Walpole administration had been merely factitious and, therefore, politically insincere he wrote in order to emphasize their political unity and significance:

In the Name of *God*, what were our perpetual Struggles against Standing-Armies, Foreign Subsidies, Votes of Credit, *Hanover*-Jobs, General Excises, Violations of the Sinking Fund, Exorbitant Taxes, Governing by parties, Oppressive Laws, and every other Ingredient that was necessary to make up one comprehensive SYSTEM of Corruption above, and slavery below?

Clearly this outburst arose from and reflected a perception of society that was anti-authority and virtually class based. Thus its author opposed strong ministerial government which he believed to be working in favour of the monied interest and against the interests of taxpayers, many of whom were landowners of the lesser sort. In the early eighteenth century at least the terms Whig and Tory implied real differences of interests and of ideology.

However, class formation in the sense of the formation of three separate classes within the ranks of the propertied was inhibited by two opposing influences. First, regional loyalties. For example, Underdown's study of Somerset in the seventeenth century shows beyond doubt that the loyalties of the ruling land-based stratum were largely regional.[7] When they talked of 'country' they meant 'county'. Further, different regions of the 'country' and different sections of the ruling stratum had different perceptions of what that

[7] David Underdown, *Somerset in the Civil War and Interregnum* (Newton Abbot, 1973).

loyalty to 'country' involved. Hence that state of social and political anarchy in that part of England in the period 1640–53 which forced the generation of another class consciousness among the artisans and small holders in the eastern part of Somerset and in Dorset marked by the rise of the Clubmen. Although, in the course of the eighteenth century regional loyalties declined in strength, regionalism continued as a divisive force into the modern period. In the eighteenth century it helped to inhibit the growth of class consciousness within many strata.

The second influence inhibiting the formation of three separate classes within the ranks of the propertied was the growth of perceptions among them about the underlying unity of interest of all men of property in the face of the propertyless. The perceptions of the latter, that ideas of Church and King and what E. P. Thompson has called the 'moral economy' of the traditional society merely kept them in subordination and without property, were also but slowly developing. This concatenation of perceptions eventually ensured that all three strata – large and lesser landowners as well as the monied interest – came to form a single ruling class as agrarian gave birth to industrial capitalism.

This short summary of the 'real' social structure of England at the turn of the seventeenth century is not significantly at odds with the account given by Marx of this period in English history. The general point is that while it describes a *class* society in process of formation it also clearly describes a society which was not yet the polarized two-class society of bourgeois and proletarians in the mature Marxian system described in chapter 2. Notably absent is the big industrial millionaire of the *Communist Manifesto* to whom Marx referred when he wrote, 'The bourgeoisie, historically, has played a most revolutionary part', and in that sense it confirms what Laslett wishes to say about the absence of a bourgeoisie and class conflict in this period. However, since it does describe a *class* society in process of formation, particularly in the agricultural sector, it also confirms what Marx had to say when he wrote:

The history of landed property, which would demonstrate the gradual transformation of the feudal landlord into the landowner, of the herediory, semi-tributory and often unfree tenant for life into the modern farmer, and of the resident serfs, bondsmen and villeins who belonged to the property into agricultural day labourers, would indeed be the history of the formation of modern capital.[8]

This quotation also shows how Marx saw the English landowners almost as surrogate or proto-bourgeoisie. But that, of course, was all they were, for their capitalistic development was by no means assured. According to Marx, the spread of capitalistic production in agriculture was repeatedly being interrupted in such a way that the, 'peasantry [was] always being reconstituted, although in smaller numbers and invariably under worse conditions'.[9] This was so because 'Not until large scale industry, based on machinery, comes, does there arise a permanent foundation for capitalist agriculture. Then the enormous majority of the rural population is fully expropriated; and therewith is completed the divorce between agriculture and rural domestic industry.'[10]

Clearly Marx's perception of the economic and social structure of England in this period was one which could accommodate the fact that vestigial 'feudal' landlords lived alongside modern landowners, that capitalist farmers employing wage labourers worked next to the remnants of a peasantry, and that capitalists and labourers in domestic industry worked in the interstices of a predominantly agricultural society, but in an agricultural society experiencing significant economic and social change. Nevertheless, he could also see that the consolidation of capitalism and, therefore, the emergence of the bourgeoisie in the form described in the *Communist Manifesto* had to wait upon industrialization based on machine technology. Furthermore, as we have already noted, Marx was also aware that in the mid-nineteenth century, when industrialization was well under way, the most extreme polarity between the propertied and the propertyless was still in the agricultural sector. And we are also aware that Marx was conscious of the absence of *class* consciousness among workers, especially agricultural labourers, at that time, and therefore that Marx was clear that scarcely any of these classes were *classes*. However, Marx also added the state and its attendant bureaucracy to his picture of the early eighteenth century, and he was aware that the developing

[8] Karl Marx, *Grundrisse*, pp. 252–3.
[9] Karl Marx, *Capital*, pp. 829–30.
[10] *Ibid.*, p. 830.

consciousnesses that were influencing political and economic events were also complex. Thus, he wrote:

With few exceptions it is the struggle between 'moneyed interest' and 'landed interest' which fills the century from 1650 to 1750, as the nobility, who lived in the grand style, observed with disgust how the userers were devouring them, and, with the building up of the modern credit system and the National Debt from the end of the seventeenth century, lording it over them in legislation etc. Already Petty [1661] speaks of the land-owners' complaints over the fall in rents in spite of land improvements. He defends the usurer against the landlord and puts money rent [interest] and land rent on the same footing.[11]

Marx himself regarded the usurer and the monied interest as principal agents in the primitive accumulation of capital through the share they took out of the revenues of landowners. However, the monied interest was important mainly at moments of the creation of capital and was characteristic of early capitalism. In the late seventeenth and early eighteenth centuries industrial and com-mercial capitalists, as new men, aligned themselves behind the landowners against the monied interest; according to Marx they went 'more or less hand in hand with the landowners against this antiquated form of capital'.[12] Therefore, the state which acted as a commanding midwife to the new capitalist society was not a state representing or reflecting the interests of the big industrial capitalists or bourgeoisie described by Marx in the *Communist Manifesto*. The notion that it was not such a state is also supported by Marx's opinion that the industrial capitalists of the Industrial Revolution were still parvenus in the late eighteenth century. Their increase in numbers paralleled the expansion of factory industry and the enlargement of the sphere of fixed or, in Marx's ter-minology, constant capital. During the period 1650–1750 the state acted more on behalf of the monied interest than any other single

[11]Karl Marx, *Theories of Surplus Value*, trans. G. A. Bonner and E. Burns (London, [1954]), p. 30, Cf. Marx to Annenkov, 28 December 1846, K. Marx and F. Engels, *Selected Correspondence* (London, 1956), p. 41: 'Hence burst two thunderclaps – the Revolutions of 1640 and 1688. All the old economic forms, the social relations corresponding to them, the political conditions which were the official expression of the old civil society, were destroyed in England.' For a modern biographer's view of the class nature of the struggle between Whig and Tory see H. T. Dickinson, *Bolinbroke* (London, 1970).
[12]*Theories of Surplus Value*, p. 30.

interest group. It seems to me that what we have here is the final heroic phase of primitive accumulation.

In short, my description of the real social structure of England in this period and Marx's notions about that society have much in common and they both point to a far more complex version of the Materialist Conception of History than Laslett appears aware of and to a far more complex transformation of social structure than can be encompassed or made to come alive through the use of his simple twofold division into pre-industrial and industrial, one-class and multi-class societies.

Perhaps the point that I am attempting to make is best grasped by recognizing two things about Marx's history. First, according to the principle of the Marxian dialectic, capitalism with its accompanying class relations that were not yet *class* relations was inherent in feudalism, particularly its English form and therefore feudalism was a progressive mode of production when compared with other modes of production and forms of society. Secondly, the transition from feudalism to capitalism was the result of long, slow, uncertain processes as society changed as a result of its own internal contradictions and generated from within itself a bourgeoisie which only became a class for itself some time *after* 1750. Thus, it is not, as Laslett would have it, that Marx believed that 'Capitalism changed the World', but that change in the Western world *was* Capitalism. And in that change of word order lies a world of difference.

Laslett's concept of a two-stage classification, pre-industrial/industrial is of little help in thinking about recent history. It is far cruder, for example, than Rostow's five-stage[13] model which has come under such devastating attack. It is also much inferior to Marx's typology of modes of production which can also be said to leave the period between 'Feudal' and 'Capitalist' societies inadequately conceptualized. For example, if, as Laslett urges them to, historians were to adopt a simple twofold division into pre-industrial and industrial epochs, they would have to equate twelfth-century England with early eighteenth-century England, since both would have to be classified as pre-industrial. Yet it is a truism that there are vast differences between the two

---

[13]W. W. Rostow, *The Stages of Economic Growth* (Cambridge, 1960).

periods, differences which by the eighteenth century had prepared the ground for industrialization: it is precisely because there are such differences that historians can hold conflicting views about the nature and processes of the intervening period. Accordingly, while it is clear that English society in the late seventeenth and early eighteenth centuries was not feudal, however one defines that term, it is equally clear that it was not industrial. Yet it was capitalist. Because it was so, the social systems and social structures in these centuries were in a state of flux. And it seems to me that comparative social statics as employed by Laslett cannot encompass what social historians would need to say to describe or account for seventeenth- and early eighteenth-century England. On the other hand a dialectical system, Marx's system when understood as Marx wrote it and not as most social historians, including Laslett, interpret it, can adequately and summarily encompass the transformation which took place. Unfortunately there is no space to enlarge on this theme in this book, and I refer interested students to my contributions to *Feudalism, Capitalism and Beyond*.[14]

Earlier I said that a one-class society would seem a contradiction in terminology. Indeed, it might be better to call Laslett's 'one-class society' a 'classless society', as Perkin does, and it is to Perkin's account of the early eighteenth century in England that I now turn.

In his account of 'The Old Society' in *The Origins of Modern English Society 1780–1880*, Harold Perkin describes Peter Laslett's 'Lost World' in terms very similar to Laslett's. However, Perkin bases his account on the work of the sociologist R. Aron instead of on Weber or Runciman, and describes the pre-industrial England of the early eighteenth century as a 'classless society'. By using this term he means to convey the idea that the political, economic and social power of the community was concentrated in a unified elite, the landed aristocracy. This unified elite stood at the head of an otherwise fragmented society; a society divided vertically into interest groups on the basis of property and patronage – the twin pillars of eighteenth century society. In Perkin's eighteenth-century society property, landed property, determined all. Landed property

[14] Eugene Kamenka and R. S. Neale (eds), *Feudalism, Capitalism and Beyond* (London, 1975).

was familial, not personal and, bound as it was by the legal constraints of the classic settled or entailed estate, it was dynastic.
Landed property gave wealth as well as status, gave entry into local
and national politics, and created opportunities for the exercise of
patronage and the binding of man to man in vertical relationships
and in what the eighteenth century called 'friendship'.

In this description of society Perking isolates and emphasizes the
regionalism of eighteenth-century society referred to earlier and, in
commenting upon Professor Habakkuk's view that 'consequently
one might suppose that England was a federation of country
houses', he asserts, 'And so indeed it was.'[15] Moreover, in Perkin's
view these regional vertical relationships based on property and
patronage were the permanent bonds of society. He opposes his
perception of eighteenth-century society as permanently bound by
these vertical regional relationships to the structure of horizontal
relationships which characterized the emergent class society of
early nineteenth-century England to which I will refer in chapter 4.
Perkin's views on the nature of eighteenth-century society are
worth examination.

Despite his claim that eighteenth-century England was classless,
Perkin is conscious of the fact that in some areas of pre-industrial
society, particularly in industrial relations, class-like relationships
characteristic of a mature capitalist society were developing.
Nevertheless, he believes in general that *class* was a weakly thing for
which men had yet to invent a word and which was not yet
manifest in the myriad political movements and factions of the
time.

Writing of patronage he sums up his perception of the social
structure of this pre-industrial England in the following:

Patronage, however, was more than a device for filling jobs, fostering
talent, and providing pensions for the deserving and the undeserving. In
the mesh of continuing loyalties of which appointments were the outward
sign, patronage brings us very close to the inner structure of the old
society. Hierarchy inherent not so much in the fortuituous juxtaposition of
degree above degree, rank upon rank, status over status, as in the permanent vertical links which, rather than the horizontal solidarities of
class, bound society together. 'Vertical friendship', a durable two-way

[15] Harold Perkin, *The Origins of Modern English Society 1780–1880* (London 1969),
p. 42.

relationship between patrons and clients permeating the whole of society, was a social nexus peculiar to the old society, less formal and inescapable than feudal homage, more personal and comprehensive than the contractual, employment relationships of capitalist 'Cash Payment'. For those who lived within its embrace it was so much an integral part of the texture of life that they had no name for it save 'friendship'.[16]

Perkin's observation that 'friendship' was a social nexus peculiar to the old society, 'less formal and inescapable than feudal homage, more personal and comprehensive than the contractual, employment relationships of capitalist "Cash Payment"', plus his awareness of the development of class-like relationships, at least between employers and employees, suggest that he is a little uneasy about the image that his description of the vertical structure of early eighteenth-century society as rigid and permanent might generate. For example, since the social structure *did* change, and Perkin aruges that it did, it is clear that it was in fact neither rigid nor permanent. Furthermore, the fact that Perkin describes patronage as a middle term between feudal homage and capitalist cash nexus implies a fluidity of relationships which belies the notion that there were 'permanent vertical links' binding society together. In fact it could be that the supposedly permanent links of feudal society were always characterized by impermanence. For example, the feudal bonds of Western European society were never as rigid as similar bonds elsewhere because there was always a strongly implied and frequently an actual contractual relationship in the act of fealty. Moreover, in England, at least since the Conquest, all forms of land holding were contractual in fact, therefore subject to alteration. In England there was no legal term for ownership, only *seisin*, and there were no *allods* as on the continent. (The full significance of these contractual relations for English economic history has only recently been shown by Alan Macfarlane in *The Origins of English Individualism*.) Moreover, while it may be true that the land market was tighter in the eighteenth century than in earlier periods, land did change hands and was used for a variety of economic purposes; social mobility was probably higher than ever before. Also, E. P. Thompson has recently argued that this changing landownership and land use did cause the fracturing of

---

[16] *Ibid.*, p. 49.

traditional social ties between the highest and the lowest social strata in the countryside and did produce violent social protest and consequential repressive legislation. This fracturing of social ties is also to be seen in the social consequences of the growth of cities like London and Bath in the first half of the eighteenth century and by the breakdown of corporate paternalism accompanying that growth. It is there, too, in the full sequence of Hogarth's comic histories. Indeed, the sensuality and vulgar vitality of the crowds in Hogarth's comic histories and his exploitation of theatrical themes and techniques in them as he criticized the ruling elites, lend weight to Thompson's argument that,

in practice, paternalism was as much theatre and gesture as effective responsibility; that so far from a warm household face-to-face relationship we can observe a studied technique of rule. While there was no novelty in the existence of a distinct plebian culture, with its own rituals, festivals, and superstitions, we have suggested that in the eighteenth century this culture was remarkably robust, greatly distanced from the polite culture, and that it no longer acknowledged, except in perfunctory ways, the hegemony of the Church.[17]

Also there is the evidence of the socially divisive effects of enclosure.

Perhaps the best way to emphasize the point I wish to make would be to offer some yardstick against which to measure the claims of both Laslett and Perkin about the absence of class or class-like relationships in England in the late seventeenth and early eighteenth centuries. In order to do so I follow Laslett's advice and adopt the comparative approach. To that end I will describe briefly the social structure of pre-modern Japan, by drawing principally on the work of Chie Nakane.

According to Chie Nakane in her book *Japanese Society*, Japanese society is today a truly *vertical* one. Her analysis is based on two basic but contrasting criteria; *attribute* and *frame*. She argues that in any society individuals may be gathered into social groups or strata on the bases of one or other criterion. Thus an analysis of society based on sorting people into groups or strata according to a common characteristic or attribute such as caste, size of income,

---

[17]E. P. Thompson, Patrician society, plebian culture, *Journal of Social History* **7** (1974), p. 397. See also E. P. Thompson, *Whigs and Hunters* (London, 1975). R. S. Neale, *Bath, 1680–1850: A Social History* (London, 1981), and Ronald Paulson, *Hogarth: His Life, Art, and Times* (Yale, 1971).

occupation, location in the production process and so on is one based on attribute. Such classification by attribute reflects a perception of society as structured around broad horizontal group-ings which may or may not be antagonistic to each other. Frame, however, is Chie Nakane's translation of the Japanese *ba*, which in normal usage means a special base on which something is placed according to a given purpose. Chie Nakane uses the term frame in her analysis of Japanese society to refer to a locality, an institution or a functional relationship in which it indicates a criterion which sets a boundary and gives a common basis to a set of individuals who are located or involved in it. She finds the outstanding example of a frame institution in the Japanese household or *ie*. Chie Nakane says of the *ie*:

In my view, the most basic element of the *ie* institution is not that form whereby the eldest son and his wife live together with the old parents, nor an authority-structure in which the household head holds the power and so on. Rather, the *ie* is a corporate residential group and, in the case of agriculture or other similar enterprises, *ie* is a managing body. The *ie* comprises household members (in most cases the family members of the household head, but others in addition to family members of the household head may be included), who thus make up the units of a dist-inguishable social group. In other words, the *ie* is a social group cons-tructed on the basis of an established frame of residence and often of management organization. What is important here is that the human relationships within this household group are thought of as more important than all other human relationships. Thus the wife and daughter-in-law who have come from outside have incomparably greater importance than one's own sisters and daughters, who have married and gone into other households. A brother, when he has built a separate house, is thought of as belonging to another unit or household; on the other hand, the son-in-law, who was once a complete outsider, takes the position of a household member and becomes more important than the brother living in another household. It is significant that the Japanese usage *uchi-no* which refers to one's place of work derives from the basic concept of *ie* and that physical presence in the household has greater weight than kinship in *ie* relationships. These facts show that basic social groups in Japan are formed on the basis of fixed *frames* rather than accord-ing to *attribute*.[18]

Thus *ie* refers to household but not to family or kin in the Western sense. It identifies a localized residential unit with close

[18]Chie Nakane, *Japanese Society* (Harmondsworth, 1973), pp. 4–5.

connections with production. In the *ie* dominant relationships are filial, that is they flow upwards from son to father. They are, therefore, vertical relationships and not relationships between people in equal or similar positions. These filial relationships are characterized by *on* which are obligations passively incurred, which can never be repaid in full and for which there is no limit. Thus, a son merely as son incurs unlimited obligation to his father merely as father. Historically this pattern of relationships and obligation extended to all Japanese and included relationships to the Emperor. In the modern period characteristics of *ie* and *on* have been extended into all areas of social and economic activity. As a result, Japanese industry is now characterized by recruitment by ability, promotion according to seniority and loyalty, lifetime employment, and the growth of large corporations providing a complete range of welfare benefits and leisure activities for all the different grades of employees. Thus it is difficult for the observer to categorize Japan as a *class* society divided into broad horizontal antagonistic groupings. On the contrary, the dominant relationships throughout Japanese society, in the family, the work-place and in the wider political society are deeply and funda-mentally vertical. the accompanying ethos of loyalty to Japan via a loyalty within a commitment to an enterprise are well conveyed in the Matsushita Worker's Song sung by both management and labour before the start of the day's work

> *Matsushita Worker's Song*
> For the building of a new Japan,
> Let's put our strength and mind together,
> Doing our best to promote production,
> Sending our goods to the people of the world,
> Endlessly and continuously,
> Like water gushing from a fountain,
> Grow, industry, grow, grow, grow,
> Harmony and Sincerity!
> Matsushita Electric![19]

In the pre-modern period, that is in the Tokugawa period of the seventeenth and early eighteenth centuries, these vertical regional

---

[19]Herman Kahn, *The Emerging Japanese Superstate* (Harmondsworth, 1971), p. 127. See also Ronald Dore, *British Factory Japanese Factory* (London, 1973), pp. 51–2 for the Hitachi Song.

relationships also underlay the apparent absolutism of the Tokugawa Bakufu. They were also the very conditions for the over-throw of the Tokugawa and the restoration of the Emperor Meiji in 1868. Since this is not the place to detail the history of the rise and fall of the Tokugawa we must be content with a brief sketch of the social and political structure of Tokugawa Japan.[20]

It is customary to divide Tokugawa society into six broad orders or ranks with the *Kuge* or Imperial family at the top followed in descending order according to attribute by: the *daimyo* – great lords; the *bushi* – warriors; the *no* – peasants; the *ko* – artisans; and the *cho* – merchants or traders. These orders, particularly the *Kuge* and *bushi* were further subdivided into a fine gradation of ranks each with special privileges and tasks. However, the *bushi*, divorced as they were from the land and compulsorily living in a handful of castle towns on rice stipends, were no longer true warriors. Conse-quently, *bushi* were frequently poor and without function or purpose. But as Carmen Blacker observes,

More galling than poverty and boredom was the strict feudal discipline, which stressed in almost every conceivable context of daily life the lower samurai's inferiority to the upper. A lower samurai always had to use honorific language when addressing an upper samurai, while an upper samurai addressed a lower in language which verged on the abusive. The lower samurai spoke with a different accent from that used by the upper, so that it was possible to tell to what class a samurai belonged if one merely heard him talking in the next room. In writing letters, certain Chinese characters had to be written in a particular style when a lower samurai was writing to an upper. An *ashigaru*, the lowest rank of samurai, always had to prostrate himself on the ground in the presence of an upper samurai. 'If he should encounter an upper samurai on the road in the rain', Fukuzawa recalled, 'he had to take off his wooden clogs and prostrate himself by the roadside.' Marriage between the two classes was strictly forbidden by clan law.[21]

The *no*, who made up some 80 to 90 per cent of the population, were also subdivided into ranks such that neither the 'village' nor the 'peasantry' can be thought of as homogeneous. Each village contained a few leading and relatively wealthy households most of

---

[20] The following paragraphs are based on T. C. Smith, *The Agrarian Origins of Modern Japan* (Stanford, 1965), and Paul Akamatsu, *Meiji 1868* (London, 1972).
[21] Carmen Blacker, *The Japanese Enlightenment* (Cambridge, 1969), p. 2.

whom were known as *jūkabu* or 'very important families'. Each large landholding family had satellite households of *nago* bound to the main household by grants of small amounts of land and dependent on it for capital in the form of seed, animal power and water. In return *nago* performed labour services for the main household at times of sowing, manuring and harvesting. *Nago* constituted between 56 per cent and 60 per cent of the rural population. In addition some large households included indentured and hereditary servants or *genin* to the extent of 10 per cent of the rural population. The structure of landholding in selected villages and the composition of a large household are illustrated in Table 1 and Diagram 1. Since all of these structures were permeated with the *on* of the filial relationships characteristic of the *ie*, the vertical nature of their inner structures should be clear.

Diagram 1 The composition of a family with a large holding in Shinano Province 1661 (ages in parentheses)

```
Family head    (41)
    wife       (39)
    son        (22)
    son        (17)
mother         (82)  cousin, son of paternal uncle    (67)
                         wife
                     cousin, son of paternal uncle    (61)
                         wife
                             son        (24)
                             son        (33)
                                 wife
                             son        (38)
                             wife    (34)
                                 son          (1)
                                 daughter    (12)
                                 daughter    (10)
                                 daughter     (8)
                     wife of deceased cousin, son of paternal uncle    (51)
                                 daughter    (21)
                                 daughter     (9)
                                 daughter     (7)
```

Source: T. C. Smith, *The Agrarian Origins of Modern Japan*, p. 7.

Table 1   Landholding in selected villages

Village	Province	Date	Number of holdings						Total
			0–5 koku	5–10 koku	10–20 koku	20–30 koku	30–40 koku	Over 40 koku	
Shimo	Echigo	1587	13	4		1			18
Kibuchi	Shinano	1666	1		5	10	5	2	23
Tsukiyama	Yamashiro	1694	8	2	2	1			13
Makuuchi	Iwashiro	1691	5	8	14	2	1		30

Figures show yield or Kokudaka of individual holdings: 1 koku = 4.96 bushels of rice or rice equivalents.

Source: T. C. Smith, *The Agrarian Origins of Modern Japan*, p. 3.

The vertical pattern of relationships is also apparent in the political structure and allegiance of Tokugawa Japan. By the early nineteenth century there were some 27 million Japanese living under a regime which was a mixture of the vestigially feudal and the bureaucratic absolutist. Thus, the Tokugawa clan, which had come to power at the battle of Sekigahara in 1600, exercised direct control through their own *daimyo* over about 15 per cent of the measured and productive land. Land controlled by sub-branches of the Tokugawa clan, such as the Nagoya, and the *daimyo fudai* (the faithful amongst the faithful), such as the *Li*, who were vassals of the Tokugawa, brought the area of measured land controlled by the Tokugawa and administered by dependent *daimyo* through a complex bureaucratic absolutist structure, to about 75 per cent of the total of measured land. The other 25 per cent of measured land was held by the *daimyo tozama* who were outer lords owing merely a nominal, loose allegiance to the Tokugawa. The *daimyo tozama*, such as the Maeda of Kanazawa and the Simazu of Satsuma were virtually autonomous lords with their own bureaucracies, armies and *bushi*. They held their lands mainly on the periphery, in the south, west and north of the country. The Emperor with only symbolic power resided in seclusion at Kyoto as a dependent pensioner of the Tokugawa clan. These vertical lines of political allegiance are summarized and illustrated in Diagram 2.

Thus, in the household, the village and the wider political community dominant relationships were all vertical ones reinforced by

Diagram 2   Lines of political allegiance in the late Tokugawa, Japan

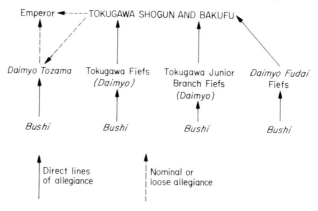

the *on* of non-contractual filial and vassal relationships. The strength of these relationships and the degree to which they still permeate the value system of contemporary Japan is evidenced in the story of the Forty-seven Ronin and the emotional appeal of *No* plays based on it.

The purpose of this excursion into the structure of contemporary and Tokugawa Japan is that it describes in stark outline the social and political structure of a society clearly articulated around true vertical relationships. In all structures these relationships flowed upwards and lasted for a man's lifetime. Contractual relationships were negligible or non-existent. The strength and exclusiveness of these vertical relationships flowed from the exercise of clearly defined functions in a location – household, village and fief – and, thereby, from what Chie Nakane refers to as frame. Today these vertical frame relationships effectively inhibit the formation of those strong horizontal relationships necessary for the formation of class institutions such as non-plant-based trades union and working-class political parties. As well they prevent the development of personal relationships going beyond the household and the work-place. Consequently, modern Japan is still a society divided by 'feudal like' factions and only held together by intensely passively dependent and localized loyalties, by the extension of the concept *ie* to the nation, and by rapid economic growth.

I remind you that my purpose in describing a truly vertical society is to use it as a yardstick for measuring the vertical nature and classlessness of English society in the late seventeenth and early eighteenth centuries.

Perhaps the first point to be made in such a comparison is one that has already been touched upon. It is that in Western European feudalism and in English landholding there was always a much stronger contractual element derivative from the development of private property in land than is made apparent in the literature on Japanese feudalism and landholding. This is one reason for regard-ing Western European feudalism as a 'progressive' rather than as a traditional, conservative socio-economic system. Certainly by the seventeenth and early eighteenth centuries the contrasts between Japan and England in respect to the spread of contractual relationships were profound. For example, in English agriculture there was nothing akin to the *nago* relationship between main and branch families. Even where farm servants lived in and where cottagers possessed a few acres, farm servants and cottagers were essentially wage labourers generally despatched to the care of the parish officers by both kin and employers when sick or too old for further useful employment. The point is that even, or, as Marx would say, especially in the conservative agricultural sector, capitalist market relations were dominant in England by the end of the seventeenth century and the conditions for a *class* society existed by that date. In other sectors of the economy market relations were overwhelmingly predominant, although tempered by vestigial Christian and humane concern.

Secondly, in matters of family life, kin ties in England were always stronger than those based on frame or location. It is true that kin and frame ties frequently overlapped since kin were often found in the same location. However, physically distant kin were still part of the family while children brought up in a distant household generally held the kin relationship to be stronger than those based on residence. Indeed, one author believes that the advent of the 'nanny relationship' in the nineteenth century, which marked the climax of the English upper-class custom of farming out their children to be brought up by others, led to the formation of separate nanny families within households. Although relationships between nanny and child were frequently very strong, the nanny institution also led to the idealization and strengthening of the kin relationship, mother/child.[22] By contrast, in Japan, after 100 years of modernization, frame relationships still take precedence over distant kin relationships as well as over class relationships.

On the other hand, English kin relationships always lacked the strength of the Japanese upward-flowing filial relationship which applied to frame relationships. Perhaps it was the relative weakness of the filial relationship in an England permeated by the contractual attitudes of a market society that led to the development of the classic settled or entailed estate which worked by legally turning eldest sons and other heirs into tenants for life! In a similar manner the patterns of 'friendship' to which Perkin refers were dependent for whatever permanence they possessed on a continuation of the patronage that formed them in the first instance; English

[22] Jonathon Gathorne-Hardy, *The Rise and Fall of the British Nanny* (London, 1974).

'frame' relationships were relatively weak. Thus Perkin's 'friend-ships' were never unlimited but were contractual and tied to patronage.

Thirdly, in the larger political world, since the early sixteenth century, no lord (except, perhaps, some Scottish lords before 1745) had either the autonomy or the capability to act like the Japanese *Daimyo Tozama*. And however powerful the appeal and ties of 'country' by the end of the seventeenth century in England, they did not approximate to the appeal and ties of fief before 1877 in Japan. The fact was that the federation of country houses referred to by Habakkuk and Perkin *was* a federation. Like all federations it required a considerable sacrifice of autonomy from its members. Indeed, such had been the sacrifice of autonomy that England was more than a federation; it was a nation ruled by a central authority and had long been so. On the other hand, Japan only became a nation with a fully effective central government after 1877 and after a long period of internal conflict and civil war.

It is never wise to press comparisons or contrasts too far but, when size of population and location in relation to other regions, as well as the locus of power are considered, then England in the second half of the seventeenth century looks more like a Japanese outer fief than Japan proper. One might more accurately claim that England was to French Absolutism as Satsuma was to Tokugawa Absolutism than that Satsuma in its relations with the Tokugawa was like an English county in its relationship to the Crown. In short, while it is possible to describe Japan in the late seventeenth and early eighteenth centuries as a society truly structured around a complex of vertical relationships in the household, the workplace, and in the wider political sphere, it is impossible to do the same for England without such qualifications as would change beyond recognition the image one would wish to create and project.

It is also true to say that any comparison of the social structure of late seventeenth- and early eighteenth-century England with that of the early twentieth century or of any other developed industrial society would also reveal vast differences between them. And all this means is what has already been said; England in the seventeenth and early eighteenth centuries was neither an industrial society nor a simple one-class or class-less pre-industrial society. It was a society in process of significant and fundamental change. I judge it to be experiencing the final heroic phase of primitive accumulation. Therefore, it was marked by characteristics and institutions of older forms of society as well as by those presaging a form of society men had yet to experience. Consequently, the late seventeenth and early eighteenth centuries were socially complicated. It is not to be wondered at that men were confused and uncertain. They were aware of changes overtaking them and of the problems of what they called 'Civil Society' but they lacked knowledge of the new world they were making and concepts with which to think about it. Historians, however, have new concepts such as capitalism, class, class consciousness, ideology, utopia as well as insights generated by Marx and others concerned with the sociology of knowledge. Consequently, in many ways historians can see more clearly than their subjects could what was happening to them. And while it is important to try to understand the past as past men understood it, it is equally important to understand their understanding in ways significant for ourselves today. Certainly there is nothing in the surviving artefacts to compel us to think about and understand the past *only* as some past men appear to us to have thought about and understood it, and nothing, not even the arguments of Mandelbaum, to prevent us from categorizing the past in ways unknown or only vaguely understood by past men.

Consider the work of Roland Mousnier in *Social Heirarchies, 1450 to The Present*. In this book Mousnier seeks to weld Weber's class, status and power into a comprehensive typology of social stratification by order, caste and class. He writes:

The division of social labour originates in a series of value judgements, more or less explicit and inspired by the desire for power, or the necessity, usefulness, importance, rank, honour, greatness of different social functions. These value judgements differ according to the society, and therefore every system of social stratification is different from every other system, although they can be classified according to types, where we can draw hierarchical concepts. In general, value judgements may be hierarchical, arranged according to the power, real or imagined in a given society, attributed by this society to such and such a social function. From this according to the society, results the pre-eminence of the priest or the warrior, of the Elder, the industrialist, or the scientist, etc.

The concept of the social stratum is a universal one that designates a type, a collection of given qualities, considered apart from the whole gamut of social attributes. It includes general concepts of social strata.

The social stratum is a 'family' which includes different 'species': order, caste and class.[23]

Thus, according to Mousnier, stratification by order occurs when people are ranked according to the esteem, honour and rank that a society attributes to social functions with little or no connection with the production of material goods. Stratification by caste, however, may be a function of ethnic or racial differences or religious belief. And stratification by class may be according to position in the production process, as in Marx, or according to other criteria connected with the production and distribution of goods. In Mousnier's view the most common basis for stratification is that based on orders or 'estates', and he attempts a classification of societies of orders. He identifies the following: the Military Order in France in the sixteenth and seventeenth centuries, the Administrative Order in Mandarin China, the Theocratic Order in Pontifical Rome in the eighteenth century and in Tibetan society, the Liturgical Order in the Muscovite State in the sixteenth and seventeenth centuries, the Philosophical Order in France in the French Revolution, in Fascist Italy and Nazi Germany, and in Communist Russia, the Technocratic Order of the twentieth century.

However, these three categories, order, class and caste, like class, status and power, are rarely completely divorced from each other. Generally there is a positive relationship between high status and wealth and between high status and control over the forces of production in order-based as well as in class-based societies. There are similar if less obvious relationships in caste societies. Nevertheless, it might be useful to make distinctions between order-based and class-based societies. Thus, in order-based societies status is ascribed, in class-based societies it hinges on private property and is achieved. In both order- and class-based societies high status gives authority over subordinates. However, in pre-industrial England from about 1650–1750, the basis of the high status of what might be called the ruling order was very closely related to land as the principal source of the production of material goods and to the development of private property. Therefore,

[23] Roland Mousnier, *Social Hierarchies, 1450 to the Present* (London, 1973), p. 20.

English society in that period cannot easily be fitted into Mousnier's classification as an order-based society. Indeed, it is worth noting that neither modern Japanese society nor English society in the period of 1650–1750 is included in Mousnier's typology of social stratification. Perhaps it would be necessary to add an Agrarian Capitalist Order to that typology to encompass English society! But this also would not do, because the high status of the ruling order in England *was* closely related to land as the principal source of the production of material goods. Thus an Agrarian Capitalist Order would not meet one of Mousnier's criteria for the definition of an order. So once again the discussion stumbles up against the question of the exact nature of English society. The fact is that it was neither pre-industrial nor industrial, neither feudal nor industrial-capitalist, neither class-less nor multi-class, neither order based nor class based, neither one thing nor the other although dialectically it was both. Indeed it is some years now since Asa Briggs drew drew attention to the fact that while a language of class began to emerge in the eighteenth century, a fact which suggests that men had begun to perceive the changes taking place around them, the predominant language was one of orders and ranks. But even longer ago Marx drew attention to the fact that it was the Scottish historians of Civil Society in the mid-eighteenth century who first employed the language of class to dissect the real nature of their society. Briggs also drew attention to the fact that the language of orders and ranks persisted well into the nineteenth century, a fact which suggests that even then not all men had perceived the changes taking place around them. In short, English society was neither one nor another clearly defined society with a fixed social structure and was not yet clearly perceived by men to be one or the other. Since this was the case the historian must choose with very great care the language he wishes to use to describe it.

In this context I draw attention to E. P. Thompson's most recent assessment of eighteenth-century English society as a case of class struggle without class which was published after the main body of this chapter was written.[24] While much of Thompson's analysis

[24] E. P. Thompson, Eighteenth-century English society: class struggle without class?, *Social History*, **3** (1), 1978, pp. 133–65.

accords well with what is written here his work focuses more upon the existence of a traditional popular culture that was rebellious because it was traditional and therefore resisted the encroachments of market forces and capitalist relationships. It is because these encroachments were widespread and experienced by many of Thompson's 'Plebs' that he sees the hitherto fragmentary nature of this traditional culture integrated by 'class'. It is, he claims, the proto-class nature of eighteenth-century society that added a new dimension to the strength of popular culture and enabled it, through its bearers, the eighteenth-century mobs (as portrayed, for example, by Hogarth) and through reciprocal relations between gentry and Plebs to win some victories against the hegemony of the men of property; the partial arrest of the work discipline, the enlarged scope of the Poor Laws, the enforcement of charities and the liberty of assembly and so on. All of which may well be true.

What is at issue, I think, is the appropriateness of using the term class struggle with its Marxian connotations to encapsulate what was going on, particularly if one has failed to distinguish *class consciousness* from class perception. For, as the argument in chapter 6 will show, the central issues of the time, namely property and power, were neither couched in a *class* terminology nor propagated within a milieu of belief and action characteristic of an urban working class as perceived by Marx – this plebian culture in the eighteenth and early nineteenth centuries even at its most articulate was essentially populist. And in this context Marx's comments upon the Critical-Utopian Socialists may have to be borne in mind.[25] Furthermore Thompson's latest position on class as popular culture seems to obscure the central role of property and power in class formation and in the development of *class* consciousness, which he sometimes seems to be writing about. For example, given that the mob, even in the Gordon Riots, expressed none of the perceptions or aspirations deemed necessary for *class* consciousness in chapter 1, what does it signify to think about its activities in terms of class struggle? Thompson's own answer seems to rest on the claim that one cannot (in the English language) talk of 'order-struggle' and on his view that class struggle precedes

---

[25] See below at the head of chapter 6.

class, that is on his belief that 'class defines itself as, in fact, it eventuates'.

Such a definition of class seems to me to claim that class is whatever is – in the terminology of this book, it is class perception. Such a neutral term, of course, takes the discussion outside the ambit of *class* and *class* consciousness as generally understood by Marxists. And that, as I have argued, is an acceptable procedure. But Thompson wishes to remain within that area of discourse as laid out by Marx. Hence his view about class struggle without class, which is to say that Thompson wishes to see his Plebs as, in some sense, unconscious proletarians and proletarians in the making, and considers himself at liberty to read class struggle into their sayings and doings. That is, he seems to claim to know these historical actors better than they knew themselves and to do so with the aid of an *a priori* analytical framework. In this respect Thompson does for his Plebs what Althusser has done for Marx – he says that they made 'class' claims without being aware of what they were doing and without the equipment of a class terminology that would help them to clarify their own consciousness and accelerate its development. The 'truth' of Thompson's position can only be settled theoretically.

This chapter began with a discussion of the views of Laslett and Perkin on the nature of English society in the period from about 1650–1750. It showed how both writers drew upon twentieth-century theoreticians for the theoretical underpinning of their notions about class in this period but noted that Laslett's working definition was similar in some respects to Marx's views on *class*. In the light of this similarity a contradiction was noted in Laslett's one-class terminology. It was also said that if this terminology were further clarified along Marxian lines that the one-class concept could be shown to be unable to encompass the real social structure of England and the changes taking place in it in the period under consideration. The social structure of England was then described to illustrate the point and to show how the Marxian position approximates more closely to the 'real' situation. The discussion then considered Perkin's perception that English society at this time was class-less rather than one-class. In particular I challenged Perkin's notion that the vertical relationships he found to be characteristic of eighteenth-century England were as permanent as he claimed, especially as he himself seemed to accept the historical fact of their impermanence. With the purpose of providing a yard-stick against which to measure the extent and strength of the vertical relationships in the social structure, and therefore, against which to measure the claims of both Laslett and Perkin about the absence of class or class-like relationships in England, I outlined the social structure of Tokugawa Japan. And, using Chie Nakane's notion of frame I showed how Japan was and still is articulated around a truly vertical social structure characterized by upward-flowing filial relationships. Compared with the vertical relationships which characterize the frame-based society of Japan, English society in the period 1650–1750 was clearly already far more a society marked by the horizontal relationships characteristic of a class-like society even though men had yet to develop a language capable of expressing these newly developing relationships. I then argued that the absence of a contemporary language which would enable men to express such relationships should not prevent historians from categorizing the past in ways unknown or only vaguely understood by men in the past. Accord-ingly I drew attention to Mousnier's typology of social stratification which concentrates upon classification by order, but I also noted that even Mousnier's typology could not adequately incorporate English society in the period 1650–1750. This is because it was neither pre-industrial nor industrial, neither feudal nor industrial-capitalist, neither class-less nor multi-class, neither order-based nor class-based, neither one thing nor the other although dialectically it was both. As such it was to be comprehended neither in Laslett's nor Perkin's nor Mousnier's, nor even Marx's typology of societies, at least as understood in the tradition of vulgar anti-Marxism in which Feudalism and Capitalism are only ever perceived as distinctively opposed categories. I concluded by referring critically to Thompson's notion that eighteenth-century English society may be thought of as characterized by class struggle without class, and pointed to further discussion relevant to this theme in chapter 6.

4

Historians, Class and the Early Nineteenth Century

> At first it [a class] is the identity of revenues and sources of income. They are three large social groups, whose components, i.e. the people of whom they consist, earn their living by wage, profit, and rent, i.e. by utilizing their labour power, capital and land ownership. However, from this point of view, say doctors, and civil servants would also constitute two classes, for they belong to two different social groups whose members' incomes flow from the same source. The same would hold for the infinite fragmentation of interests and positions which the division of labour produces among workers as among capitalists and landowners (the latter, for example, into vineyard owners, field owners, forest owners, mine owners, fishing ground owners).
>
> Karl Marx, *Das Kapital* (1865)
> new edn (Berlin, 1953), vol. III

In the last chapter I discussed the work of two historians who, confronted with the complexity of English society in the pre-modern period and apparently disillusioned with what they believe to be Marx's notion of class, have turned to other theoreticians for help and now prefer to use the terms 'one-class' or 'class-less' to describe it. The problems of such conceptualized description have already been discussed: briefly, they are those associated with positivistic simplification and reification. In the course of that discussion I drew attention to several matters central to the theme of this book which should exercise and test the judgement of historians, namely: the nature of Marx's notion of *class* and his perceptions about English society in the period; the problem of the conceptual language to be used by historians in describing it; and the usefulness and appropriateness of particular concepts such as 'one-class',

'class-less' and 'order'. In this chapter I wish to turn to the early nineteenth century to discuss the work of several historians who accept that English society at that time was, in some sense at least, a class one and who have used a concept of class as an important component in their explanations of social and political change. As we shall see, similar problems arise.

The historians to be discussed are those English historians who, in the last fifteen years or so, have written general histories of England in the eighteenth and early nineteenth centuries or who have published major works which use a particular concept of class as the pivot of their accounts of the past. Two of these authors, Harold Perkin and John Foster, have already been considered in connection with other aspects of this book, but I wish to make my first point about the early nineteenth century by reference to Asa Briggs, *The Age of Improvement* (1959). This book was published and presumably written before his essay on 'The language of class in the early nineteenth century', which, as already noted, clearly taught the necessity of learning the language of class. However, *The Age of Improvement* appears not to have benefited from these lessons. Therefore it may be used as an example of that style of historical writing in which the meaning of terms such as 'working classes', 'working class', 'middle classes' and 'middle class' is taken as self-evident, meriting no introduction, identification, description or explanation. In such writing the language of 'class' is regarded as understood. Certainly in *The Age of Improvement* these terms simply appear unexamined if not wholly unremarked. Consequently they are used in mystifying ways. Asa Briggs is quite clear that in the 1830s and 1840s 'The difference in experience and outlook of different sections of the labouring population makes it difficult to employ the term "working classes" with any degree of precision.'[1] Nevertheless, he uses the plural term 'working classes' interchangeably with the singular term 'working class'. For example, in describing the responses of the labouring population to industrialization in the 1830s and 1840s he uses the singular version of the term and writes of 'working-class reactions' and 'working-class political action'. Further, in the chapter on social cleavage he uses a quotation which includes the concept 'the people', as

[1] Asa Briggs, *The Age of Improvement* (London, 1959), p. 287.

employed by William Benbow in the early nineteenth century, as evidence of 'working-class' reaction even though he is also aware that Brougham sought to link the term 'the people' with the middle classes. In this manner Briggs seeks to subsume the perceptions of historical actors within a category generated in his own observer's mind. It could even be said that he writes as if they are identical.

This confusion of actor's perception and observer's classification is common. For example, in *Class and Conflict in Nineteenth-Century England 1815–1880* (1973), the editor, Patricia Hollis, groups contemporary writings in which appear the plural terms 'middle classes' and 'working classes', under section headings labelled 'middle class' and 'working class'. This might appear a harmless shift in terminology, the insignificance of which should be easily grasped by any student. However, it does change the concepts expressed and appears to belie the editor's explicit claim to recognize complexity in the matter of class and class conflict in the early nineteenth century. Nevertheless, the shift in terminology in this collection could be put to good use. It would be a good exercise in the study of class and class conflict to ask a student whether the material incorporated in the collection gives support to the editorial comment and terminology. In my experience good students can generally answer the question on the internal evidence contained in the collection itself. However, even the best of students is unable to decide on the reliability of the coverage, the representative nature of the material, or the 'truth' of the whole work, without access to more information or without reference to concepts and images of class which transcend the traditional two- or three-class model of social structure and social conflict.

Of course historians have recognized the inadequacies and dangers of using a class terminology as used in everyday conversation about present-day politics for the more serious business of explanation in history. One historian who has wrestled with this problem is Geoffrey Best. His solution, a favourite one among historians, merits attention. He writes:

It [*Mid-Victorian Britain 1831–75*, (1971)] will have to be judged on its merits by another group of potential readers, historically curious students in various of the social sciences and studies. To them, and to professional colleagues of the more sociological kind, I address the last part of this preface. What I have written will probably be considered social history of rather an old fashioned sort; more traditional, indeed, that I expected when I began it . . . It is probably in respect of *class* that I shall be found, by the sociological, most wanting. I have used the language of class more as it was used by Mid-Victorians than as it is used by any ancient or modern school of social theorists; i.e. I have used it continually and confusedly. Mid-victorian Society, it is hardly too much to say, was obsessed by class, and riddled with class consciousness, and generally not at all clear what it all meant . . . I was willing, when I started, to draw from the evidence as simple a class structure as the evidence would stand: the simpler, the better, since I like clear analysis as much as anyone, and am prepared to accept a Marxist structure of indelible class antagonisms if I have to. *The evidence about mid-Victorian class however has not seemed to me to make possible a simple analysis in those or any other terms.*[2]

It seems that Best agrees with Mandelbaum, and appears to believe that the 'evidence' appears before him untouched by theory or any body of concepts. Otherwise why reject all past and present theorizing about class and why plump, like Brian Harrison, for a confused contemporary terminology, the terminology of only *some* historical actors?[3] Yet one might regard this as a legitimate move, particularly if one's own purpose is the same as Best's, which is simply, 'to know what it would have felt like to be alive about 1850 and how different it would have been about a generation later'.

There are serious objections to the move, however, which must be weighed in the balance before it is accepted and acted upon. The 'simple' question to which Best seeks an answer is in fact the most difficult of all, for it raises the problem of our ability to know about men's feelings in the past, and should alert our minds to the question of the reliability of the techniques historians choose to employ in their endeavours to know those feelings. In this matter there is the problem of the accuracy with which they use contemporary terminology, for example, the use by Briggs of the term 'the people' already noted and the problem of Marx's class terminology to which we have repeatedly referred and which Best comments upon unfavourably in the preface already quoted. Best clearly rejects what he believes to be Marx's usage and prefers the more confused usage of unspecified others, yet Marx lived and thought in the period spanned by Best's book and he developed his concepts and

---

[2] Geoffrey Best, *Mid-Victorian Britain 1851–76* (London, 1971), p. xv.
[3] Brian Harrison, Review of *Class and Ideology in the Nineteenth Century*, *New Society*, 22nd November, 1972.

analyses during that time; he was as much a mid-Victorian, albeit a foreigner, as any other of Best's sources. While Marx's foreignness may be a barrier to acknowledging him as a contemporary of Best's mid-Victorians, foreignness cannot be charged against other con- . temporaries who also used a class terminology not remarked upon by Best, for example; Hodgskin, Mill and Wakefield. And about Mill I will have more to say.

Clearly Best does have a preferred best usage which may be either unconsciously or deliberately selected. But in either case, as observers of the practices of historians, we should ask for the ground of that selection. Since Best offers none of substance one might well doubt whether Best's approach will even begin to answer the 'simple' question: 'what was it like to be alive in 1850?' This is because of a further objection to this move. This is that if historians accept and adopt Best's approach they will put firm boundaries around their activities as historians. If they work *only* with the perspectives and categories of *some* past actors they necessarily shut themselves out from all other perspectives, including those of other actors, and cut themselves off from advances in knowledge and the benefit of insights of men of rare ability.

Best's approach, which is shared by many, if taken seriously, would condemn historians to the role of chroniclers able to describe and explain the past only in the terms in which some men in the past explained it to themselves. The real task of historians, to interpret in the present the content of the artefacts left over from the past and to create images of the past with the explicit aid of the most incisive conceptual tools they can devise, would be barred to them. Thus, what Berkhofer has called 'history proper' and Collingwood 'the re-enactment of past thought in the historian's mind' through the exercise of an '*a priori* imagination' could never be,[4] and the writings of historians such as Laslett, Perkin and Mousnier would have to be discarded as works of history.

Perhaps because historians such as Best recognize the inevitable duality and contradiction of their work – a wish to know the past as it was, coupled with the limitation of having to choose ways of knowing only part of it in the present – they do seek to establish the

[4]R. F. Berkhofer, *A Behavioural Approach to Historical Analysis* (New York, Free Press Edition, 1971) and R. F. Collingwood, *The Idea of History* (Oxford, 1961).

bona fides of some simple yet comprehensive interpretative framework, and, having done so, seek to knit the past together according to its pattern. This is certainly true of most of the historians mentioned so far in this book, even if the framework used by any of them is assumed rather than argued. It is even true of Best since he argues for the superiority of an unspecified contemporary usage in the matter of class.

Moreover, with the help of some concept of class as a component in their interpretative frameworks many historians seek to establish causal links between the economic and social structure of English society and patterns of religious belief, political behaviour and a myriad other aspects of culture. Therefore, they concern themselves with the sociology of knowledge. They do so in a variety of ways. For example, Kitson Clark in *The Making of Victorian England* understands class as social stratification and regards the struggle over wages as the quintessence of the class struggle. Unfortunately he works, as do many historians, within the traditional three-class model consisting of aristocracy, middle class and working class which is a very primitive and simplistic model of social structure which generally inhibits any deep penetration into the social causes of the matters Kitson Clark seeks to explain, such as, for example, denominationalism. Accordingly, when Kitson Clark writes of Primitive Methodism, he approaches an explanation of it couched in class terms derived from the three-class income-based model and believes he has proposed an explanation with real meaning when he writes: 'The differences between the revivalists and the rest, might turn into a class difference.' But, he hastens to affirm, 'The matter should not be pressed too far.'[5] Steering away from such crass economic determinism he settles instead to explain the rise and fall of sects and denominations by reference to personalities and to other 'isms', in this instance Romanticism. As we have seen, this sort of explanation is very common in historical writing, and the way in which it flows from the uncritical reification of concepts was commented upon in chapter 3.

A few historians have endeavoured to do more than use an assumed three-class model or a confused unspecified contemporary

---

[5] G. Kitson Clark, *The Making of Victorian England* (London, 1970 edition), pp. 143, 183.

usage as the framework for their historical writing. They are E. J. Hobsbawm, E. P. Thompson, R. S. Neale, Harold Perkin, J. R. Vincent, Peter Laslett and, most recently, John Foster. Hobsbawm, Thompson and Foster write firmly within the Marxist tradition and each has contributed greatly to explicating and expanding the Marxist contribution to our understanding of the history of the last 250 years in England. Laslett and Vincent have both thrown out serious challenges to that contribution, while Perkin has developed a mixed model which will provide the starting point for the next step in the discussion.

We have seen how, in his *The Origins of Modern English Society 1780–1880* (1969), Perkin begins his analysis of the transformation of English society with a notion based on the work of the sociologist R. Aron that leads him to argue that England was a class-less society for most of the eighteenth century. And in the last chapter I commented upon his notion that it was an hierarchical society based on property and patronage, 'characterized by horizontal antagonism between vertical interest pyramids, each embracing practically the whole range of status levels from top to bottom of society'.[6]

Perkin also argues that a class society emerged sometime between 1789 and 1833, or, more precisely, between 1815 and 1820. This class society was characterized by, 'class feeling, that is, by the existence of vertical antagonism between a small number of horizontal groups, each based on a common source of income'.[7] 'The great conflicts of the age', he claims, 'were all at bottom struggles for income.'[8] However, these antagonisms did not completely destroy the old vertically-based society nor tear apart the new, instead they gave birth to a 'viable class society'; one which, although riddled by antagonism and class feeling, developed institutions capable of resolving or containing conflict. 'Violence', he writes, is 'the mark of an immature class society.'[9]

Although Perkin asserts that at bottom classes were in conflict about income he also argues that the actual observed conflicts were not couched in material terms. He argues this on the basis of his

[6] Harold Perkin, *The Origins of Modern English Society 1780–1800*, p. 176.
[7] *Ibid.*, p. 176.
[8] *Ibid.*, p. 219.
[9] *Ibid.*, p. 342.

agreement with T. H. Marshall, who wrote: 'The essence of social class is the way a man is treated by his fellows (and, reciprocally, the way he treats them), not the qualities or the possessions which cause that treatment.'[10] Therefore, says Perkin, the vertical antagonism between classes and the feeling of solidarity in each class transcended the common source of income which supported them. In place of divisions and conflicts based on differences in income there developed a struggle between 'ideals' which were couched in idealistic, particularly sectarian terms.

By the mid-nineteenth century, he says, there were three major classes, 'something like compact entities', each with its combatant ideal; the entrepreneurial, the working class and the aristocratic. But there was also a fourth class, 'The forgotten middle class'. This was composed of professional men, virtually 'above the economic battle'. Able to rely on a steady income less subject to competition than rent, profits and wages, these men were able to choose their 'ideal' from among those available. Nevertheless, they did have their own 'ideal' for society. It was a functional one based on expertise and selection by merit. Furthermore, via the mainstreams of nineteenth-century social thought men from the 'forgotten middle class' attempted to sublimate the economic interests of the other three classes into morally and intellectually coherent social philosophies. This fourth class also provided ready-made 'social cranks'. These were men who were able to free themselves from their own class 'who could be relied upon to come to the aid of any class but their own'. It is true that they came from all three major classes but they were drawn mainly from the free choosing members of the 'forgotten middle class'.

As Perkin's argument progresses the class ideals appear increasingly separated from their basis in conflict over income. They are progressively reified until the mid-nineteenth century is made to appear as a perfect market in ideas or 'ideals' in which no one group or class derived any advantage from power, position or wealth. Perkin writes: 'It is not so much that the ruling class imposes its ideal upon the rest, but that the class which manages to impose its ideal upon the rest becomes the ruling class.'[11]

[10]Quoted in Perkin, *ibid.*, p. 176.
[11]*Ibid.*, p. 271.

There is much more in Perkin's book and his interpretation of the modernization of England than I have space to record here. Nevertheless, what I have said does state the core of what he has to say about class in the early nineteenth century. Restated as concisely as possible his argument runs:

1 There were three major social classes defined by source of income.
2 Stratification by income gave rise to class feelings antagonistic to other classes. Class feelings, however, transcended concern with income differences.
3 Class feelings gave rise to 'ideals'.
4 Conflict was between 'ideals' rather than social classes.
5 Moreover, 'ideals' were frequently formulated by class outsiders or 'social cranks' from a fourth class.
6 This fourth class was to a considerable extent outside the prevailing economic system. It generated its own rational and moral 'ideal' as well as ideologues and spokesmen for all the other 'ideals'.

Thus summarized the discussion of class in Perkin's book appears traditionalist. The definition of three classes by source of income is that handed down to us by the classical economists and the dominant tradition of the nineteenth century. It is almost vulgar Marxist in its simplicity, except that by emphasizing the income and behavioural elements in class formation it ignores and obscures those objective power relations which are central to Marx's own class analysis. The traditionalist aspect of Perkin's model is emphasized rather than diminished by his recourse to the notion of a fourth class. This is so because the fourth class is viewed as in some sense lying outside the economic system but vital for the production of social cranks as outsiders and ideologues. It seems that it is only in this way that Perkin is able to explain the sources of political activity and energy of men like James and John Mill, Thomas Hodgskin, John Gray, Robert Owen and Thomas Malthus, plus the fact that there were more than three 'ideals', without abandoning too much of the three class model.

Although this device is a convenient one it is untidy and inaccurate. These shortcomings flow from the fact that Perkin's perception of class formation in the nineteenth century has as its basis income distribution. Power relations are only latent in or peripheral to his analysis. For example, he argues that the eighteenth-century ruling class, which he dissects so well in the first part of his book, had no special advantages in the 'battle of the ideals' in the nineteenth century and that a ruling class emerged, as it were, after the event. Further, the content of the class feeling which is held to transcend income-based classes is not elaborated to embrace perceptions of power relations and the frustration they generated, nor the overt conflict to which these perceptions gave rise. According to Perkin, conflict resolution by violence is the mark of an immature class society, the mature (English) version of which, in the nineteenth century, was not marked by conflict but was a 'viable' class society in which classes, although separated by deep objective and subjective differences, nevertheless lived in a state of peaceful co-existence under the general umbrella of a successful entrepreneurial ideal. Thus, Perkin offers a notion of a class society which is fundamentally at odds with that advanced by Marx and Marxist historians.

What Marx had to say about *class* has already been described in some detail in chapter 1. In this section of this chapter we will seek to add to that knowledge some understanding of the ways in which recent Marxist historians have attempted to use their own notions of Marx's system. This will be done through a brief discussion of the general position of E. P. Thompson and John Foster. In *The Making of the English Working Class* (1963), Thompson defines class as:

an historical phenomenon, unifying a number of disparate and seemingly unconnected events, both in the raw material of experience and in consciousness. I emphasize that it is an *historical* phenomenon. I do not see class as a 'structure', nor even as a 'category', but as something which in fact happens (and can be shown to have happened) in human relationships.[12]

Thompson then argues that while class experience is largely determined by the productive relations into which men enter, and can be thought of as *determined*, the class perceptions of men with a particular experience of class, their class consciousness, is not. Since class consciousness and not income or productive relations or

[12] E. P. Thompson, *The Making of the English Working Class* (London, 1963), p. 9.

any other definition by category, is the essence of class, his book is about the development of a working-class consciousness. Since a working-class consciousness is the product of perceptions of relationships between capital and labour, between exploiters and exploited, it is essentially a two-class model of social relations which he considers and the gradual development of a two-class society which he describes. He writes:

In the years between 1780 and 1832 *most* English working people came to feel an identity of interests as between themselves, and as against their rulers and employers. *This ruling class* was itself much divided, and in fact only gained in cohesion over the same years because certain antagonisms were resolved (or faded into relative insignificance) in the face of an insurgent working class. Thus the *working class presence was, in 1832, the most significant factor in British political life* [my italics].[13]

Such is the essence of Thompson's position on class. Discussion on some aspects of the verisimilitude of these notions about the formation of a working class by 1832 will be postponed until chapter 6. However, one point in regard to class consciousness is worth noting at this point; it is that Thompson's notion does not touch upon Marx's own notion of *class* consciousness (see chapter 1). In this respect, what Thompson refers to as class consciousness seems to be that which workers actually perceived and thought; their personal and collective psychology. This might best be thought of as a 'class perception', which certainly fell short of Marxian *class* consciousness. Indeed, Thompson admits the deviation of the class perception of his subjects from *class* consciousness on the last page of his book where he writes, 'Hence, these years appear at times to display, not a revolutionary challenge, but a resistance movement, in which both the Romantics and the Radical craftsmen opposed the annunciation of Acquisitive Man.'[14]

In his emphasis on class as relationship or a 'happening' rather than as a 'category' or 'structure', Thompson does focus upon class consciousness as an important aspect of the concept of class. It is this aspect of class which Perkin also attempts to isolate by his use of T. H. Marshall's behavioural definition of class and in his concentration upon 'ideals' rather than the income distribution with which he begins his analysis. However, it is clear that Perkin and

---

[13] *Ibid.*, pp. 11–12.
[14] *Ibid.*, p. 832.

Thompson attribute a different content to the class consciousness they attempt to distinguish. It will also become apparent that class consciousness in Foster and Marx are different again. These differences of meaning pose almost insurmountable problems for historians for, while it is perfectly legitimate to do as did Humpty Dumpty, and make a word mean anything one chooses, there can be no doubt that private languages inhibit effective communication. Therefore, it would be helpful if historians could agree to use the term *class* consciousness in Marx's sense and refer to other levels of class awareness as class consciousness or, preferably, class perception. Also it would be desirable to agree that classifications made according to objective criteria such as income and wealth should be referred to as stratification and the groups so classified referred to as strata rather than classes. This would leave the term *class* for use according to more significant definition as, for example, in Marx or Dahrendorf. If this could be done then Perkin's classes would become strata and the problem of attaching his class 'ideals' or class perceptions to different strata would become more immediately apparent. However, to expect this is to cry for the moon. The second best solution would result if historians familiarized themselves with each other's terminology, as well as with that used by Marx.

The theme of the development of a Marxian *class* consciousness is taken up by John Foster in his *Class Struggle and the Industrial Revolution: Early Industrial Capitalism in Three English Towns* (1974) and some criticism of his position has already been offered. However, because Foster's account of the first fifty years of the nineteenth century in England is presented within an explicit and sophisticated Marxian framework which focuses upon *class* consciousness as the crucial issue in that analysis and attempts to isolate and account for it in a very technically competent way, his main argument must be stated.

The basic aim of his book is said to be 'to further our understanding of how industrial capitalism developed as a whole'. But, its central theme in fact 'is the development and decline of a revolutionary class consciousness in the second quarter of the century'.[15]

---

[15] John Foster, *Class Struggle and the Industrial Revolution: Early Industrial Capitalism in Three English Towns* (London, 1974), p. 2.

The place on which Foster concentrates is Oldham, a cotton-spinning town with a population of about 50,000 at mid-century. He argues that between 1790 and 1860 the working population of Oldham passed through a sequence of consciousness: labour consciousness – a form of trade union consciousness; *class* consciousness; and liberalized consciousness. *Class* consciousness in Foster means a revolutionary consciousness which posits the necessity for the overthrow of the existing political state. All other states of consciousness were variants of false consciousness. The main factor generating and sustaining varieties of false consciousness were levels of consumption. He writes: 'The patterns of culture that define any group's identity are not arbitrary but *concrete*, based upon particular historically determined levels of consumption.'[16]

However, as groups tried to preserve their identities by maintaining their levels of consumption they created political conditions favourable to the creation of a collective *class* identity incompatible with the existing order. According to Foster this state was reached in Oldham in the 1830s and 1840s, particularly amongst spinners.

Foster's argument is as follows. By 1780 Oldham had already passed through the phase of primitive accumulation in which money accumulated through the exploitation of private property rights in land had been used to put labour to work. As a result, by the turn of the century, the economy of the town had developed to the point where wage labour was extensively used in the manufacturing stage of capitalist development. In this stage the rhythm of work and men's experience of life was determined not by harvests or climate but by the trade cycle. The main consequence of the trade cycle was periodically to force employers to maintain profit margins through enforcing wage cuts. As this practice developed, workers' consciousness changed. Their major concern ceased to be the prices of the things they consumed and became instead a concern to maintain or improve the real price of their own labour. This led to the development of a labour consciousness particularly among weavers.

During its second phase of economic development, from the

[16] *Ibid.*, p. 5.

second decade of the century until the early 1840s, Oldham became a centre of factory industry. This process, particularly apparent in spinning, led to the growth of a large body of semi-skilled and unskilled factory workers who rapidly became conscious of themselves first as a communtiy, then as a class antagonistic to the locally dominant bourgeoisie. Furthermore, throughout the 1830s and 1840s industrial crises intensified, profit margins fell and wages were squeezed. As this happened, levels of consumption fell and workers, particularly the spinners who were already strongly unionized, inclined to revolutionary ideas and practices and approached true *class*, i.e. revolutionary, consciousness. The high point in this development was the politicization of industrial issues in the strike of 1842.

By the late 1840s Oldham had entered upon a third phase of economic development characterized by the growth of the machine-making industry and a general dependence on overseas markets. The growth of machine making produced a new labour stratum, an aristocracy of labour distinguished by function and levels of consumption from the previously undifferentiated mass of factory workers. They provided a breeding ground for a new false consciousness. Further, the experience of the bourgeoisie in the preceding period of *class* consciousness had led them to take stock of their own precarious situation. Having, as it were, received notice of revolution they decided to exploit the new economic situation and buy off sections of the hitherto *class*-conscious proletariat, including important sections of its leadership, and attach them to a new liberalized ideology. The key move in this process was the Ten Hour Movement. Thus, Foster argues, 'liberalization (akin to Perkin's viable class society) was in fact a collective *ruling-class* response to a social system in crisis and integrally related to a preceding period of working-class consciousness'.[17]

Foster writes as a Marxist. However, there is an important difference in chronology between his history of the nineteenth century and Marx's as it affects the notion that under Economic Imperialism the ruling class could and did buy off sections of the working population, e.g. by the Ten Hour Movement. This notion

---

[17] *Ibid.*, p. 3.

is Leninist rather than Marxian. And, in order to make his case, Foster has to write the history of Oldham with the help of a compressed amalgam of Marx's ideas on Capitalism and Lenin's on Imperialism. Thus, he telescopes developments, which in Marxism/Leninism were spread over some 150 years from about 1750 to the turn of the twentieth century, into less than half that time and completes the whole historical sequence before 1850. Only in this way is he able to explain the 'liberalization' of the mid-nineteenth century within a version of the Marxist/Leninist framework.

Apart from the early chapters of his book, in which he examines briefly the genesis of capitalism in the Oldham area and acknowledges the crucial role of landowners in it, Foster uses a two-class model of society throughout his analysis. *Class* means to Foster something akin to that which it means to Thompson. That is, it does not mean stratum, occupation or income group but refers to *class* consciousness. But this is a *class* consciousness of a particular kind compared with which all other notions of class consciousness might have to be thought of as class perceptions.

The distinguishing feature of *class* consciousness in Foster's account is 'intellectual commitment'. By this he means that to be *class* conscious workers have to have passed beyond mere trade union activity and blind protest to an awareness of the political nature of their struggle to exist and preserve their identity. This means that they must have come to recognize a need for revolutionary solutions and to have done so in thought, consciously and clearly. He writes:

If, therefore, one wants to distinguish between the two periods (1770s to 1820s and 1840s) it does seem to have been this permanence of intellectual commitment which was the really decisive factor. And while it is easy to criticize the movement's theory – its somewhat unsystematized economic analysis and its lack of Leninist rigour about state power – the key point is that it worked. As far as the northern factory population is concerned it passed the test of practice. It succeeded in the most difficult task of relating the struggle for a non-capitalist society to the immediate experience of working people. It took the system's apparently most insoluble failings – its inability to function without periodic bursts of over-production and wage cutting – and turned them into political issues: political issues whose solution was barred by the existing state-power set-up. It was this which was the great achievement of the campaign on poor law, police and above all factory reform.[18]

Since Foster's notion of *class* consciousness in relation to Marx's system has already been criticized in chapter 1, I make no further comment. Instead I will conclude this one by drawing attention to a perception of the sources of conflict in early and mid-Victorian England which denies the explanatory value of a Marxian analysis for that period.

J. R. Vincent in *Pollbooks: How Victorians Voted* (1967) bases his perception of conflict in nineteenth-century England on the work of the sociologist Ralf Dahrendorf, who argues that class conflict has its roots in the unequal distribution of power and authority rather than in differences in property, income or consumption. The first step in Vincent's argument is his claim that industrialization did not simply produce two classes – employers and workers – who would inevitably polarize into the two great antagonistic classes, bourgeoisie and proletariat as postulated by Marx. He says:

As a working hypothesis which at least fits a number of phenomena which would otherwise be puzzling, it may therefore be suggested that while the Industrial Revolution produced some proletarians in some factory districts, over the country in general the economic growth with which it was associated worked for quite a long time in favour of a wider distribution of small property and a diminution of the relative power of large property.[19]

On the basis of this notion and his analysis of the poll books, Vincent argues that political behaviour, as instanced by voting behaviour, was not determined by economic class in a Marxian sense nor by social stratification according to income. He believes, instead, that:

The essential division was between distributed property (mainly urban) and concentrated property (mainly rural), between capitalist agriculture and distributist petty production and exchange, between an urban 'free peasantry' and the great capitalists who ruled the only real Marxian Proletariat that England had, the labourers in husbandry.[20]

[18] *Ibid.*, p. 148.
[19] J. R. Vincent, *Pollbooks: How Victorians Voted* (Cambridge, 1967), p. 7.
[20] *Ibid.*, p. 25.

Therefore, the great and crucial conflicts were between agrarian capitalists and urban petty manufacturers. Vincent's model like Foster's is essentially a two-class one.

Apart from the assumption that agricultural labourers can properly be thought of as 'a real Marxian proletariat' especially in regard to *class* consciousness, a question on which *Captain Swing* (1969) by E. J. Hobsbawm and George Rudé has thrown substantial light, there is a crucial assumption about class relations and class perception which Vincent has to make in order to sustain his argument. First, he claims that the characteristic relationship in urban areas 'was that of vendor and customer, not employer and employee'. Consequently, no groups were tied together 'by the cash nexus, or by relations of production, and there was no constantly recurring conflict arising through the antagonisms of differing groups competing for the rewards of the general flow of production in which they participated'.[21] Vincent claims that his challenge to what he calls the Marxian notion of class conflict is firmly grounded in empirical studies of the distribution of votes according to occupation. These studies are based on analyses of the poll books. Vincent finds that in general the votes of urban dwellers, whether tailors, builders, shopkeepers, merchants or gentlemen, were distributed among parliamentary candidates and political factions and parties in such a way as to show that there was no *class* basis for voting behaviour. To arrive at this conclusion, however, Vincent has to equate occupation as listed in the poll books, which is really a stratum, with class, and insist upon the homogeneity of occupational groups as classes and the homogeneity of their perceptions. Writing of shoemakers he says:

Though their fortunes might vary considerably upward or downward, *all* shoemakers shared in a body of social opinion about what kind of people shoemakers were, which in turn derived from an objective economic homogeneity natural to skilled small producers competing in a free market.[22]

The proposition that there was an 'objective economic homogeneity' among shoemakers depends on the notion that shoemakers were all independent producers and were, like tailors

---

[21] *Ibid.*, pp. 24–5.
[22] *Ibid.*, p. 6.

and other craftsmen and producers, members of an urban 'free peasantry' with homogeneous class perceptions derived from the fact that they were all petty vendors in a market dominated by big agrarian capitalists. It is a proposition which merits careful consideration based on the kind of detailed empirical inquiry reported on in *Class and Ideology in the Nineteenth Century* (1972). This detailed report on one constituency commented upon by Vincent shows that there was no 'economic homogeneity' among shoemakers and other urban artisan groups in Bath. It shows, on the contrary, that stratification along a spectrum rich to poorer was undoubtedly an important factor influencing their voting behaviour.[23] However, if further detailed inquiries show Vincent's claims about the enfranchised to be true, the fact that in the 1840s only about 6 per cent of the population had a vote means that his argument can have no bearing on the question of the class perception of those masses of the population written about by Marx, Thompson and Foster.

Unfortunately an important descriptive account of London artisans by Iowerth Prothero appeared too late for me to incorporate a discussion of the significance of his evidence and argument into this chapter. Prothero's thesis is important because he believes that the artisans of Western Europe as a whole demonstrated the same characteristics as the London men,[24] namely, that while their self perception centred upon the notion of respectability and their sense of independence, they did not see themselves opposed as a class to their employers nor to the middle-classes generally.

This chapter began with a discussion of the number of ways in which historians of recent English history have used the concept class. The purpose of the discussion was to show that there are real problems of conceptualization and terminology and, therefore, real problems and differences of interpretation as well as underlying differences of opinion about the nature of the historians' task. The discussion has not settled the issues raised nor did it seek to do so. Indeed, while my own bias and preferences may be apparent, I have so far attempted to leave the issues open and have merely

[23] R. S. Neale, *Class and Ideology in the Nineteenth Century* (London, 1972), p. 73.
[24] Iowerth Prothero, *Artisans and Policies in Early Nineteenth Century London: John Gast and his Times* (Baton Rouge, LA, 1979). However, see my forthcoming review in *The Journal of Modern History.*

pointed to some significant differences between the various categories of historical writings on class.

This discussion suggests that it is possible to draw up a fivefold classification of historians according to their approach to class. The first category includes those historians who assume that class and its related concept class consciousness are wholly understood by their readers. These historians use the terminology of the conventional three-class model as if there were no problems of substance associated with such usage. The second category includes those who, while they recognize that there are problems, tend to mix up contemporary with current usage and those who, although attempting to define their terms, do so within the conventional three-class model and according to current usage. In practice many historians locate themselves in both categories, sometimes making implicit assumptions about the meaning of terms and sometimes defining their terms according to the conventional three-class model. The third category includes those historians who choose to adopt an exclusively contemporary and admittedly confused usage. My guess is that most historians use a mixture of these first three ways when they think and write about class.

The fourth category consists of those who attempt to interpret the past with the help of an explicit and basically two-class Marxian model which directs attention to the importance of *class* consciousness for any *class* interpretation of recent English history.

The fifth category includes those historians who have attempted to construct explicit sociological models of class and class consciousness as alternatives to or an improvement upon Marx's system. This is a rather heterogeneous category since it includes Perkin and Vincent as well as Neale, whose views have yet to be discussed, for while there are similarities between Perkin's 'forgotten middle class', Vincent's 'urban free peasantry' and Neale's 'middling class', there are crucial differences between the total models of which they are parts. Two of these models, Perkin's and Neale's, also direct attention to the importance of class consciousness or class perception in their analysis.

In short, in this chapter as in chapter 3 I have attempted to emphasize the fact that class is a difficult and complicated concept for an historian to use and that different historians use it differently. I have also suggested that historians would do well to agree on a common terminology and have pointed to the necessity for dist-inguishing stratum, occupation, class and class consciousness as well as re-emphasizing differences between Marx's notion of *class* consciousness and what is better thought of as class perception.

In the next chapter I will outline the system of Ralf Dahrendorf which has been used by a number of historians, including Laslett, Vincent, as well as myself, to give some theoretical underpinning to their explanations of social and political change. This will lead to an exposition and further defence of my own five-class model.

5

The Five-class Model

I have introduced, as a structural determinant of conflict groups,
the category of authority as exercised in imperatively co-
ordinated associations. While agreeing with Marx that source
and level of income – even socio-economic status – cannot usefully
be conceived as determinants of conflict groups, I have added to
this list of erroneous approaches Marx's own in terms of property
in the means of production. *Authority is both a more general and a more
significant social relation.*

Ralf Dahrendorf, *Class and Class
Conflict in an Industrial Society*
(London, 1959), p. 172 (my italics)

As we saw in chapter 3, Mousnier's classification of societies of
orders is virtually a classification based on power. In this classification the basis of power lies in the exercise of some highly valued
service or function such as military or religious service or in
ideological purity and activism, which is justified in terms of the
cultural orientation of the society described, but not necessarily
associated with control over the means of production. Further,
Mousnier considers that such order-based societies constitute the
most common form of society. On the other hand he holds that
class societies characterized by elite power groups deriving their
power from private ownership of the means of production or from
other criteria connected with the production and distribution of
goods are to be found only in the Western world in the recent past.
However, it has to be borne in mind that Mousnier's societies of
orders are not therefore orderly. In fact they can be seen to be
involved in civil conflict and internal war just as much as Marx's
class societies are held to be in a state of *class* struggle. In these conflicts their separate orders clash over matters of status, prestige,

esteem and privilege. They clash, therefore, over the power which is the source of these desired goods. But, as I have already suggested, this is precisely what happens in *class* societies in Marx's system – men struggle over status, prestige, esteem and privilege which is to say that they struggle over the value or human worth that society grants to persons as well as over access to a range of desired material and non-material goods. It is the mark of *class* consciousness when men understand that their struggles are really conflicts over the sources of power from which these things flow and which, under capitalism, is property. Thus, in Marx's system, whatever appearance might show, the reality is that the contending groups are always the oppressors and the oppressed who conflict with each other over matters of power and authority. Even in that most simple of his polemical works, the *Communist Manifesto*, Marx sketched the essence of the complexity of the meaning he attached to the statement that, 'The history of all hitherto existing society is the history of class struggles'. He wrote:

Freeman and slave, patrician and plebeian, lord and serf, guild-master and journeyman, in a word, oppressor and oppressed, stood in constant opposition to one another, carried on an uninterrupted, now hidden, now open fight, a fight that each time ended either in a revolutionary reconstitution of society at large, or in the common ruin of the contending classes.

In the earlier epochs of history, we find almost everywhere a complicated arrangement of society into various orders, a manifold gradation of social rank. In ancient Rome we have patricians, knights, plebeians, slaves; in the Middle Ages, feudal lords, vassals, guild-masters, journeymen, apprentices, serfs; in almost all of these classes, again, subordinate gradations. The modern bourgeois society that has sprouted from the ruins of feudal society has not done away with class antagonisms. It has but established new classes, new conditions of oppression, new forms of struggle in place of the old ones.

Our epoch, the epoch of the bourgeoisie, possesses, however, this distinctive feature; it has simplified the class antagonisms. Society as a whole is more and more splitting up into two great hostile camps, into two great classes directly facing each other: Bourgeoisie and Proletariat.

We see, therefore, how the modern bourgeoisie is itself the product of a long course of development, of a series of revolutions in the modes of production and of exchange. Each step in the development of the bourgeoisie was accompanied by a corresponding political advance of that class. An oppressed class under the sway of the feudal nobility, it became an armed and self-governing association in the mediaeval commune; here independent urban republic (as in Italy and Germany), there taxable 'third estate' of the monarchy (as in France); afterwards, in the period of manufacture proper, serving either the semi-feudal or the absolute monarchy as a counterpoise against the nobility, and, in fact, cornerstone of the great monarchies in general, the bourgeoisie has at last, since the establishment of Modern Industry and of the world-market, conquered for itself, in the modern representative State, exclusive political sway. The executive of the modern State is but a committee for managing the common affairs of the whole bourgeoisie.

The bourgeoisie has played a most revolutionary role in history.[1]

In this extract we can see that Marx referred to conflict between a variety of oppressor and oppressed groups within the one society, identified conflict as 'now hidden, now open', and stated that the outcome of these varied conflicts was indeterminate. He also identified the 'complicated arrangement' of pre-industrial societies and used the following terms interchangeably to describe them: order, rank, gradation and class. It should be clear that to Marx, pre-industrial societies were complex and that the conflicts in them were not carried on between two great homogeneous classes. Such a simplification and clarification of class conflict is the distinctive feature of the epoch of the bourgeoisie. Furthermore, Marx was also perfectly clear that the bourgeoisie did not appear fully grown as a nationwide phenomenon but that it developed unevenly and in different forms in different parts of Europe – remember his views about English society and state in the early eighteenth and mid-nineteenth centuries – and that the conflicts in which its members were involved at various times could be viewed as intra-class as much as inter-class conflicts. Therefore, unless one adopts the naive view that Marx saw *class* conflict in pre-industrial capitalist societies as identical in nature, extent and intensity with *class* struggle within industrial capitalist societies, it would seem that Marx's system can encompass Mousnier's notion about order-based societies in the pre-industrial era as well as Laslett's notion about the intra-class nature of conflict in that era. The terminology may be different but the concepts have much in common. Indeed, since Marx's system is dialectical rather than merely descriptive, it provides a framework for both a richer description and an analysis

[1] Karl Marx, *Selected Works*, vol. 1, pp. 33–5.

of the complexity of English society in the early eighteenth century and the origins of change in that society, a description and analysis which Perkin's work amplifies but does not destroy. In fact, Marx's work is untouched by the criticism of it contained in the work of Laslett, Perkin and Mousnier, whether it be explicit or implicit, just as it remains untouched by the earlier criticism of J. D. Chambers about the creation of a labour force under capitalism.

Perhaps Marx's mistake lay not in his account of the past but in his universalizing of his identification of power with private property in his own time. Moreover, the form in which Marx presented his views frequently led to the idea that he believed implicitly in the positivistic notion that the mere dissolution of legal titles to private property would abolish *class* and *class* conflict in their entirety. Whereas, as the discussion in chapter 2 revealed, Marx's ideas about the possibility of *class* consciousness and Communism focused upon the idea of the total transformation of a system based on private property, which would incorporate revolution and a need for *Class* consciousness understood as the development of autonomous human consciousness. Nevertheless Marx's anarchist contemporaries and many others since have pointed out that the abolition of legal titles to private property could not be expected to abolish *classes* and *class* struggle because power and conflicts about power also have their roots in, or are attached to, other aspects of social organization such as those military, religious, racial, ideological and technological ones noted by Mousnier and commented upon by Ralf Dahrendorf:

> The dogmatic conjunction of classes and effective private property documents in itself a betrayal of sociology. Perhaps a Marx without the Marxian philosophy of history would have realized that power and authority are not tied to the legal title of property. Marx himself could not realize this, and certainly could not admit it, for had he done so, his philosophical conception of the class-less society would have become impossible both empirically and intellectually.[2]

In his own model of class and class conflict in industrial society Dahrendorf recognizes the overriding importance of power and authority in generating class conflict but he rejects what he regards

[2] Ralf Dahrendorf, *Class and Class Conflict in Industrial Society* (London, 1959), p. 31.

as Marx's own narrow identification of power with private property in capitalist societies. He writes:

I have introduced, as a structural determinant of conflict groups, the category of authority as exercised in imperatively co-ordinated associations. While agreeing with Marx that source and level of income – even socio-economic status – cannot usefully be conceived as determinants of conflict groups, I have added to this list of erroneous approaches Marx's own in terms of property in the means of production. *Authority is both a more general and a more significant social relation* [my italics].[3]

And, in commenting upon the possibility of empirically testing his model, a problem of some importance to historians, he says: 'Empirically, group conflict is probably most easily accessible to analysis if it be understood as a conflict about the legitimacy of relations of authority.'[4]

Since the loci of relations of authority in Dahrendorf's model are what he refers to as 'imperatively co-ordinated associations' it is important to understand what he means by the term. An imperatively co-ordinated association is an association of men held together by an authority structure resting ultimately on the force of law. Thus, a nation is an imperatively co-ordinated association, as is a closed corporation, a parish, an industrial enterprise, a landed estate, a farm, an established church, a trade union, a military organization, a university, a school, a family and so on. Each of these associations has an authority structure in which some exercise authority and give orders, and the rest are subordinate. Although, in the last resort this authority is legitimized by the force of law, authority for as long as it works or appears to work in the interests of all, is also legitimized by convention and deference. However, men are also aggressive and covet power – power over themselves as well as over others – and there is a good deal of latent conflict as well as overt hostility and aggression in all imperatively co-ordinated associations.

Conflict in any industrial society consisting of many imperatively co-ordinated associations is likely to be most intense when all the authority/subordinate positions of most men and women place them in the same position, i.e., are superimposed. The fact was, in

---

[3] *Ibid.*, p. 172.
[4] *Ibid.*, p. 176.

the industrial-capitalist societies of the nineteenth century described by Marx, the chief determinants of all positions of authority and subordination *were* the positions people occupied in the production process. In the industrial-capitalist system, therefore, all authority/subordinate positions were superimposed, hence Marx's notion about the polarization of *classes* and *class* struggle. However, in present-day industrial society, characterized as it is by the growth of corporate and government enterprise and a massive explosion of knowledge giving rise to whole new technical-bureaucratic groups, the authority/subordinate positions held by many people may not be superimposed; consequently although conflict is sometimes intense it is frequently diffused. What Dahrendorf refers to as class conflict rarely turns into *class* struggle in a Marxian sense. Which is to say, from Marx's viewpoint, that false consciousness has many disguises.

The mechanics of Dahrendorf's model are as follows. The allocation of people into groups according to the positions of authority and subordination held by them in imperatively co-ordinated associations places them in what Dahrendorf calls quasi-groups. These quasi-groups are recruiting grounds for interest groups which Dahrendorf regards as 'the real agents of group conflict'. That interest groups are a real category and not merely an analytical concept can be demonstrated empirically, which is to say that what Dahrendorf refers to as the manifest interest of interest groups, which is similar to Marxian *class* consciousness, can in principle be discovered by interview techniques. Whether interest groups with a manifest interest become conflict groups will then depend upon a variety of technical, political, social and psychological prerequisites, that is, upon the whole social ecology of the society under scrutiny and upon the availability of those ideological and utopian modes of thought described by Mannheim. In short, Dahrendorf's model does not provide a single simple blueprint for tracing the passage from quasi-groups based on positions of authority and subordination to those conflict groups which Dahrendorf consciously chooses to call 'classes'. Consequently, social historians are still left with the problem of what methods to use as substitutes for interview techniques and which words to use to contain the concepts and perceptions they wish to convey to others.

Dahrendorf refers to conflict groups based on positions of authority and subordination as classes. He does so for three reasons. First, he considers the category conflict group to be too general. For example, there appears to be no reason why the contending parties in conflicts between Protestants and Catholics, negroes and whites, town and country, Christian and Muslim should not also be called conflict groups. However, Dahrendorf believes that such a neutral designation would convey nothing of the nature or cause of conflict. On the other hand, the term class would limit the conflicts explained by his model to conflicts over authority and subordination, i.e., conflicts over power. The term class is a limiting factor.

The problem with this argument of Dahrendorf's is that in the real world in which social historians have to work all the types of conflict mentioned above do include elements of conflict over positions of authority and subordination and may, therefore, be thought of as class conflicts. Since they also contain elements of conflict about property and positions in the production process they may also be thought of as *class* conflicts in a Marxian sense. This problem of terminology cannot be resolved by asserting dogmatically that some conflict groups are not class conflict groups.

Dahrendorf's second reason for calling conflict groups classes is his view that the term *class* conflict as used by Marx was used to encompass conflicts over the existing arrangements of society, particularly those concerned with power and authority, and that there is no other concept which expresses this purpose with equal clarity.

His third reason is that there exists a tradition of sociological usage which identifies a shift from property to power as the determinant of class conflict and that his work is in that tradition. However, Dahrendorf is also aware of contrary arguments and considers that his decision to call conflict groups classes could be reversed.

In spite of my strictures on Dahrendorf's reasons for preferring the term class to conflict group his reasons do focus attention upon two aspects relevant to the theme of this book which have already been touched upon. First, in his model the crucial determinant of classes is the distribution of authority and, therefore, of power in society. And this reminds us of Marx's own concern with power and authority in his system (see chapter 1).

Secondly, they challenge the view that class is an 'historical concept' inseparably tied to a definite historical entity such as the industrial proletariat or to an historical epoch such as the nineteenth century – a view which is frequently used to confuse discussion about past and present societies. But this is not to say that all societies, past, present and future characterized by quasi-groups, interest groups and conflict groups should be thought of as 'class' societies. Such a conclusion would run counter to the view expressed in chapter 3 which claimed that there is some point in attempting to distinguish between order- and class-based societies according to whether status is regarded as ascribed or achieved, the one being the mark of a society with little social mobility such as Tokugawa Japan, the other the mark of a society with high(er) social mobility such as early nineteenth-century England.

Surely, if men in one society perceive themselves as bound to place and rank within a traditional system of upward-flowing vertical relationships while men in another society perceive themselves possessed of the norms of private and contractual right in a society otherwise characterized by broad horizontal relationships, it would be misleading to use the same term, whether it be order or class, as an aid to describing them. Which is to say that a society is not only what historians say that it is but also what contemporaries believed it to be – Marx, with his concepts of *class*, false consciousness and *class* consciousness, attempted quite rightly to conflate the two. Therefore, while I agree with Dahrendorf that it is probably best not to think of class as an 'historical concept', I do consider that there is real conceptual and heuristic value in dist-inguishing order-based from class-based societies along the lines already mentioned. In chapter 6 I will take up the point again in connection with contemporaries' perceptions of the nature of English society in the period 1750–1840.

Perhaps the most significant point about Dahrendorf's model is that it shifts the emphasis in discussion about class away from approaches to class based on notions about the primacy of classifications based on income, source of income or economic interest; those notions which underpin the analyses of most historians allocated to the first three categories in chapter 4 as well as some others. Instead he draws attention to the authority structure of a society and people's perceptions about it as the key to class formation. His model and analysis reinforce comments in chapter 1 on the place such perceptions had in Marx's analysis.

However, because of the preferences of so many historians there appears to be a continuing need to re-focus attention upon this aspect of Marx and to suggest to historians and students alike that perceptions of the authority structures of society, which in industrial societies are dominated by property relations, might have more to do with the development of class consciousness than either social stratification or merely economic aspects of class formation. And so we come to the five-class model.

One recent author in surveying the field of writers on class notes that a three-class model, based on economic criteria such as income, source of income or economic interest 'is the most natural way to think about class in an industrial society' and, in his discussion of the five-class model, argues that models or explanations not 'based on the sort of convergence of economic and ideological interest which is essential to class formation'[5] must be in 'error'. And that is the fateful verdict he passes on the five-class model. Another critical commentator on the five-class model, Gertrude Himmelfarb, also condemns it. She considers the explicit borrowing from Dahrendorf, with its emphasis on the authority structure of society, sufficient to give the five-class model the kiss of death. Such a use of sociological theory, she says 'can hardly be helpful. At best it plays no part in his [the historian's] research, at worst it distracts him from attending to the *actualities* of the historical situation'[6] Indeed, since the first appearance of the five-class model it has been critized for explicitly combining theory and history and its author has been found guilty of the crime of not acting properly as an historian (others accuse him of using the wrong theory!). In Himmelfarb's attack he becomes an archetypal scapegoat. Stripped of his 'moral imagination', his badge of office as an historian, he is loaded with all the sins of sociology and consigned to an intellectual

---

[5] R. J. Morris, *Class and Class Consciousness in the Industrial Revolution 1780–1850* (London, 1979), pp. 32 and 34.
[6] Gertrude Himmelfarb, Social history and the moral imagination, in *Art, Politics, and Will*, ed. Anderson, Donadio. Marcus (New York, 1977), p. 36.

wasteland. On the other hand some sociologists note that he does not always use the concepts he uses in the manner intended by the theorists he borrows from, notably Dahrendorf and Lockwood. They, too, charge him with not using the concepts of a favoured theorist, for example, Weber. Therefore, the time has come to set out the five-class model as simply and as clearly as possible and to state more completely than hitherto what I think a theoretical/conceptual framework does or could do for historians.

As Mannheim has shown, all thought, including historical thought, is structured within some *a priori* system of attitudes and values; a standpoint. Without such a structuring, the world of things and of thoughts would be incomprehensible. Standpoints, which are unexamined positions which people simply have, may be analysed for consistency, coherence, logic, content and explanatory power – including the opposite of all these terms. This may be done piecemeal according to the needs of the moment and accepting all the nuance of language, the untold assumptions of argument, and the constraints of existing systems of value, which often allow the thought to dance away like a will o' the wisp. Or it may be done systematically with the clear purpose of establishing what is being said and what we are being persuaded to agree with.

The clear formulation and statement of a theory or concept(s) should allow for no doubt about the nature and structure of the argument. This is important for historians because, as I have already said, in their search after the unique (which purpose itself flows from a standpoint about the nature of history) they cannot help but use abstract terms, such as 'class', 'democracy', 'capitalism', 'nation', 'culture', 'family', 'urban' and so on, which are terms generally ill-defined yet reified. What is more, historians cannot help but use words like, 'most', 'many', 'majority', 'typical', 'often', 'some' and 'rarely', all of which imply classification and which, through the nuance of language, send out value-loaded signals implying quantitative judgements – frequently when no measurement has been carried out. Finally, they cannot avoid using the range of theoretical explanations offered to them by other disciplines without cutting themselves off from the main intellectual, creative and aesthetic currents of their day, and without pretending not to exist. In short, historians, unlike Mannheim's *Freischwebende Intellegenz*, cannot avoid using implicit interpretative frameworks or explanatory systems in writing history; even the mere chronicler must arrange his data along a linear time scale and the antiquarian has to believe that he is not required to render orderly or meaningful the formless material he displays. But, when historians and students do not make clear the system of thought they use they can easily make *ad hoc* changes in terminology and concepts. The result is that much historical writing is rhetorical, elusive and mystifying.

The special problem with the concept class is that while it is used to describe and to help explain the cause and course of economic as well as of social and political change it is also an important component of the changes to be explained. Moreover, as Himmelfarb so rightly observed, it is morally highly charged. This moral component in class is undoubtedly part of the cultural heritage of everyone in a class society. Nevertheless it is likely to be perceived differently by members of is component classes. This raises the problem that the historically determined and morally charged conceptual language we use places obstacles to and limitations upon arriving at a knowledge of the past and upon the thoughts we can express about it. Which, is a long-winded way of saying that the past always enters the present and necessarily shapes our perceptions and, thereby, shapes our perceptions of the past itself – hence the observation that the three-class model appears the 'natural' way of thinking about class and the truth of Stedman Jones's claim that since Weber 'the word "class" has been domesticated into the historian's vocabulary'[7]

The alternative open to us is not to pretend to an objectivity similar to that of Mannheim's *Freischwebende Intelligenz*, which we cannot have, but to make explicit our concepts and explanatory systems. My argument is not that this will guarantee objectivity. It will not. What it should do is focus attention on the structure of an argument, enable us to know what is said and to know the grounds for agreement or disagreement with what is said. It should also help us to know how far we are constrained by past thought.

Accordingly, the five-class model is a very simple one. Furthermore, although it has been used by others as the starting point for a

---

[7]Gareth Stedman Jones, From historical sociology to theoretical history, *The British Journal of Sociology* **27**, 1976, p. 301.

more general theory of class it was intended only as a shorthand way of describing class formation in England in the early nineteenth century during the formative phase of industrial capitalism. This means, therefore, that it is not necessarily in conflict with Marx's description of England at mid-century nor with his analytical formulation of a two-class model based on position in the production process. Indeed, in regard to class consciousness as the significant factor in class formation, the five-class model will be seen to comprise two classes.

Heuristically and didactically the purpose of the five-class model is also to challenge the hegemony of the three-class model and of economist positions in regard to class formation.

The five-class model uses Dahrendorf's concept of an imperatively co-ordinated association and focuses upon relationships of authority and subordination as the bases of classes in the early nineteenth century. Underpinning these relationships are property relations as perceived both by those with and those without property. One might say, in the structuralist terminology of Althusser, that I argue for the relative autonomy of class consciousness, the chief components of which are perceptions of power in an order-based social structure under threat of dissolution from transformations in the economic structure of society brought about by industrial capitalism.

I also distinguish four other concepts: social stratification, social class, class consciousness and political class.

Social stratification is probably best thought of as determined by some objective, measurable and largely economic criteria such as source and size of income, occupation, years of education or size of assets. Some aspects of stratification, however, are more likely to be identified by other less easily quantifiable criteria, i.e., by things like values, social custom and language. Many of these criteria will be particularly difficult to identify since, in addition to the problem of measurement, they may exist in the minds of members of a social stratum only as norms which are not always matched by behaviour.

Social class, thought of as a conflict group arising out of the authority structure of imperatively co-ordinated associations, may be objectively identified, at least in part, by setting out the authority structure of associations. But this in itself will not be enough for the identification of a social class as a conflict group. At best it will produce a sorting of people with similar authority or subordinate positions into what Ginsberg and Dahrendorf called quasi-groups. In this connection, in 1972, I wrote about the categories of the five-class model

> ... that, I would prefer to regard all those groups called social classes as quasi-groups at different levels of social class consciousness, and therefore at different levels of political activity such that in the early 1820s only the upper-class and the middling-class were political classes. I would also be content to label these quasi-groups, A, B, C, D and E![8]

Nevertheless these quasi-groups function as recruiting fields for classes.

Whether such a quasi-group produces or becomes a social class depends upon the technical, political and social conditions of organization and the generation of class consciousness within it. These, in turn, depend on the specific historical conditions. Nevertheless, the formation of a social class as a conflict group will always have much to do with the growth of sensations of collective identity of interest among individuals in a quasi-group *vis-à-vis* other groups or social classes, and much to do with relationships of authority and subordination as felt and experienced in a quasi-group. The crucial notion to grasp is that there is a distinction between social stratification and social class, and that social classes are conflict groups derived from perceptions of relationships of authority and subordination.

Class consciousness in the five-class model, therefore – in the terminology of this book – is class perception and not Marx's *class* consciousness. For all classes but especially for members of the middling-class – about which more later – it must embrace a consciousness of position in a set of relationships of authority and subordination, i.e., a consciousness of the nature and distribution of power in society and one's place in it, accompanied by sensations of a collective identity with people in similar positions. It is at this point that perceptions about connections between property and power are important for class consciousness.

The existence of social class as a political class is most easily inferred from the existence of continuously organized political and/or industrial action.

[8]R. S. Neale, *Class and Ideology in the Nineteenth Century* (London, 1972), p. 11.

Since class consciousness or class perception as defined is the crucial determinant of collective action or inaction, the five separate classes of the five-class model are identified by a mixture of objective position – social stratification – and class consciousness. Which is to say that I deliberately conflate objective and subjective criteria but, like Marx, I give greater weight to subjective criteria (the relative autonomy of class consciousness). In attempting this I use the words 'proletarian', 'deferential' and 'privatized' or 'individuated' to distinguish types of class consciousness. The first two terms are readily understood. By 'privatized' I hope to identify the consciousness of those whose work situation is socially isolating and whose consciousness approximates most nearly to a pecuniary model of society in which contract and the cash nexus is seen as the dominant relationship between individuals. Such a class consciousness also embraces notions of a high need for personal achievement and demands for the protection of property in one's labour and for small property.

The component groups in the five-class model are:

1   *Upper class*, aristocratic, landholding, authoritarian, exclusive
2   *Middle class*, big industrial and commercial property-owners, senior military and professional men, aspiring to acceptance by the upper class, deferential towards the upper class because of this and because of concern for property and achieved position, but often individuated or privatized.
3   *Middling class*, petit bourgeois, aspiring professional men, other literates and artisans, individuated or privatized like the middle class but collectively less deferential and more concerned to remove the privileges and authority of the upper class in which, without radical changes, they cannot realistically hope to share.
4   *Working class* A, industrial proletariat in factory areas, workers in domestic industries, collectivist and non-deferential and wanting government intervention to protect rather than liberate them.
5   *Working class* B, agricultural labourers, other low-paid non-factory urban labourers, domestic servants, urban poor, most working-class women whether from working-class A or B households, deferential and dependent.

Also I emphasize that a society as status conscious as England in the early nineteenth century

will appear to be cramped even within a five-class model. If, however, it is borne in mind that this approach to the ranking of people is concerned not with social classes as defined above but simply with social stratification (according to status), and if it is realized that each of the five social classes can embrace more than one social stratum however delineated, and if women are recognized as a sub-group in each social class, then the model could be made complex enough even for those historians who deny the usefulness of the concept of class.[9]

In diagram 3 I reproduce the five-class model as it first appeared in 1966 not because I believe it to describe any 'reality' nor because, as has been said, I find words a burden, but because it adds a visual dimension to the words I use. That dimension is somewhat akin to the purpose of a painting by Magritte. The more it disturbs and the more historians are disturbed by the model's lack of a 'catchy terminology'[10] the more successfully will it have achieved its purpose. The core of that purpose is to identify the emergence of a

Diagram 3   The five-class model

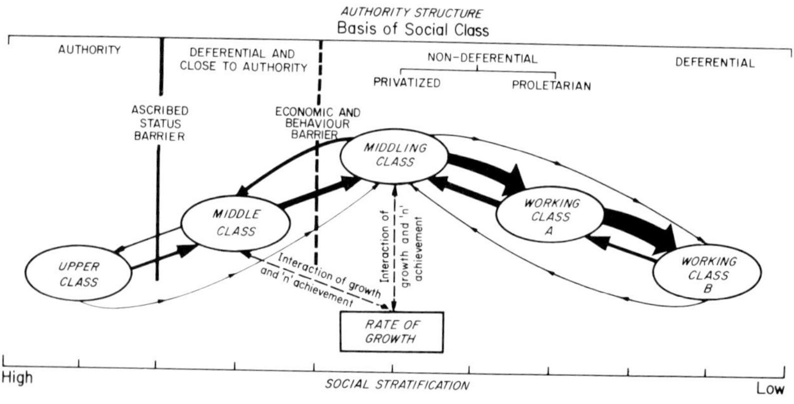

Arrows indicate direction of flow. Thickness of line indicates guessed probability of moving from one class to another circa 1800.

Reproduced with permission from *Victorian Studies* **12**, 1968.

[9] *Ibid.*, p. 29.
[10] *Ibid.*, p. 11. Comment by F. M. L. Thompson. Perhaps I should mention here that the mathematical bit referring to a Markov chain analysis was added to satisfy one of the readers for *Victorian Studies*!

middling class as the central, most unstable and most significant political class in England in the period from 1800 to the 1840s. In the model this class undergoes continuous replacement from a variety of sources: from successful occupants of upper socia strata in working class A, although very rarely from working class B, from less successful occupants and their children, of the upper and middle classes, as well as from its own natural increase. It also loses population to all other classes. Consequently the middling class itself displays divergent political and social tendencies. In times of rapid economic growth and when traditional ascriptive relationships of authority and subordination are weak or absent there is likely to be a shift of many people to higher social strata and social classes. Where, however, traditional relationships of authority and subordination remain strong, men may move from low to higher social strata without any effect on their authority positions. In this circumstance there will develop a strong middling-class consciousness, the essence of which is that it is individuated and non-deferential. The political class engendered by this class consciousness will struggle with established authority for a greater share in political power. At other times the political way in which the disparate, because individuated or privatized, elements of the middling class will jump, will depend on specific historical conditions.

It is my contention that by the 1820s enough people in the social strata covered by the middling class had generated sufficient similar social class consciousness to develop as a political class at least in some regions. The upper and middle classes were also class conscious and productive of political classes. Working class A was beginning to develop a distinctive proletarian social class con-sciousness, again in some regions, and was beginning to emerge as a political class. Working class B, however, was a long way from developing a social class consciousness that was anything other than deferential, and a long way from appearing as a distinctive political class.

The model, in contrast with the three-class one, represents an attempt to formulate a conceptual apparatus which focuses atten-tion on a number of crucial aspects of early nineteenth century England. These are: the existence of a middling class identified by its class consciousness; the dynamic political and economic roles of this class; movement between social strata rather than classes; and the rise and fall of political classes associated with uneven economic growth.

The model, as an heuristic device, helps to elucidate some of the 'stuff' of history. It enables one to see that the debate over the significance for class/*class* consciousness of the initial preparation of the Charter is at best misdirected, at worst, a non-issue.[11] It helps to locate the 'class' appeal of Philosophic Radicalism and the attraction of Systematic Colonization. It focuses attention on groups otherwise omitted from psychologist 'explanations' of Victorian sexuality. And I have used the model to open up lines of research into the backgrounds of governors and members of executive councils in the Australian colonies, into the origins of the 'Victorian' ballot, and into the significance for working-class consciousness of the suffragette movement.[12] The model has been used by others as the historical basis for a more general theory of class formation.[13]

Perhaps the most important idea to emerge from the five-class model is that of the middling class – a political class identified by political action based on privatized and achievement-oriented consciousness and clear perceptions about the bases of power in what appeared to its members to be a traditional order rather than a class-based society. Its perception and programme were rooted in a long Radical tradition extending from Paine and Cartwright, through the Corresponding Societies, the Hampden Clubs, the inspired agitation of Henry Hunt and the campaign for Parliamentary Reform in the late 1820s and early 1830s. Some of its spokesmen recalled the Saxon myth and others, in the West Country, revived memories of the Monmouth Rebellion and the bloody reaction of Judge Jeffreys. For a time, throughout the 1830s, both in and out of Parliament, they held the centre of the political stage in opposition to the upper class and its satellite middle class, and looked set to

---

[11] D. J. Rowe, The people's charter, *Past and Present* (36), 1967, pp. 73–86. I. Prothero and D. J. Rowe, Debates. The London Working Men's Association and 'The People's Charter', *Past and Present* (38), 1968, pp. 169–76.

[12] R. S. Neale, *Class and Ideology in the Nineteenth Century.*

[13] Frank Beckhofer and Brian Elliott, Persistence and change: the petite bourgeoisie in industrial society, *European Journal of Sociology* **XVII** (1), 1976, pp. 74–99.

transform the political structure of England. It is England's tragedy that they failed.

As already suggested, response to my general approach to historical inquiry and my formulation of the five-class model has ranged from enthusiastic welcome, through considered rejection and off-hand dismissal to outright hostility. I am pleased by the enthusiastic welcome, appreciative of the considered rejection and intrigued by the off-hand dismissal and downright hostility. It seems that in trying to shift perspectives and in arguing against the conventions of traditional social history I have offended against the canons of faith rather than the procedures of an intellectual discipline. The roots of hostility may lie here.

Some of the issues involved may be brought into sharper focus by commenting upon one of these hostile responses rather than by taking an overview of all of them, particularly since the author (Gertrude Himmelfarb) locates the critique within the context of a methodological debate and puts forward her own alternative method of handling the question of class in the early nineteenth century.

Gertrude Himmelfarb, in her paper, 'Social history and the moral imagination', agrees that I have not written nonsense and concedes that there is one important virtue even in the diagram: 'it offers an alternative to the traditional three class model'.[14] Moreover, she does not query the substantive argument developed around the model. What she does take exception to is the attempt to reduce what I have to say to the form of a diagram and, thereby, to supplement words with a visual impression. I have earlier, in 1972, admitted to at least one serious weakness in the diagram and I am not emotionally attached to it. In fact I wrote, of the whole schema: 'If, as I hope, teachers and students of history confronted by my use of the model become dissatisfied with it and seek to clarify their own terminologies and conceptual frameworks, so much the better.'[15]

Himmelfarb, however, seeks to open up a schism in social history similar to that which, in the 1960s, separated traditional economic history from the 'new' economic history. Thus, she begins her

[14]Gertrude Himmelfarb, Social history and the moral imagination, p. 34.
[15]R. S. Neale, *Class and Ideology in the Nineteenth Century*, p. 3.

criticism of the diagrammatic form of the five-class model by locating it in a context in which 'a generation of historians is being trained to write a kind of history that is as nearly devoid of moral imagination as the computer can make it'.[16] She attributes to this generation a preference for facts perceived as 'hard' data, precise and unambiguous. And she contrasts this with her own preference for the moral imagination which examines attitudes, beliefs and ideas. Without actually saying so she equates this new generation of historians with Arnold's 'barbarians' and 'philistines'.[17] Himmelfarb denies the need for explicit theorizing and concept-making. She attacks social historians who feel there is something to be learned from other disciplines and subjects and is vehemently opposed to model-building, sociological historians and their notions of class.

I am then identified as the archetypal sociological historian and model-builder distinguished by all the hallmarks of that breed; burdened by language, lacking a moral imagination, seeing only 'facts', and believing that theorizing and picture-making solve the problems of class when class has been 'objectively identified'. When I am so forcibly branded as a positivist I am reminded of another East European story. A raven flying leisurely over the Russian border spots a rabbit running westwards for its very life. The raven flies down and asks, 'Rabbit, why do you run so fast?' The Rabbit, gasping for breath, replies, 'They have just decreed that all crocodiles are to be executed.' The Raven, slow witted, circles away. But then flies back and says, 'Rabbit, you are not a crocodile.' 'You try telling them', says the Rabbit and keeps on running.

I am not a crocodile and I intend to stay put. What Himmelfarb says shows that whereas she claims the ability to get inside Carlyle's mind, she has failed utterly to get inside mine. Himmelfarb's failure to understand my position may be my fault. I should write more clearly. But, there is also a theoretical explanation of her failure which points to a reason for doubting the usefulness of her own historical methodology. It flows from the possibility that her pre-existing conceptual framework or the set of her mind

---

[16]Gertrude Himmelfarb, *social history and the moral imagination*, p. 30.
[17]*Ibid.*, p. 30.

prevents her from so doing. Simply, Himmelfarb has already made up her mind, she has adopted a standpoint. Himmelfarb writes:

To the sociological historian, however, language is a 'burden' in the worse sense. Having made a great virtue of precise and explicit definitions, he often proceeds to formulate definitions that are either so obtuse as to be incomprehensible or so tautological as to be useless. For the sociologist, there may be some meaning or utility in the definition of social classes as 'conflict groups arising out of the authority structure of imperatively coordinated associations'; its abstractness may be appropriate to his purpose, which is to describe the phenomenon of class in its most general, universal, abstract sense. But for the historian, interested in the particularity of a historical situation (or in the particularities of a number of related situations), such a definition can hardly be helpful. At best it plays no part in his research; at worst it distracts him from attending to the actualities of the historical situation. What it does do is give him the illusion that by virtue of some such definition, he has 'objectively identified' the concept of class. It is this illusion, this claim to objectivity, that is the driving force behind the enterprise of sociological history.[18]

In this passage Himmelfarb identifies her main concern and her misreading of my purpose. But first, I draw attention to some 'hidden' concepts. Himmelfarb's argument posits the existence of two abstract and homogeneous classes of historians. Each of the two classes is identified by certain fixed kinds of behaviour; historians study abstract 'historical situations', sociological historians use abstract definitions which, by definition or assertion, can play no part in research. From her observation of the behaviour of sociological historians, which runs counter to her definition or assertion of the proper role of historians, Himmelfarb infers an intentional cause, their claim to objectivity. Since the class of sociological historians is homogeneous, the author of the five-class model also claims objectivity. This claim to objectivity is an illusion. It is also the driving force behind this kind of history.

These hidden concepts, definitions, abstractions and assumptions and the behavioural analysis within which they are employed show that Himmelfarb, like everyone else, thinks within a pre-existing conceptual framework made up of concepts, definitions, abstractions, assumptions and theoretical modes of procedure. The theoretical and methodological difference between Himmelfarb

---

[18] *Ibid.*, p. 35.

and myself is that I consciously seek to clarify my concepts, definitions, abstractions, assumptions and theoretical modes of procedure. I may not do it very well but I do believe that it is a necessary step in coming to grips with the complicated reality – the construction of the past in the present. Himmelfarb seems to prefer working in the dark. That I do seek clarification of concepts and the rest is because – as much of the argument in this book will have shown – I *know* that I am not objective, just as I know that Himmelfarb is not objective; and no pretence of objectivity on her part will persuade me otherwise (see chapter 2). I believe I can even find some support for my position in Trilling whose work is so much admired by Himmelfarb. Trilling wrote,

> The refinements of our historical sense chiefly mean that we keep it properly complicated. History, like science and art, involves abstraction: we abstract certain events from others and we make this particular abstraction with an end in view, we make it serve some purpose of our will. Try as we may, we cannot, as we write history, escape our purposive-ness. Nor, indeed, should we try to escape, for purpose and meaning are the same thing.[19]

Whether, in consequence of this view Trilling is a relativist, I do not know. I am not. Like Mannheim I believe there is an historical truth to be found and that some descriptions and explanations of it are better than others. Since these descriptions and explanations may be based on flashes of insight, creative leaps, or some bold formulation of an idea and since there *are* choices to be made between them, I also believe that theoretical and conceptual clarification is an essential aid in making them, especially for those who may not have experienced the flash of insight, taken the creative leap, or made the bold formulation.

It seems to me that Himmelfarb, too, is not an intentional relativist, just as she is not an intentional behaviourist, and that she also believes that some explanations are better than others and, maybe, that there is an historical truth to be found. If she does not believe that some explanations are better than others, for example, that the moral imagination is a better way of explicating class in the early nineteenth century than the five-class model, I cannot see what all the fuss is about – she should let me write my history

---

[19] Lionel Trilling, *The Liberal Imagination* (New York, 1951), p. 188.

unmolested and go on writing hers and leave the customers in the historiographical supermarket to decide between us.

In the explication of the paragraph from Himmelfarb I re-wrote what she said with the object of emphasizing its theoretical and conceptual structures and focusing upon the 'logic' of her argument. But I also previously claimed that her mode of procedure mirrored her general historical method and that gave grounds for doubting its overall usefulness. It is time I explained myself.

Himmelfarb's position is similar to that of thinkers and historians who may be thought of as Historical Idealists such as Croce, Dilthey and Collingwood. (Also it seems to place her in the same category as Best above.) Her 'Moral Imagination' is akin to Collingwood's 'Historical Imagination' although I am less certain that, like the latter, it incorporates the notion of an *a priori* imagination.

Historical Idealists all insist upon a radical distinction between the human sciences and the natural sciences and the kinds of phenomena they study. They argue that while covering laws are appropriate in the natural sciences the human subjects of the human sciences do not, characteristically and essentially, act in accordance with general laws. Human beings are autonomous agents and their actions must be understood in terms of their own perceptions of themselves and their world, hence, in terms of their ideas, attitudes and beliefs. This means that historians must study individuals and that history is the study of the unique made without reference to general laws. Therefore, history is *sui generis*. Moreover, since only external behaviour can be observed, it is unintelligible except by reference to unobservable occurrences in the historian's mind, for example, Collingwood's 'Historical Imagination'. These occurrences consist of some sort of empathetic apprehension of the inner workings of another mind, or *Verstehen*. Consequently historians do not properly explain events, rather, they seek to understand the unique episodes of the past in the terms in which men in the past understood their own society. As Danto put it: 'Historians' explanations do not include laws for the simple reason there are no historical explanations.[20]

This method is always in danger of dissolving into subjectivism.

[20] Arthur C. Danto, *Analytical Philosophy of History* (Cambridge, 1965), p. 206.

Indeed, this was Collingwood's own verdict upon it. He wrote:

> I began by considering a theory according to which everything is given: according to which all truth, so far as any truth is accessible to the historian, is provided for him ready made in the ready made statements of his authorities. I then saw that much of what he takes for true is not given in this way but constructed by his *a priori* imagination; but I still fancied that this imagination worked inferentially from fixed points given in the same sense. I am now driven to confess that there are for historical thought no fixed points thus given: in other words that in history, just as there are properly speaking no authorities, so there are properly speaking no data.[21]

But, Collingwood rescued his *Verstehen* approach by falling back upon a Kantian transcendental consciousness. This is a notion that there is an *a priori* activity of the human mind which organizes the world of objects and their relations and gives to the mind's observations and relationships a form of objectivity. It was in accordance with this notion that Collingwood saw his 'Historical Imagination' as an *a priori* construct or activity of the mind which

> can give the historian his criterion of historical truth. That criterion is the idea of history itself: the idea of an imaginary picture of the past. That idea is, in Cartesian language, innate; in Kantian language, *a priori*. It is not a chance product of psychological causes; it is an idea which every man possesses as part of the furniture of his mind, and discovers himself to possess in so far as he becomes conscious of what it is to have a mind. Like other ideas of the same sort, it is one to which no fact of experience exactly corresponds. The historian, however long and faithfully he works, can never say that his work, even in crudest outline or in this or that smallest detail, is done once for all. He can never say that his picture of the past is at any point adequate to his idea of what it ought to be. But, however fragmentary and faulty the results of his work may be, the idea which governed its course is clear, rational, and universal. It is the idea of the historical imagination as a self dependent, self-determining, and self-justifying form of thought.[22]

There is no evidence in Himmelfarb that her 'Moral Imagination' has any such *a priori* nature. Consequently her system moves inevitably along the path of subjective relativism already well trodden by those Historical Idealists who, historically, have been the cause of concern to thinkers as intellectually apart as

[21] R. G. Collingwood, *The Idea of History* (London, 1961), p. 243.
[22] *Ibid.*, pp. 248–9.

Mannheim and Mandelbaum and, in our time, as Theodore Adorno and Louis Althusser.

Certainly, as Himmelfarb says, we should read Carlyle and Disraeli but, as we read them, we should bear in mind that Himmelfarb's identification of them as the exemplars of class is entirely subjective. Further, her attempt to cajole us into accepting her choice according to the great-man principle, and her contention that it was Carlyle's association of the moral idea of work with class that made class 'dangerous', are not convincing. The first ignores the fact that 'greatness' is as much bestowed as earned – it is already subjective – and the second ignores the real experience of class and class conflict that made class dangerous.

The quite arbitrary nature of her choice is made clear in her own words. 'If', she says, 'we refuse to indulge the current prejudice against greatness, we may choose to consult on the question of class – Thomas Carlyle.[23] Indeed! But only on condition that we admit to indulging some other prejudice. A prejudice, perhaps, in favour of 'greatness'? If so why not choose J. S. Mill and his five-class model? Why not Marx and his far more complicated schema? On the other hand why choose greatness at all, particularly if one wishes to get inside the minds of the less than great? Why not Charles Hall? Why not Thomas Hodgskin? Why not William Hone and his moral perception of Derry Down Triangle in *The Political House That Jack Built*? Why not the working-class delegate from the Bristol Political Union who spoke at the inaugural meeting of the Bath Union on the morrow of the slaughter accompanying the Bristol Riots? Why not?

The answer is that Historical Idealism, in the absence of an appeal to something like a Kantian transcendental consciousness, has no answer. Consequently one is free to suggest that historians can only really get inside minds which, in a sense, they are already inside. For the rest they merely report on the product of some minds and do not know the actual thought itself. This immediately raises the problem of the unconscious and also the structuralist position which suggests that the way in which people see themselves and their intentions may not actually represent the reality of their existence and their behaviour. Intentions, in other

[23]Gertrude Himmelfarb, 'Social history and the moral imagination', p. 38.

words, need not always be explicitly expressed nor even consciously evident to the actor. It is not clear how Himmelfarb or other Historical Idealists would address this problem. Therefore, instead of allowing idealist historians to clothe themselves in the nuance of language they should be exposed for what they are, theoretically naked in a cold epistemological world. Perhaps *Verstehen* is itself an illusory remedy for the anomie of bourgeois society!

Yet, when we get to the end of Himmelfarb's attack on the five-class model, we find there is not much in it at all, merely a call for 'an exercise in modesty'[24] – a call to take ideas, beliefs, principles, perceptions and opinions of contemporaries seriously. If that is all then we have been dragged through a storm in a tea-cup, for who takes ideas, beliefs, principles, perceptions and opinions of con-temporaries more seriously than a historian concerned about the truth of class and class consciousness in early nineteenth-century England? The problem is, which contemporaries and why?

Let me, therefore, offer the following account of a contemporary political analysis which has a very close affinity with that of the five-class model even though it does not apply the identical terminology to the groups identified. It is based on J. S. Mill's analysis of the electoral basis for a united Reform or Movement Radical Party which appeared in the *London and Westminster Review* in 1839 and to which I referred only briefly in 1968.

The background to Mill's article was the Reform Act of 1832 and the three elections of 1832, 1835 and 1837. In the days of heady enthusiasm following the first two of these elections ultra-radicals like J. A. Roebuck, H. S. Chapman, George Grote and Sir William Molesworth believed that Toryism was virtually dead and Move-ment Radicalism just around the corner. And, for a time at least, some of them, including Mill and Chapman, believed they had a leader, a 'Napoleon Ideologue', in Roebuck. However, at the 1837 election the radical faction in Parliament was virtually annihilated and Roebuck was defeated in the 'Drunken Election' at Bath. Moreover, Roebuck had turned out to be too waspish and extreme for most of the radicals. His *Pamphlets for the People*, published throughout 1835 and 1836, had offended many of them. Conse-quently, Movement Radicalism was in disarray and some radicals,

[24] *Ibid.*, p. 55.

including J. S. Mill, were looking for ways of uniting all the radical movements and factions in Parliament and in the country. Fortunately, or so Mill thought, Lord Durham, known to some as 'Radical Jack' because he had proposed a ballot clause in the 1832 Reform Bill, and to others as 'King Jog' because he had once expressed the view that he thought it possible to jog along on £40,000 a year, was the best hope for a parliamentary leader of a united radical party. That this hope was to prove a forlorn one is beside the point. What matters here is the political analysis Mill used to support his belief.

Mill began his analysis by arguing for the importance of two parties which would represent in Parliament two broad social groups which he labelled (a) the 'Privileged' or 'Satisfied Classes' and (b) the 'Disqualified Classes'. His use of the plural form 'classes' in both cases should make it clear that the terms 'Privileged' and 'Disqualified' were not meant to describe two homogenous economic classes in a simple two-class model of society and social conflict. Thus Mill's reference to two parties does not necessarily imply that he believed in the existence of such economic classes. In fact, Mill's essay was aimed at bringing several oppositional or radical classes or strata into an effective united political party. Since such a party would have to be politically effective in Parliament, he gave only very cursory treatment to working-class movements based on social strata without the franchise. Clearly, the word 'classes' as used by Mill in the terms 'Satisfied Classes' and 'Disqualified Classes' was to be thought of as referring to a notion of political class. The basis for the development of the class perceptions of these two political classes was either the possession or non-possession of political power. Accordingly:

The Privileged Classes are all those who are contented with their position; who think that the institutions of the country work well for them; who feel that they have all the influence, or more than the influence, in the present order of things, which they could expect under any other: who enjoy a degree of consideration in society which satisfies their ambition, and find the legislative prompt to lend an ear to their complaints and if they feel anything as an inconvenience to endeavour to devise a remedy for it. All, in short, who feel secure that the interests of other people will be postponed to theirs, compose the conservative body. Those who feel and think the reverse of all this are the Disqualified Classes. All who feel oppressed or unjustly dealt with by any of the institutions of the country, who are taxed more heavily than other people, or for other people's benefit, who have, or consider themselves to have, the field of employment for their pecuniary means or their bodily or mental faculties unjustly narrowed: who are denied the importance in society, or the influence in public affairs, which they consider due to them as a class, or who feel debarred as individuals from a fair chance of rising in the world; especially if others, in whom they do not recognise any superiority or merit, are artificially exalted above their heads: these compose the natural Radicals.[25]

Even those radicals who had, perhaps, developed radical sentiments because of low wages, low profits or unemployment had done so, according to Mill, because they either imputed their situation to the actions of government or believed that government could remedy it. Their perceptions were, therefore, based on perceptions of power.

However, Mill was clear that underlying the political power nature of the two political classes were the social circumstances, interests and life-style of the respective social groups or, as he calls them, classes, which comprised the two political classes. He wrote:

For our part we have hardly any belief in reaction, and but little in any growth of political opinion, whether Radical or Conservative but the growth in numbers, intelligence, and wealth, of the classes who are already, and from the circumstances of their position, Radicals or Conservatives.[26]

His subsequent analysis of the component classes of the 'Privileged' and 'Disqualified', terms which, as we have seen, connoted distinctions of power, therefore, had its starting point in groups based on circumstances and interest, or in what I prefer to call stratum.

Each of the two parliamentary political classes comprised several distinct political classes based on a similar number of strata. For example, although the 'Privileged' comprised two strata, the very rich and the landed interest, the landholders predominated. Thus:

The landholders as a class are generally unqualified Tories; those who are not so, mostly belong to the conservative Whigs, differing from Tories in little but in hereditary personal connections and in name.[27]

---

[25] J. S. Mill, A letter to the Earl of Durham on reform in Parliament, by paying the elected, *London and Westminster Review* **XXXII**, 1839, pp. 478–9.
[26] *Ibid.*, p. 477.
[27] *Ibid.*, p. 450.

Although landholders formed the main strength of the 'Privileged' Mill also included 'nearly the whole class of very rich men'. In this stratum he included all those of great monied, manufacturing or mercantile wealth, particularly those in the protected trades; the shipping, timber and West Indian interests. This very rich stratum also included the leaders of the professions; the army, navy and law, and the beneficed clergy of the Church of England. Together these strata comprised the 'Privileged'.

The other political class, the 'Disqualified', was largely drawn from the 'middle classes'. This amorphous group, however, comprised several strata. First, the bulk of the manufacturing and mercantile population except, as mentioned above, those who were very rich. According to Mill this stratum of small capitalists consisted of those rendered disqualified and radical by the restricted field of employment and the falling rate of profit. Their economic predicament was exacerbated by the operation of the Corn Laws. Secondly, a stratum embracing 'almost all the skilled employments, those which require talent and education but offer no rank – what may be called the non-aristocratic professions'.[28] Thirdly, a stratum comprising small landed proprietors, prosperous farmers and market gardeners, particularly those close to towns and obviously dependent on the prosperity of the manufacturing sector. The fourth group was made up of nearly all electors in Scotland and Ireland. All four of these strata were potential sources of electoral strength for a united Radical party.

Nevertheless, the main political strength of the party of the Disqualified was to be drawn from the most class-like stratum of ten-pound electors in the towns. According to Mill:

They are the greatest sufferers of all by low profits, and an overcrowded field of employment. They belong almost universally to the 'uneasy classes'. They are nearly all of them struggling either against the difficulty of subsisting, or against that of providing for their sons and daughters. They have no common interest or fellow feeling with the aristocracy; under no circumstances can they hope to be participators of aristocratic privileges.[29]

Many of this stratum were active in the new town corporations and

[28] *Ibid.*, p. 486.
[29] *Ibid.*, pp. 485–6.

many more were Dissenters: 'Between them and the aristocracy, there is a deeper gulph fixed than can be said of any other portion of the middle class; and when men's consciences, and their interests, draw in the same direction, no wonder that they are irresistible.'[30] Finally, men in this stratum were men with a high need for achievement, 'men of active and aspiring talent, indeed, in all classes, except the highest, are Radicals everywhere; for what is Radicalism, but the claim of pre-eminence for personal qualities above conventional or accidental advantage?'[31]

Any additional source of support for a united parliamentary party representing all of the 'Disqualified' lay in 'the whole effective political strength of the working classes'. However, with less than 6 per cent of the population possessing the franchise the *effective* political strength of the working classes was slight and they carried little weight. Mill argued that this did not matter since the united radical party would rule in the interest of the whole, especially, therefore, it would rule in the interests of the working classes, until political reforms could safely be ventured upon. The motto of Radical politicians, he said, should be 'Government *by means of* the middle for the working classes.'[32]

In arguing for the unity of interest between the proposed united parliamentary radical party and the working classes Mill distinguished clearly between what he called 'The Oastlers and Stephenses [who] represent only the worst portion of the Operative Radicals, almost confined, moreover, to a narrow district in the North', who asserted the rights of labour against the claims of capital, on the one hand, and the intelligent leaders of the working classes in the London Working Men's Association, on the other. These latter were the men 'who framed the People's Charter, who originated the agitation for it; who have some of their members present at every meeting which is held for it in any part of the country; and who represent the best and most enlightened aspect of working class Radicalism'.[33] However, Mill qualified his approval of these men because many of the best of them still 'entertain

---

[30] *Ibid.*, p. 486.
[31] *Ibid.*, p. 486.
[32] *Ibid.*, p. 494.
[33] *Ibid.*, p. 497.

notions in political economy with which we by no means coincide'. Consequently, he allocated to all the working classes a merely subordinate role in the united radical party of the 'Disqualified'.

When simplified and represented schematically Mill's class analysis of England in 1839 appears as shown in Diagram 4.

The similarity between Mill's class analysis and the basic elements of the five-class model may be seen by referring to p. 133 above. The difference between the two schemes arises from the fact

Diagram 4   Mill's class analysis of England in 1839

PRIVILEGED CLASS = The politically dominant class

Stratum	*Characteristics*
1) Landowners	Aristocratic, privileged, satisfied
2) Very rich; leaders in the professions of army, navy, law and beneficed clergy of the Church of England	Sharing in and benefiting from legislative privilege, aspiring to landownership but otherwise satisfied

BARRIER OF ECONOMIC AND POLITICAL POWER AND PRIVILEGE

DISQUALIFIED CLASS = The politically subordinate class

	Stratum	*Characteristics*
THE MIDDLE CLASSES	1) Ten pound electors 2) Non-aristocratic professionals 3) Small capitalists	Struggling, dissatisfied, aspiring, uneasy, frequently dissenters, opposed to aristocratic privilege and power
	4) Small landed proprietors, prosperous tenant farmers, market gardeners 5) Electors in Scotland and Ireland	Opposed to aristocratic privilege and power
THE WORKING CLASSES	6) Working class	London based, intelligent, dissatisfied, opposed to privilege and power including the power of capitalists
	7) Working class	Northern based, basically anti-capitalist, also dissatisfied and anti-Poor Law

that the five-class model involves some reorganisation of the component strata in Mill's scheme. Thus, Mill's 'London-based' working class plus the ten-pound electors, the non-aristocratic professionals and the small capitalists represent those strata which, in the five-class model, produce the middling class. His 'Northern based' working class is the equivalent of those strata producing the working class A of the five-class model. However, strata making up working class B were not discussed by Mill for obvious reasons. The upper class and middle class of the five-class model are virtually identical with Mill's landowners and the very rich. However, the five-class model does not distinguish as a separate class the small landed proprietors, prosperous tenant farmers and market gardeners isolated by Mill. That is, perhaps, an error in the five-class model.

These re-groupings and labellings are of little significance compared with the characteristics both Mill and I seek to emphasize. Namely, that the most politically radical, indeed, the almost revolutionary political class in England in the 1830s had its basis in several strata in the towns: small capitalists, including producers, traders and shopkeepers; professionals; and artisans. The consciousness of all these groups was sharpened by their perception that they were antagonistic to and in conflict with aristocratic power and privilege and by their sense of being blocked in every circumstance and aspiration of their lives by that aristocratic power and privilege. This consciousness was beyond doubt class consciousness, a class consciousness which was given political expression in Philosophic Radicalism particularly in its emphasis on the secret ballot. Its carriers were to be found both in and out of Parliament. It blossomed among those who feared the onset of the stationary state and those who supported and advocated Movement Radicalism and Systematic Colonization. This consciousness was the consciousness of aspiring but blocked men oppressed by aristocracy and beginning to suffer from the emergence and competition of men of large capital.

That this class was a transitional one lacking a consciousness which could culminate in a compacted, collectivist, *class* consciousness, and a class overtaken by industrialization and the emergence of other classes and class consciousness is also true, but no reason, therefore, for dismissing it as of no account in political developments in the first four decades of the nineteenth century. For, while the historical present always contains the future, a fact which we allow to determine the linear form of the histories we write, it also exists as the culmination of other historical pasts. Historians must attempt to understand it as such.

J. S. Mill, from the standpoint of the economic and political milieu in which he moved, was certainly conscious of the stirrings of this political class and used several terms to describe it; the uneasy classes, ten-pound electors, natural radicals, the Disqualified. The five-class model also seeks to highlight its existence by reviving a term, middling class, well known and used in the 1830s and 1840s by, for example, John Gray and William Thompson. In fact it was so well known and used that in a letter addressed to the Imperial Chartists in the *Northern Star* in 1842 Feargus O'Connor used a plural form of the term to describe the same social phenomenon which the five-class model seeks to highlight. In this letter he attacked every suggestion of an alliance between Chartists and other political parties and used the term 'middling classes' to refer to members of those groups who, throughout 1841 and 1842, had sought to bring about a union between Radicals and Chartists, the sort of union which returned Roebuck as MP for Bath against the national swing of votes in 1841 and brought about the Sturgeite conference in Birmingham in 1842. There can be little doubt that O'Connor sought to identify the same radical social groups described by Mill which are also subsumed in the term middling class in the five-class model. O'Connor wrote:

Many attempts are now being made to win us, weak as we are: but all will fail. Some mushroom leaders would win you by pointing out the great advantages which a union with the middling classes would confer upon you, and to insure those advantages, would tempt you into a general union with that order, as a body; others would point out the great benefits to be gained by a distinct union with the Corn-Law League Party.[34]

O'Connor's equation of the plural term 'middling class' with the singular term 'order' in this passage suggests some continuing confusion in his mind about the homogeneity of the class he sought to

---

[34] *The Northern Star*, 5th November 1842. See also O'Connor's letters addressed 'to the Industrious Portion of the Middling Classes' in *The Northern Star*, 15th June to 13th August 1842.

describe and also indicates the survival in political thinking in the middle years of the nineteenth century of the language of 'ranks' and 'orders' of an earlier form of society.

In any case Mill's identification and analysis of a widespread, even if not nationwide, political class comprising many strata, which was at odds with the aristocracy and the very rich, but which was neither middle class nor proletarian, plus O'Connor's reference to those strata as the 'middling classes', lends additional evidential support to the main message of the five-class model, namely, the existence of a political class that was neither middle class nor proletarian in consciousness and whose members in some constituencies sought to distinguish themselves from Tories, Whigs and Liberals on the one hand and from working-class Chartists on the other. The fact that none of the historians mentioned in chapter 4, except, perhaps, J. F. C. Harrison, refers to or comments upon Mill's class analysis, and the fact that historians who prefer to use contemporary usage and publish for student consideration extracts on class which take no cognizance of Mill on class, are acts of omission and rejection as striking as the general rejection by historians of Marx on class.

I began this chapter with a reference to the importance of power in Mousnier's classification and I recalled Marx's own perception about the importance of power relationships in *class* formation. Then I introduced Dahrendorf's idea that Marx was misleading because of his narrowing of power relations to those arising from property relations. I followed this with an account of Dahrendorf's own explanation of class conflict, which centred upon his concept of an imperatively co-ordinated association. Although I commented critically upon some aspects of his system, notably in regard to maintaining a conceptual distinction between order- and class-based societies, I approved of it because it shifted the emphasis in discussion about class away from economist classifications to ones based on the distribution of power. I also noted that Dahrendorf conceded that under industrial capitalism *the* major determinant of power relations was the capital/labour relationship in a system of private property. Because of historians' preferences I thought it necessary to emphasize this and to state once more the importance of theorizing and concept-making for the practice of history.

I then introduced the five-class model. I emphasized that what it pointed to was the existence of a middling class identified by a class consciousness arising out of perceptions of the nature and distribution of power in society and of people's places in it. It was a political class identified by political action based on a privatized and achievement-oriented consciousness and clear perceptions about the basis of power in what appeared to its members to be a traditional order rather than a class-based society. Thus the core of the five-class model is a two-class one. In presenting the case I reproduced the diagram (Diagram 3) of the five-class model for pedagogic reasons.

The account of the five-class model was followed by Himmelfarb's criticism of it. Since this criticism was methodological rather than concerned with matters of substance, although the thrust of the methodological criticism would be to introduce other substantial data, the chapter continued with a renewed discussion on historical method. This time it involved a discussion of Historical Idealism and the method of *Verstehen*. The conclusion was that *Verstehen*, unless carefully handled within some clear theoretical framework, degenerated into subjective relativism. Nevertheless, it is a path that historians concerned with the truth of class and class consciousness in our period must tread. As an example of a contemporary analysis which 'confirms' the theoretical appropriateness of the five-class model I summarized the theoretical argument put forward by J. S. Mill in 1839. But that is only one path. In the next chapter I will attempt to lay down several other trails.

6
Class and Class Consciousness, or The Right to the Whole Product of Labour

The significance of Critical-Utopian Socialism and Communism bears an inverse relation to historical development. In proportion as the modern class struggle develops and takes definite shape, this fantastic standing apart from the contest, these fantastic attacks on it, lose all practical value and all theoretical justification. Therefore, although the originators of these systems were in many respects, revolutionary, their disciples have, in every case, formed mere reactionary sects. They hold fast by the original views of their masters, in opposition to the progressive historical development of the proletariat. They, therefore, endeavour, and that consistently, to deaden the class struggle and to reconcile the class antagonisms. They still dream of experimental realization of their social Utopias, of founding isolated 'phalansteres', of establishing 'Home Colonies', of setting up a 'Little Icaria' – duodecimo editions of the New Jerusalem – and to realize all these castles in the air, they are compelled to appeal to the feelings and purses of the bourgeois. By degrees they sink into the category of the reactionary conservative Socialists depicted above . . .

They, therefore, violently oppose all political action on the part of the working class . . .

Karl Marx, *Communist Manifesto*

O'Connor's address to the Imperial Chartists finished with the words:

My beloved friends, I will *join no party*. I will remain firm as the rock, and will cheerfully accept the cooperation of all who will join you and me in breaking the oppressor's head.[1]

Since he was writing for a very diverse group O'Connor may have been deliberately vague – his letter is almost an invitation to his readers to choose their own oppressors and then to join with all others in breaking heads. Unfortunately for historians of class they

[1] *The Northern Star*, 5th November 1842.

cannot, or ought not, to write like politicians. Not only are they obliged to identify oppressors and oppressed they must also identify who the oppressed saw as their oppressors and seek to understand the ideas and attitudes characteristic of the class consciousness of both classes. In this respect Himmelfarb's comments on Carlyle and Disraeli are apt – at least if one is looking for the class consciousness of those in positions of power and influence – and my observations on Mill are relevant for any conclusion about the actual class perception or class consciousness of the middling classes in England. But, if one is interested, as many historians have been, in either verifying or falsifying Marx's notion of *class* consciousness by reference to 'reality' one has to look elsewhere.

This problem, the attribution of class perception or *class* consciousness to different social strata is, perhaps, the most pressing as well as the most difficult task facing social historians. It will test their 'Moral' and 'Historical Imaginations' to the very limit. It will demand, therefore, that they get their theoretical procedures right.

If, like historians of class in the eighteenth and nineteenth centuries, the historian is principally concerned to identify the class perception and the developing *class* consciousness of the mass of the population, the first problem, one that goes without saying, is that he is immediately disadvantaged because most of his subjects have left no record of either act or thought. Secondly, the records in which there is some trace of his subjects – Poor Law, criminal, trade union, company, church, chapel, hospital, local government and government records generally – raise all the problems of a behavioural approach to history. For the most part these records record behaviour connected with applications for relief and sickness, involvement in riots, petty crime, strikes, the payment or non-payment of rates and taxes, enrolment of apprentices, and voting behaviour. Since people may be involved in strikes, crime and riots – and cast their votes – for many individual reasons, inferences about class perception and especially *class* consciousness from collective acts of isolated groups are fraught with immense obstacles. And I have already expressed scepticism about the significance for the existence of *class* consciousness *before* 1840 of the evidence displayed by Foster: seizure of control of vestries, police, and Poor Law by working men, exclusive dealing, and opinions on the Crimean War.

This problem of the behavioural approach is exacerbated by the fact that very many of the extant records have to do with the social pathology of a people. For example, I have recently discovered from records of business before the Mayor and Justices of Bath that between 1787 and 1793 about 1:20 persons in any year was involved in a case of personal assault either as complainant or as defendant and that the ratio of assaults varied inversely with movements of real wages. I could conclude from this that summonses for assault were the tip of the iceberg and that personal violence was characteristic of life among the labouring population in Bath and 'explain' it by reference to the anomie of urban life, or I could argue that 95 per cent of the population in any year were not involved in an assault and that that is evidence of an orderly society if not evidence of community.[2] In each case my explanation would have to be theoretically structured and not merely left as a matter of opinion. This must be so since the theoretical is the *only* way to argue from behaviour to consciousness. This problem and its necessary theoretical resolution weaken all arguments about class perception/*class* consciousness based on criminal statistics and records of transportation. The fundamental cause of the problem is that without knowledge of either individual or collective intent nothing of substance *can* be said about consciousness.

It is also true that expressions of intent not manifest in action may not be interpreted as *class* consciousness. Hence Foster's concern with the issue of intellectual commitment to the actions carried out by his subjects as evidence of *class* consciousness.

Because of the problem of interpreting behaviour as a manifestation of either class perception or *class* consciousness I will not linger long over those historians who have worked at the problem from this direction except to refer the reader to the relevant parts of *Class and Ideology in the Nineteenth Century* and to Morris's comments in *Class and Class Consciousness in the Industrial Revolution 1780–1850*. I will say, however, that for every historian who has focused upon a given series of events as evidence of class perception there is another one who could add more. Not to be outdone I add that there is much to be said about perceptions of property/propertylessness manifested

---

[2] R. S. Neale, *Bath, 1680–1850: A Social History* (London, 1981).

in the Gordon Riots, 1780, the Wiltshire Shearmen's Strike, 1802, the Bristol Riots, 1831, and the national strike of shoemakers in 1803/4 none of which are mentioned in Morris's discussion of the evidence.

Since class consciousness, whether it be thought of as class perception or *class* consciousness, is clearly a matter of the mind it is to products of minds that we must look. Moreover, since *class* consciousness is an intellectual business (chapter 1) it must be sought not merely in attitudes and beliefs but in the production of systematic thought and in the forms of utopian thought generated by response to perceptions about the distribution of power in a society characterized by private property. The ensuing problem will be that of knowing how widespread those perceptions were.

The first step I would like to attempt is to consider ways in which men and women in the eighteenth century perceived their own society and particularly to ask, to what extent did they see their world as order based and did they see it structured around relations of authority and subordination based on a division between those with and those without property. I will attempt this by displaying some of the conscious products of minds that, by all accounts, were widely bought, read and looked at. Some at least of the anonymous masses must have shared the perceptions of the authors of the works they admired.

The theme of antagonism between property and liberty, which had been recognized by the Levellers, Gerrard Winstanley and the Diggers between 1647 and 1652, clearly survived in popular memory in the eighteenth century even though it seems to have faded from standard history for nearly 300 years. The theme is revealed in Plate 1 from the *Catchpenny Prints*. These prints were published *c*. 1780 as popular broadsheets and children's chapbooks by the firm of Bowles and Carver at No. 69 St Pauls Churchyard.[3] They were very popular and widely read. In Plate 1, property and liberty are depicted as a pair of fighting cocks. The animals and birds in the surrounding pictures all evoke rural and, therefore, landed imagery. Except for the baboon. This may be a purely random choice of subject. On the other hand, in other prints in the collection, baboons and apes are sometimes dressed in clothes worn

---

[3] *Catchpenny Prints* (Dover Publications, New York, 1970).

Liberty and Property, A Pair of Fighting Cocks, c. 1780. By general permission of Dover Publications, *Catchpenny Prints*, 1970.

by the aristocracy and military officers. This association of apes with a decadent aristocracy is also a common theme in Hogarth's comic histories.

Hogarth's work generally may be regarded as bitter moral criticism of the ruling elites in a society based on private property and absolute self-interest stated from the standpoint of a petit bourgeois. Indeed, his earlier prints, including *An Emblematical Print on The South Sea Scheme*, 1721, *The Lottery*, 1721 and *Some of The Principal Inhabitants of Ye Moon: Royalty, Episcopacy and Law*, 1724, reflected the critical standpoint of a London craftsman yet to reach the ranks of the petit bourgeois. His perception and critical position, undoubtedly shared by many, may be shown very clearly through an analysis of the last of these prints. In *Royalty, Episcopacy and Law*, Royalty is represented as a shroud with no corporeal substance and a crownpiece for a face. The moons displayed on the king's orb and sceptre are emblems of inconstancy. Episcopacy, seated higher than Royalty, has a jew's harp for a face and, with every twang of the harp from a hand raised in a blessing, works a money pump in the form of a church steeple also topped by another emblem of inconstancy, a weathervane. The bishop's coat of arms is a carving knife and fork. Law, with a mallet for a face, is without a left arm to hold the scales of justice and carries a gigantic sword in his right hand. The judge is flanked by two symbols of the dilettantish, aristocratic society; the woman has a teapot for a face, a glass for a neck and a fan as a torso. Her companion has a mirror for a face and two decorated fan sticks for legs. The king is flanked by courtiers with mirrors for bodies and money as heads and by soldiers in the garb of firescreens. As if the context was insufficiently critical, Hogarth set the scene within the circular frame and cloudy surroundings favoured by the baroque history painters whose products lauded their wealthy and propertied patrons. It is a penetrating satire on Thornhill's Greenwich Hospital painting of William and Mary, or of George I and his family. But, above all, it is an uncompromising criticism of all fractions of the ruling elite from a lower-class perspective.[4] All that is lacking is an explicit reference to property. Yet one may doubt that his customers needed any such reminder.

As anyone who knows Hogarth's work must realize, his world and his representation of it, unlike the world as it appears in the work of most historians writing on class, included women. His portrayal of them shows the degree to which he saw their subordination and exploitation tied to property and power. They were the most exploited class. For example, while *A Harlot's Progress*, 1732, may be understood as a simple tale of corrupted innocence, a knowledge of Hogarth's allusions and emblems shows his perspective to be subversive. His message in the print is that an attractive girl from an artisan or petit-bourgeois family, such as Moll Hackabout, had little control over the course of her life. Rather it was determined by society. Through its prevailing materialist mores, based on property, self-interest and self-indulgence, this society emphasized conspicuous consumption and the luxury of outward show and appearance – it was, after all, the heroic age of primitive accumulation in England. And, through the growth of centres of consumption, such as London and Bath, the social system invited labourers,

---

[4]There are many versions of Hogarth's prints but see especially, *Engravings by Hogarth*, ed. Sean Shesgreen (New York, 1973). See, also, R. Paulson, *Hogarth: His Life, Art and Times* (New Haven, 1971) and F. Antal, *Hogarth and his Place in European Art* (London, 1962).

Royalty, Episcopacy and Law, 1725: Hogarth's Satirical Comment on Power in the Eighteenth Century. By permission of the British Library.

both men and women, to emulate their betters and to be mobile in search of higher earnings – why else would a country seamstress arrive unmet in London? In these circumstances the only alternative open to Moll, indicated in plate one as a life of domestic drudgery and, thereby, of total subordination, was no choice at all.

Moreover, whatever marginal choice there might have been was effectively blocked by the attitudes and behaviour of the wealthy and powerful who set themselves up as models of society but did all in their power to seduce girls like Moll to their own ways and then to punish them for being seduced. This made it even more difficult for Moll to choose a life of drudgery at the start or to renounce her trade once embarked on it. At the same time the effect of legal decisions and the practice of the Church created role models in the form of successful criminals and self-regarding parsons which reinforced the original impulse to emulation and the consequences of the initial act of seduction. In a word, in the civil society portrayed by Hogarth everyone preyed on everyone else except, as he suggests, the loyal servant class; Moll's bunter was faithful to the end.

Stylistically, also, there is a starkness and gloominess about *A Harlot's Progress* that reinforces the oppressive and despondent mood of its content. Moreover, the strong verticals in plate one become more pronounced as the series progresses until, in the final plate, the assembled company is as boxed in it as Moll is in her coffin.

But life was no better for a woman at the other end of the social scale. In *Marriage à La Mode* the fate of two young people is decided against their wills by the noble institutions of family and landed property coupled with the social aspirations of those who had neither. In short, a wealthy bourgeois sells his petulant, plebian daughter to a noble of ancient lineage as a wife for his disinterested, dandified son. This act, in the interest of property, destroys both young people for whom there is no choice. Furthermore, the way in which each is destroyed is conditioned by the values of the social class to which each belongs. The young man, already marked by a 'beauty' spot, seeks his pleasure in debauching young girls like Moll in *A Harlot's Progress*. The girl, his wife, surrounds herself with all the pleasures and trappings of the aristocracy. She takes a lover and is surprised in bed with him by her husband. In the ensuing fracas the husband, an ignoble victim of his own dual sexual standard, is killed by the lover in self-defence. The lover is caught and executed. The girl takes laudanum and dies. Her only child, a crippled girl, is also marked by her father's beauty spot. The aristocratic line is dead. This series is a savage and unrelenting attack on all the institutions and values of both aristocratic and bourgeois society from a lower-class/order perspective.

In fact, in his individual prints and his comic histories Hogarth directed a continuous stream of criticism at the social values and behaviour of the ruling elite. As indicated in chapter 4, this included great agrarian capitalists, court and government functionaries, place-hunting politicians and clerics, and stockjobbers and dealers in money and credit, all of whom were creatures of the economic changes they helped to produce, which are best subsumed under the Marxian concept of primitive accumulation. In this system Hogarth was himself a petit bourgeois with origins in the ranks of London's artisans, a member of one of those classes developing in the interstices of agrarian capitalist society referred to in chapter 3. Hogarth was a self-made man; the product of talent, work, successful marriage and, in the end, the new mass market for art generated by the spread of economic prosperity in England.

That prosperity was built on a society based on private property, self-interest and the growth of individualism. And the separation between self and society brought about by this new world, epitomized by Christian in *Pilgrim's Progress* and by Robinson Crusoe, also marked the beginnings of a new sense of alienation from society and a need to find ways of overcoming it.

Hogarth's art grew out of these new opportunities and the tensions they created. This was a new sort of world and Hogarth's art a new kind of art. It should be accommodated within the account of any historian concerned with class consciousness in the eighteenth century. Yet the fact is that general economic and social historians as well as those concerned with class in the eighteenth century rarely, if ever, include Hogarth's work in their analyses. When they do so it is to illustrate either some facet of a general European enlightenment, or to claim Hogarth as a patriot and a living example of John Bull.[5] Significant work on Hogarth has been left to art historians, principally Antal and Paulson, but they, working

---

[5] Hogarth is not referred to in the major writings of E. P. Thompson, Harold Perkin or Peter Laslett. He is also ignored by cultural historians such as Norman Hampson and Basil Willey. According to Peter Gay, *The Enlightenment: An Interpretation*, vol. 2 (London, 1970), p. 218, Hogarth was the carrier of generalized, enlightened 'values of industry, sobriety and humanity'. According to David Jarrett, *England in the Age of Hogarth* (London, 1974), p. 22, 'He was also himself an archetype of the freeborn Englishman, coming close in many ways to that most basic and influential of archetypes, John Bull'.

within the framework of the three-class model, seem content to locate him within an aristocratic/middle-class relationship.[6]

Law is undoubtedly a product of minds. As E. P. Thompson and his colleagues have shown, eighteenth-century law both reflected and embodied a class perception of English society. Law revealed not only the perceptions of those in power but also identified the existence of groups hostile to certain aspects of the behaviour of those in power and against whom the powerful tested and developed their own class consciousness. For example, the year before Hogarth published *Royalty, Episcopacy and Law*, the men of property who had benefited from the Revolution of 1688 and who enjoyed the fruits of great property safe in the justification of it provided by John Locke, enacted in four weeks the Black Act which created at one legislative stroke some fifty new capital offences. The occasion for the passing of this Act was an outburst of 'Blacking' in which men on horseback and on foot armed with guns and accompanied by dogs took deer, rabbits, hares, gamebirds and fish, broke down fences and fishponds and took timber from the Royal Forest at Windsor and from forests in Hampshire belonging to the Crown and the Bishopric of Winchester. The 'Blacks' claimed that they were simply exercising customary rights in these forests. The Crown and the Bishops claimed that these were offences against property. Because the authorities found it increasingly difficult to protect the rights of private property they sought to intimidate and terrorize the local population. The result was the Black Act. In the first few years of its operation at least sixteen men were hanged, an unknown number died in Newgate and Reading gaols, many more were transported or imprisoned and some forty or more became outlaws. The Black Act remained on the Statute Book for more than 100 years.[7] Its clauses merit reading with some serious consideration by those who claim that England was a 'class-less' or a 'one-class' society in the early eighteenth century.

Adam Smith, who might be thought of as knowing his world better than historians, had no doubt that England was divided into

---

[6] Antal, *Hogarth*, and Paulson, *Hogarth: His Life, Art and Times*.

[7] The Black Act, 1 George II, 1723; see E. P. Thompson, *Whigs and Hunters* (London, 1975). Also, E. P. Thompson (ed.), *Albion's Fatal Tree: Crime and Society in Eighteenth-century England* (London, 1975).

two contending classes or orders. It was because it was so divided that he found the expenses of justice in the protection of property a legitimate component in the expenses of the Sovereign necessary for the growth of the wealth of a nation. The basis for this view was that property, which gave to some the right to appropriate the product of the labour of the majority, was the key to wealth. However, Smith also recognized that a corollary of great property was propertylessness and great inequality. This could be expected to incite indignation among the labouring population and result in threats by them against property such that 'The acquisition of valuable and extensive property, therefore, necessarily requires the establishment of civil government.'[8] Indeed, Smith was so persuaded of the necessity of property that he wrote: 'Civil Government, so far as it is instituted for the security of property, is in reality instituted for the defence of the rich against the poor, or of those who have some property against those who have none at all.'[9]

Some writers and publicists believed that property and attitudes associated with it and flowing from it permeated everything with the hegemony of property such that it just was a fact of life. In this genre Jane Austen's novels are all about property and *Mansfield Park* may be read as an essay on property and alienation. William Blake, in his poem 'London' also reduced life to the hegemony of property. Only this time it was property seen as the economic and political rights of the Corporation of the City of London as granted to them by the Crown – even the Thames was 'chartered' and the inequality of property and power permeated every crevice of human life.

LONDON
I wander thro' each charter'd street,
Near where the charter'd Thames does flow
And mark in every face I meet
Marks of weakness, marks of woe.

In every cry of every Man,
In every Infants cry of fear,
In every voice; in every ban,
The mind-forg'd manacles I hear.

[8] Adam Smith, *The Wealth of Nations*, Everyman edn (London, 1947), vol. II, p. 199.
[9] *Ibid.*, p. 203.

How the Chimney-sweepers cry
Every blackning Church appalls,
And the hapless Soldiers sigh
Runs in blood down Palace walls.

But most thro' midnight streets I hear
How the youthful Harlots curse
Blasts the new-born Infants tear
And blights with plagues the Marriage hearse.[10]

In *The Rights of Man* Tom Paine also generalized about property and traced its illegal origin to William the Conqueror and his descendants who, having conquered the country, 'parcelled out the country in this manner, and bribed some parts of it by what they call charters to hold the other parts of it the better subjected to their will'.[11] In saying that and although he used natural rights arguments similar to those of John Locke he directly challenged Locke's justification of great property. Moreover, instead of applauding the Revolution of 1688 as the great achievement it seemed to Locke to be, Paine regarded it as eclipsed by the advance of reason and the revolutions in America and France. According to Paine the Bill of Rights, which was a constitutional product of the Revolution of 1688, was a Bill of Wrongs. Thus, in the writings of Tom Paine, property was the illegitimate product of power and incompatible with liberty.

That there were other people who shared the perceptions of Blake and Paine and those other, possibly humbler writers yet to be discussed in the remainder of this chapter is shown by the anonymously written *Political Creed* published in 1794. It is brief enough to speak for itself:

Political Creed

I believe that God is the impartial father of the whole human race; that the rights of all men therefore must be equal; and that he who tamely resigns those rights, wrongs his posterity, degrades himself, and ought to be ashamed to live.

I believe that no authority can be legitimate but that which is delegated by free voice of the people; and that the representative system, founded on frequent elections and universal suffrage, is the perfection of political wisdom.

[10] William Blake, *Songs of Innocence and Experience* (Oxford reprint, 1967), plate 46.
[11] Tom Paine, *The Rights of Man* (London, 1937), p. 39.

Yet, even in a government thus constituted, to allow any individual the power of waging war, on rendering abortive the general voice, appears to be preposterous; because it presumes that the intellect of one man is superior to the consolidated intellect of a nation.

As those who govern ought to possess integrity and abilities and as integrity and abilities cannot be transmitted from sire to son, I therefore believe that hereditary kings, and hereditary legislators, are hereditary —

Religion, I believe to be an affair between the conscience of man and his Creator, and that it ought to be as free as the atmosphere in which we breath; that all national churches are national defects, and that the state which compels me to contribute to any teacher, particularly to a teacher whose doctrines I can not approve, is guilty of a robbery. The mind is seated far above coercion. Hypocrites may be produced by force; proselytes never.

I believe that all unequal laws must necessarily be unjust, and that every country in which one description of men are privileged, and another debased, in which one man may sweep over the fields and fences of his neighbour and kill his hare in triumph, whilst another who destroys the animal in the act of plundering his little garden, shall be doomed to fine or imprisonment; in which one man may loll on the lap of pleasure, and for a few scrapes of the pen receive thousands on thousands annually from the coffers of the nation; whilst another shall be dragged from his dearest connexions, and compelled to fight the battles of a weak or a wicked minister for a few pence per day – Every country in which these and the like enormities are found, however free the forms, or however the tongue of prejudice may sound its praise, I firmly believe to be in a state of slavery; and therefore to be a miserable residence for men of liberal souls.[12]

And so to William Hone and his lampoon, *The Political House that Jack Built*. William Hone was a printer and bookseller and a former member of the London Corresponding Society. In 1817 he was tried three times for publishing blasphemous libels in the form of parodies of the Catechism, Litany and Creed. According to E. P. Thompson these three trials 'are some of the most hilarious legal proceedings on record'.[13] Needless to say the London juries brought down verdicts of 'Not Guilty' and Hone was at liberty in 1819 to publish his most renowned lampoon which went on sale at one shilling a copy. The fact that it ran to forty-six editions by 1820 is testimony to the popularity of the work which is reputed to have sold 100,000

---

[12]Anon., *Liberty – Scraps* (London?, 1794).
[13]William Hone, *The Political House that Jack Built*, forty-sixth edn (London, 1820).
E. P. Thompson, *The Making of the English Working Class* (London, 1963), p. 721.

copies. It takes only a few explanations to make its message as clear today as it was when first published. Thus; the Dandy of Sixty was the Prince Regent, the Doctor was the Home Secretary, Lord Sidmouth, and the Spouter of Froth By The Hour was the President of the India Board, George Canning, who became Prime Minister in 1827. The notorious Derry Down Triangle was the Foreign Secretary, Lord Castlereagh, so-called because of his active part in the brutality of the Irish repression of 1798. The peaceable meeting for Reform was 'Peterloo' held in Manchester in 1819, at which eleven people were killed and over 400 wounded by an unannounced and uncontrolled charge of the Yeomanry. *The Political House that Jack Built*, which identified the Wealth that lay in the house that Jack built as Magna Charta, the Bill of Rights and habeas corpus as well as a great chest overflowing with money, also identified the Vermin,

> That plunder the Wealth
> That lay in the House,
> That Jack built

as flunkeys, soldiers, clergymen, tax collectors and lawyers. Throughout the lampoon they are supported by the coercive power of the state. The result: 'The People, all tattered and torn, -who curse the day wherein they were born.' *The Political House that Jack Built* was the irreverent apotheosis of Locke's, *Two Treatises of Government*. Property was inimical to liberty.

The foregoing instances refer to a people's perception of their society. It suggests that some on both sides of the property divide saw their world as divided between those with and those without property and saw clearly that property determined the relations of authority and subordination in that society. Yet, in all probability, their thought was still more structured by perceptions of orders than of classes. Thus Hogarth, Jane Austen and probably even Hone looked to peaceable improvements arising from a morally regenerated ruling elite – their watchword was not revolution but reform.

In laying out this brief selection of evidence I mentioned none of the problems that arise in connection with the identification of the sort of systematic thought and forms of utopian thinking which would be necessary to settle the question of the existence or

———" Not to understand a treasure's worth,
Till time has stolen away the slighted good,
Is cause of half the poverty we feel,
And makes the world the wilderness it is."

THIS IS

THE WEALTH

that lay
In the House that Jack built.

The Wealth of England in 1817: Its Political Constitution. From *The Political House that Jack Built*, William Hone, 46th edition, London, 1820.

——— ——" A race obscene,
Spawn'd in the muddy beds of Nile, came forth,
Polluting Egypt: gardens, fields, and plains,
Were cover'd with the pest;
The croaking nuisance lurk'd in every nook;
Nor palaces, nor even chambers, 'scap'd;
And the land stank — so num'rous was the fry."

THESE ARE

THE VERMIN

That plunder the Wealth,
That lay in the House,
That Jack built.

The Opponents of the People in 1817. From *The Political House that Jack Built*, William Hone, 46th edition, London, 1820.

emergence of *class* consciousness, at least among leaders. And it is to that question I turn again by reference to Foster's work. I do so because in his work Foster has come closer than most other historians to arguing for the fact of *class* consciousness by 1840 – a proposition, incidentally, to which it is not necessary for a Marxist historian to adhere.

Foster claims that the really significant development in Oldham pointing to *class* consciousness was the intellectual commitment of the spinners and their politicization of an industrial dispute in 1841. But, as I have already said, what has to be shown is that the objectives of the revolutionaries went beyond mere bread and butter ones conceived in the interest of a particular section of society but were more touched with Marx's notion of the proletariat as the dissolution of all classes than coloured by mere bourgeois or petit-bourgeois notions of equal right. It is in this latter respect that the intellectual commitment of Foster's radical working-class leaders can be seen to be most defective.

A crucial notion, central to the development of *class* consciousness, is that the labourer has a right to the whole product of his labour. Yet this notion was not peculiar to Marx. It sprang from a long tradition of ideas about equal rights to property which came to be systematically formulated in the writings of Ogilvie, Spence and Hall and can probably be traced to its intellectual origins in the work of John Locke. These ideas were available in pamphlet and book form in the first three decades of the nineteenth century.

The lack of discussion by Foster about the notion of labour's right to the whole product of labour and its consequences for action is a vital omission. This is so because any claim about the development or existence of a working-class *class* consciousness of a Marxian kind *must* demonstrate the germination of something more than a merely revolutionizing or politicizing consciousness. It must demonstrate that the purpose of revolutionary and political activity was to transform the capital/labour relationship according to arguments and principles arising from the labour theory of value. It is according to such claims that capitalists may be said to have no moral right and only a legal right to profits earned on capital which is legally but not morally theirs. This is not to say that early forms of working-class consciousness must only be defined in terms of Marx's mature theory, only that an embryonic working-class *class* consciousness must be touched by some primitive form of it.

Of all the working-class leaders discussed by Foster it is only the Owenite Socialists who came at all close to formulating policies based on notions about labour's right to the whole product of labour. But, only four out of fifty-seven of Oldham's working-class leaders, active in 1832, 1842 and 1848 are listed by Foster as Owenite Socialists and he does not discuss their ideas!

Other historians, however, *have* taken up this theme of the importance of beliefs about labour's right to the whole product of labour. The classic statement about it was made by H. S. Foxwell in his introduction to Anton Menger's, *The Right to the Whole Produce of Labour*. According to Foxwell, Menger

Conclusively proves that all the fundamental ideas of modern revolutionary socialism [he was writing in 1899] and especially of the Marxian socialism, can be definitely traced to English sources. It was a handful of English writers, brought up in the classic country of capitalistic production, and reflecting upon the terrible wreckage of the early pre-regulation period, who laid down the broad lines of thought upon which socialistic criticism of capitalism has ever since proceeded. Original, independent, trenchant and radical as they were, this little school of writers stand apart, clearly distinguishable from the various groups of contemporary social reformers, as well as from that English socialism whose form was determined by foreign influences. Not content, as the common English habit is, to attempt to palliate the miseries of the time by specific and detailed legislation, they challenged the very principles upon which the system of society rested; and while others were absorbed in the advocacy of social utopias, they devoted themselves to asserting the inherent defects and injustice of the existing system, and demanded that these defects should be dealt with by radical and preventive, rather than by regulative and remedial methods.

Of this English School, the chief names are undoubtedly those of Godwin, Hall, Thompson, Gray, Hodgskin, and Bray. It will seem to many that Robert Owen should be added to this list. But though it is impossible to exaggerate the importance of the Owenite movement as a propagandist and remedial agency, and as a means of giving asylum and resonance to socialist ideas, Robert Owen himself was not remarkable as a militant and destructive thinker. Thomas Spence and Tom Paine, and even William Cobbett in some respects, might have a stronger title to be regarded as leaders of the revolutionary movement. Much more, I think, may be said . . . for the claims of William Ogilvie.[14]

Foxwell also argued that it was Ricardo not Owen who gave productive inspiration to English socialism. This inspiration came

[14]Anton Menger, *The Right to the Whole Produce of Labour*, introduced by H. S. Foxwell (London, 1899), pp. xxvi-xxvii.

to them via the labour theory of value from which these socialists derived the idea that labour had a right to the whole product of labour. This, said Foxwell, 'was the real intellectual origin of revolutionary socialism and it is for this reason I have called it Ricardian'.[15]

Subsequently historians of ideas, such as George Lichtheim, have challenged the more extreme claims of Foxwell and Menger and have pointed out that Marxian Revolutionary Socialism had at least three points of origin: French Revolutionary Socialism, German Socialism and Ricardian Socialism. As well it depended upon Marx's use of the synthesizing capacity of Hegel's system of thought. Further, according to this view, English socialism was never revolutionary nor truly socialist.

Nevertheless, English historians with greater awareness of the complexity of the real world and more concerned with the lateral history of moments in time than with linear histories of thought have been attracted, and rightly so, by the writings of the Ricardian Socialists, and in their search for evidence of working-class *class* consciousness in the early nineteenth-century they refer to the thought of the Ricardian Socialists and thereby to the indigenous origins of English socialist thought and its proto-Marxist character. For example, at the end of his great work on *The Making of the English Working Class*, E. P. Thompson writes:

When Marx was still in his teens, the battle for the minds of English trade unionists, between a capitalist and a socialist political economy, had been (at least temporarily) won. The winners were Hodgskin, Thompson, James Morrison and O'Brien; [all advocates of the idea that labour had a right to the whole product of labour]; the losers were James Mill and Place . . .

From 1830 onwards a more clearly defined class consciousness, in the customary Marxist sense, was maturing, in which working people were aware of continuing both old and new battles on their own.[16]

Harold Perkin also writes:

Whenever it [the idea of the right of labour to the whole of its product] succeeded, it transformed the working class movement from an ameliorative one which accepted the basic structure of the new class society into a revolutionary one which rejected it altogether . . .

[15] *Ibid.*, p. lxxxiii.
[16] E. P. Thompson, *Making of the English Working Class*, pp. 829 and 712.

Chartism was more than a movement for Parliamentary Reform: it was an attempt to restore by political means the worker's right to the whole produce of labour.[17]

Moreover, Perkin believes that a mature working class sprang into existence sometime between 1815 and 1820.

More recently David Jones in his *Chartism and The Chartists* has written:

Another popular idea [of the Chartists] which Thomas Hodgskin, Owen, Henry Hetherington and a whole battalion of anti-capitalists placed at the centre of their philosophy, was that the distribution of wealth should be regulated by the labour theory of value.[18]

Nevertheless, both Thompson and Perkin qualify their conclusions. Thompson observes that the victory in the battle for the minds of trade unionists was only of two years standing. He also admits that the total content of the collective working-class *class* consciousness he describes, even when it incorporated ideas about the labour theory of value and labour's right to the whole of its product, was so mixed and confused that he was led to doubt its very existence as a collective consciousness. In the penultimate paragraph of his book he says: 'These years [the 1830s] appear at times to display, not a revolutionary challenge, but a resistance movement, in which both the Romantics and the Radical Craftsmen opposed the annunciation of Acquisitive Man.[19] Harold Perkin similarly qualifies his initial strong positive assertion about the nature of working-class *class* consciousness and the influence on it of ideas about the rights of labour to the whole of its product. These qualifications lead him to interpret demands for political reform and systems which merely encouraged workers to opt out of the competitive capitalist system as revolutionary responses. He concludes 'The fragmentation of the [working-class] ideal in practice as well as theory was its fundamental weakness'.[20]

And so we come to the Catch 22 in the proposition I have advanced.

[17] Harold Perkin, *The Origins of Modern English Society* (London, 1969), p. 236 and 389.
[18] David Jones, *Chartism and The Chartists* (London, 1975), p. 36.
[19] E. P. Thompson, *Making of the English Working Class*, p. 832.
[20] Harold Perkin, *Origins of Modern English Society*, p. 237.

Evidence of ideas about the right of labour to the whole product of labour can point to the emergence of *class* consciousness in workers. Further, a working-class *class* consciousness of a Marxian kind cannot be said to exist in their absence. On the other hand evidence of ideas about the right of labour to the whole of its product will not provide sufficient grounds for making firm statements about the existence of a working-class *class* consciousness of a Marxian kind. In this respect Foxwell's introduction is misleading. Foxwell called his little school 'Ricardian Socialists' and did so because he attributed the essence of their thought, their ideas about the labour theory of value, to Ricardo. Then, because Marx derived his original version of the labour theory of value from Ricardo, Foxwell saw these English authors as proto-Marxists. Yet it is by no means certain that all the members of Foxwell's school of Ricardian Socialists got their ideas from Ricardo nor that their followers saw their ideas as dependent upon Ricardo's labour theory of value. In fact it can be shown that the thought of many of these English forerunners of Marx also antedated that of Ricardo. And it can be shown that they drew their inspiration and perception from other sources which were themselves the products of a pre-industrial form of society. Thus, while the society which bred their response was indeed capitalist, it was agrarian and commercial capitalist rather than industrial. In that different form of capitalism and in perceptions arising from it lies a world of difference with great significance for our identification of *class* consciousness.

Menger identified a most significant characteristic of these early English theorists when he wrote:

In no country in the world is the whole economic life so completely dominated by that system of production which since Louis Blanc has been called capitalism, as in England. We should therefore expect to find the socialist campaign directed mainly against so-called *mobile capital* (*Mobiles Kapital*). In point of fact, the exact opposite is the case. Those socialist systems which have as yet attained any great degree of popularity in England direct their attack against landed property and rent, and concern themselves but little with profits and property in capital.[21]

Menger's explanation for this phenomenon was a political one. He argued that concentration of landed property had reduced the

[21] Anton Menger, *Right to the Whole Produce of Labour*, p. 146.

actual authority of landlords to negligible proportions while parliamentary reforms had substantially reduced their political power.
Therefore, he said, they were a declining force suitable and ripe for
attack. Hence the development of theories attacking landed
property. While there may have been something in this argument
when Menger wrote in the 1880s it is inadequate as an explanation
of the generation of the theories themselves some sixty or a hundred
years earlier. And it is to an account of the origin of those ideas that
we must turn.

The case against property, originally and especially a case
against landed property, had its roots in the eighteenth century in a
society conscious of the antagonism between property and liberty
described earlier in this chapter and in a stream of thought
expressed in the writings of William Ogilvie, William Godwin,
Charles Hall and Thomas Spence. Of these writers Ogilvie and
Spence in the eighteenth century wrote independently of any
influence from Adam Smith's version of the labour theory of value.
Further, in the early nineteenth century, Ricardo's version of the
labour theory of value cannot be held to have influenced the views
of many writers on socialism. For example, John Gray, one of the
'school' referred to by Foxwell, acknowledged no debt to Ricardo in
his *Lecture on Human Happiness* but did draw heavily on Colquhon
and Owen. Furthermore, the *Articles of Agreement of the London Co-
operative Society* (1825), prepared for the foundation of a co-operative
community, reflected the views of Godwin and William Thompson
more than they did those of Owen. They showed no influence of
any kind flowing from Ricardo. Only in the work of Charles Hall
writing at the very end of the eighteenth century did this stream of
thought connect with the labour theory of value of the classical
economists. But it did so through reference to Adam Smith's idea
that property was power over labour rather than through the work
of Ricardo. In fact, Ricardo's theory could not have influenced
anyone writing before 1817. Furthermore none of these writers was
referred to as a socialist until after 1827.

In the writings of Ogilvie and Spence the oppressors in the
eighteenth century were identified as landlords. They were a class
of idle men occupying all the available land and living on an
unearned income extracted from it. This they protected against the
propertyless with all the force of laws of their own making.

Therefore, said Ogilvie and Spence, the form of oppression experienced by the propertyless was deprivation of property and, therefore, deprivation of the means to a full and independent life. According to Ogilvie this was an offence against natural law which gives to every man an equal share of the soil in its original state. He said: 'This title to an equal share of property in land seems original, inherent, and indefeasible by any act or determination of others, though capable of being alienated by our own. It is a birthright which every citizen still retains.'[22] Spence, too, believed in the fact of an equal natural right to property in land.

Nevertheless, these two writers based their separate solutions to the problem of the distribution of property on an acceptance of the fact of unequal property. Therefore, their solutions were 'non-revolutionary' solutions designed only to modify the system of landholding. However, had their solutions been implemented the new systems of landholding would have produced 'revolutionary' consequences. For example, Ogilvie in his progressive agrarian law granted to every citizen over twenty-one years of age the right to claim land up to forty acres in perpetuity and to pay a fixed perpetual rent to the private landlord. The new property owner was to live on the farm and have power to transmit it to his heirs. However, he was not to have powers of alienation whether by lease or will, nor rights of common on the manor. All who acquired property under this law were to perform service in the county militia and pay to the lord of the manor, the landlord 'certain aids and services of a feudal nature, so regulated as to produce that degree of connection and dependence which may be expedient for preserving order and subordination in the country without danger of giving rise to oppression and abuse'.[23]

There was more to Ogilvie's proposals than briefly reported here although what is reported is sufficient to show that Ogilvie's utopia, like all eighteenth-century utopias, was a backward-looking one. His perception of the proper arrangement for society was that it should be firmly based on a prosperous peasantry who were to be capable of bearing arms but bound to larger landowners by ties of

---

[22] William Ogilvie, *An Essay on the Right of Property in Land* (London, 1782), p. 9.
[23] *Ibid.*, pp. 99–100.

connection and dependence. It was essentially an arcadian and organicist solution to the impending breakdown of society.

Spence's utopia was also arcadian. One difference between it and Ogilvie's was that collective landownership was to replace private landlordism. Thus, parish land was to be let in small lots at public auction and the rents due paid into the parish treasuries. Parish officials would then use the income to pay the parish's share of central government costs, poor relief, official salaries and to provide a fund for defraying the cost of necessary local public works. The whole was to come under the control of democratically organized parish meetings. As Spence's plan changed with time his parishes took on more and more the appearance of parish republics bound together by a central government to which they would be subordinated. Nevertheless, 'Spensonia', his utopian island, kept its arcadian image as he described it as a paradise of gardens, meadows, pastures and orchards, in which everything was 'neat and indicative of domestic happiness . . . the habitation of rational beings worthy the approbation of the Deity . . .'.[24] This Spensonian system could never be overthrown by force because all Spensonians were to be soldiers serving in a citizen army in which promotion was to be by merit. Spence's view of the ideal society was a rather more egalitarian one than Ogilvie's.

The writings of Ogilvie and Spence were widely read and discussed during the second half of the eighteenth century and, no doubt, oral tradition carried their ideas in various forms into the early years of the nineteenth. But, it was Charles Hall's *The Effects of Civilization* (1805, 1813, and 1849) which linked eighteenth-century themes concerned with property and the distribution of wealth, as set out in the work of Ogilvie and Spence, to those of the first English 'Socialists' of the early nineteenth century. For example, the 1849 edition of Hall's book was brought out by John Minter Morgan who had been an ardent admirer of Hall in the early 1820s. Indeed, Hall's ideas had influenced Morgan in the writing of his own *The Revolt of the Bees* (1825). In this book, and like John Gray in his *Lecture on Human Happiness*, Morgan recommended his readers to the proposal for a co-operative community contained

[24] Thomas Spence, *Pig's Meat*, ii (1794), p. 214.

in the London Co-operative's Articles of Agreement and it seems
likely that *The Revolt of the Bees* was well known to the early co-
operators. Further, the fact that Minter Morgan once employed
William Lovett to make a model of an industrial village for him,
probably in 1828, indicates that at least one member of the future
LWMA also knew his work and through him the writing of Charles
Hall. Charles Hall's ideas were also known to Francis Place as well
as to Spence with whom Hall had disagreed over Spence's neglect
of the problem of inequality of forms of property other than landed
property and for his retention of too much of the existing economic
system in his schemes.

In short, I think there can be little doubt that Hall's book was
well known, at least to those who played leading roles in the formation of ideas which served as triggers in the growth of working-class
perceptions. Indeed, Foxwell singled out Hall as especially significant in the history of the labour theory of value and Max Beer,
although rejecting Hall's conclusions and proposals, considered his
position as 'an intermediary one between natural law or ethical
socialism and proletarian or revolutionary socialism. It is the first
interpretation of the voice of rising labour'.[25]

More recently, however, historians have given scant attention to
Hall, remarking only upon his classification of society into rich and
poor and his notion, derived from Adam Smith, that wealth was
power over labour. Yet Hall, a Devonshire doctor, is important in
our present inquiry not only because of the influence of his ideas
but also because he had a clear perception of the structure of the
society in which he lived and worked which led him to suggest a
visual model for thinking about it.

In this model he identified clearly the source of power and
oppression in early nineteenth-century society as he saw it and set
out clearly his own utopian vision as a remedy.

Hall wrote:

The people in a civilized state may be divided into many different orders;
but for the purpose of investigating the manner in which they enjoy or are
deprived of the requisites to support the health of their bodies and minds,
they need only be divided into two classes, viz., the rich and the poor.[26]

---

[25] Max Beer, *History of British Socialism* (London, 1920), vol. 1, p. 127.
[26] Charles Hall, *The Effects of Civilization on the People in European States* (London,
1805), p. 3.

Asa Briggs believes that when Hall made this statement using the language of class he 'stated clearly for the first time the central proposition of a class theory of society'.[27] But this claim by Briggs about the significance of Hall's work, which is similar to that made by Beer and Foxwell, is misleading because Hall also used the language of orders and ranks when he wrote:

He would naturally therefore, divide the people . . . into two orders, viz. the rich and the poor. We shall make the same division; and as the different conditions of the people are among the greatest effects of civilization, shall inquire into the situation of each of these orders separately.[28]

Further, since Hall also described at least three sub-classes or degrees of the order or class of the rich it is clear that he used the languages of 'order' and of 'class' interchangeably[29] and did not reserve the term 'class' for use only in a two-class model.

In fact Hall used a two-order model of society more frequently than the two-class one with which he is credited. And rightly so. Hall's concern was the unequal division of power in society which resulted from inequality in the distribution of wealth. Therefore, following Adam Smith, he defined wealth as that which gives power over and commands the labour of the poor. He believed that the kind of power that wealth gave to the rich over the poor in the early nineteenth century was similar to and originated with 'that which antiently the great allodial lords, and the feudal barons of almost all Europe exercised over their vassals'.[30] Thus in Hall's analysis the source of power in the early nineteenth century was wealth derived from landed property, the unequal distribution of which divided society into possessors and non-possessors and deprived the latter of the means of life itself, to mental and spiritual improvement, and to happiness.

Having established this relationship between land, wealth and power, Hall then proceeded to show how all forms of government, whether monarchical or republican, were in fact ruled by an

---

[27]Asa Briggs, The language of 'class' in early nineteenth-century England, first published 1969. Reprinted in M. W. Flinn and T. C. Smout (eds), *Essays in Social History* (Oxford, 1974), p. 157. See also J. R. Dinwiddy, Charles Hall, early English socialist, *International Review of Social History* **XXI**, 1976, pp. 256–76.

[28]Charles Hall, *Effects of Civilization*, p. 2.

[29]See, for example, the discussion, *ibid.*, pp. 137–9 and p. 43.

[30]*Ibid.*, p. 50.

aristocracy of the landed rich. In his discussion of the nature of monarchy he used a conical image of society to project his order-based perception of its social and political structure. This perception is another by a contemporary to add to that of J. S Mill. I leave him to describe it in his own words:

I have often imagined that the first stage of things (monarchy) might be aptly represented by a cylinder of a great length, but whose thickness or base was too small for it, when placed perpendicularly, to continue in that position. Around this towering royal cylinder, other cylinders, about two thirds of its height, are placed; these may represent the late princes of the blood in France: to these another row is put, somewhat shorter, composed we may say, of dukes, archbishops, etc.: next follows a circle of cylinders, which we call counts, barons, bishops: after this another of knights, and other men of great landed estates: then a row of cylinders representing merchants, master manufacturers, wholesale dealers, lastly, one of lesser landholders, etc., etc.; each succeeding row lessening in height. The individuals of each row standing close to each other, and every inferior one closely encircling the next above it; and having now acquired a broad basis, it stands firm and immovable against the utmost efforts of all the rest of the people, how superior so ever they may be in numbers. This conical figure would equally resemble a republic, if the first cylinder was a little shortened.[31]

As a model of one man's perception of society as it was structured in the early nineteenth century it was clearly order- rather than class-based and was one in which the subordinate groups were thought to be more dominated by aristocratic landholders than by a bourgeoisie or a middle class of capitalists.

According to Charles Hall the economic and social consequences to the poor of this land-dominated and order-based structure of wealth and power arose from the distortion of production brought about by the power of demand for luxuries exercised by the rich. Whereas Mandeville had praised luxury as the fount of national greatness Hall denounced it as the cause of the degradation of the poor.

The economic analysis underpinning his opinion began with a discussion of the causes of the great scarcity and high price of corn in the years 1800–1. He argued that the reason for this scarcity was an insufficiency of labour in agriculture brought about by a cause of

[31] *Ibid.*, pp. 75–6.

a moral nature. This moral cause was the diversion of labour from agriculture into manufacturing brought about by a luxury demand emanating from the wealthy, idle, non-producing and powerful fraction of the population. This diversion of resources into manufacturing was also encouraged by a luxury import trade generated by this same ruling group. In order to pay for these imported luxuries English labour was diverted from production for the domestic market to production for export. Therefore production, especially agricultural production, was lost to domestic consumers. Then there was war. This was an additional burden, the brunt of which was borne by the poor as consumers, taxpayers and soldiers. In short, the essence of Hall's argument was that the pattern of production was determined by income distribution and that income distribution was the result of the unequal distribution of power in a society structured and supported as shown in the conical order-based model. Hence the overall deficiency in agricultural output and the suffering of the poor which gave rise to the vital question whether '500,000 souls shall perish annually, and that eight-tenths of all the others should be pinched, distressed, and diseased, in order to furnish this small number with the superfluities?'[32]

Hall's answer to his own question was an unequivocal, No! His solution was two pronged. In the short term he wished to abolish the laws of inheritance, to ban the import of luxuries other than necessary medical supplies, and to employ more labour in agriculture. In the long term his utopian solution required the nationalization of all land and its equal division into unalienable freeholds of three and one half acres and a cow per family. Following this redistribution no horses were to be kept' 'till we can get rid of the prejudice that prevails against eating them'.[33] Furthermore, once the land had been equally divided and the rich destroyed, 'the inhabitants of a parish would seldom be led out of their parish for anything wanted; every place would produce everything that there was a real occasion for'.[34]

[32] *Ibid.*, p. 129. Cf. this account of Hall's work with that in J. T. Ward, *Chartism* (London, 1973), p. 33 and especially p. 47 where Ward claims that Ricardian labour value theories were developed by Charles Hall.

[33] *Ibid.*, p. 301.

[34] *Ibid.*, p. 170.

Although it is possible to separate Hall's analysis from his conclusions and thus to comprehend his work as an expression of class
feeling in an industrial capitalist world the inseparability of his
analysis and conclusions in his own mind is clearly indicated in his
correspondence with Spence. In this correspondence he chastized
the latter for keeping too much of existing commercial relationships
in his new Spensonian world and demonstrated beyond all doubt
his penchant for small-scale peasant agriculture as the basis for his
arcadian utopia. He wrote:

I think what we should each aim at would be to go back a good way
towards our natural state, to that point from which we strayed, retaining
but little of that only (to wit of the coarser arts) which civilization has
produced, together with certain sciences . . . when people became more
numerous so as to require all the land in the then known method of
agriculture to support them, they divided the lands, not letting one person
have more than another. To this state we should return as being the most
natural and simple . . . your plan seems to be too complicated.[35]

It is difficult to comprehend such a proposal as in any way a
manifestation of *class* consciousness.

Hall's book was republished by Morgan as late as 1849 and
Morgan in his own *Revolt of The Bees* portrayed his utopia in Hall's
agrarian image. So did virtually all the leading social critics of the
time even though the details of the organization of their utopias
might have varied, Spence, Gray, Morgan, the first London Co-
operative Society, Owen, even Thompson, Bray and O'Connor, all
saw that the source of oppression lay in the institution of private
landed property and all perceived the oppressors in society as an
aristocracy based on landed power. Even those who perceived the
dual nature of power in the agrarian capitalist society in which they
lived were very conscious of the subordinate and dependent role of
capitalists. Hall's position has already been made clear. As
examples of other views I offer the following. According to William
Thompson:

It seems inaccurate to say that the capitalist and moneyed aristocracy
have supplanted in Britain the old feudal aristocracy, or inherited its
power. Both species of aristocracy, the capitalist and the feudal, the old

[35] Charles Hall to Thomas Spence, quoted in Olive D. Rudkin, *Thomas Spence and
his Connections* (London, 1927), p. 133.

aristocracy of *open force* and the new aristocracy of *chicane*, have formed a *coalition* against the Industrious Classes. The old aristocracy has been too wise to force capitalists into the ranks of, into sympathy with, the industrious ... The new baron of chicane is amalgamated with the old baron of force.[36]

As I have already argued, J. S. Mill thought things were little different in 1839.

This opinion about the perceived source of oppression is also supported by the popularity of Hone's lampoon, *The Political House that Jack Built* in 1820 and twenty years later by many of the titles and themes of the protest poems written by Chartists. For example, 'What is a Peer?' unequivocally located the perceived source of oppression in the aristocracy:

WHAT IS A PEER?

What is a peer? A useless thing;
A costly toy, to please a king;
   a bauble near a throne;
A lump of animated clay;
A gaudy pageant of a day;
   An incubus; a drone!

What is a peer? A Nation's curse –
A pauper on the public purse;
   Corruption's own jackal;
A haughty, domineering blade;
A cuckold at a masquerade;
   A dandy at a ball.

Ye butterflies, whom kings create;
Ye caterpillars of the state;
   Know that your time is near!
This moral learn from nature's plan,
That in creation God made man;
   But never made a peer.[37]

The titles and content of other Chartist poems also convey the impression that the source of oppression was seen to lie with the traditional, land-based authority; 'The Tory Squire', 'How to be a

---

[36]William Thompson, *Labour Rewarded: The Claims of Labour and Capital Conciliated, or How to Secure to Labour the Whole Product of its Exertion* (London, 1827), pp. 9–10.
[37]Y. V. Kovalev (ed.), *An Anthology of Chartist Literature* (Moscow, 1956), p. 4.

Great Lord', 'The Judges are Going to Gaol', 'The Brave Old King', 'The Strength of Tyranny', 'The Royal Bounty', and so on.

Other widely read writers, notably Richard Carlile, also attacked the priesthood for their share in the oppression exercised by the landed aristocracy and there can be little doubt that the established Church was widely perceived by working men to be an enemy of the common man. In short, the opinions of leading radicals and these expressions of opinion by many supporters of the Chartist movement, the most working-class *class* consciousness of the protest movements of the early nineteenth century, lend much weight to the view advanced here, chiefly on the basis of the writings of leading theorists, that the chief perceived source of oppression in early nineteenth century England was the power and privilege of a land-based aristocracy rather than an industrial-based class of capitalists. These perceived sources of oppression, as I have described them, seem to have significantly influenced the policies advocated by the various writers. For reasons touched upon in the discussion of Historical Idealism, I am less sure that they reveal their intentions – I do not claim to have entered into their minds merely to have reported the thrust of their argument.

It appears that at least two divergent conclusions could follow from arguments based on the idea that labour had a right to the whole of its product. The first recommended legislative action to establish peasant cultivation based on equal and small-scale landownership. Such a reconstructed peasant society might be virtually self-sufficient as in Hall's utopia, or allowed to provide the basis for parish republics as in Spence, or form the starting point for petty competition as in Thompson. The second recommended voluntary co-operation. This was Gray's preferred solution and the solution preferred by many others in the first half of the nineteenth century.

According to Thompson, the ultimate choice between individual competition and voluntary co-operation ought to be based on experience. By the time he came to publish *Labour Rewarded*, in 1827, he had himself become a committed co-operator. The reason for his change of opinion was his growing conviction that co-operation was the *only way* to ensure that labour would receive the value of the whole product of labour. Moreover, he believed that this could only happen in a voluntary community (a collective) with equal remuneration and communal use of communal property. Although Thompson was well aware of the great expansion of industry and commerce in the early nineteenth century, the communities he advocated were, nevertheless, to be primarily agricultural with manufactures merely attached to them mainly to supply the community's needs for clothing and furniture. Indeed, anti-consumerism was a feature of his thought. Consequently, only surpluses were to be exchanged with other communities and both consumption of inessentials and exchanges were to be severely restricted. Thompson called these communities 'Agricultural and Manufacturing Associations' and he envisaged the country dotted with such associations, each one consisting of some 2,000 persons; his utopia, also, was still overwhelmingly arcadian.

The many advocates of voluntary co-operation soon came to be dominated by Owen, and the co-operative movement as a whole was monopolized by the Owenite socialists. As a result the ideas of Spence and Thomas Holcroft and of those other land reformers, Ogilvie, Hall and Morgan, are now rarely mentioned in general histories or ever discussed as indicators of actual class perceptions. It is necessary, therefore, to say a little about Owen's opinions.

Owen's initial co-operative proposals sprang from his concern with the problem of poor relief in the County of Lanark. He proposed that the poor should be employed in largely self-supporting Villages of Co-operation which would be primarily agricultural and based on spade husbandry with manufacture as an appendage. These communities would exchange their surplus products with each other. Since they would be based on rational principles of education and make provision for the education of the young in those principles they would not compete but co-operate with each other. Their aim would be to train good citizens as well as to relieve the poor. Since Owen's ideas were also tinged with atheism his followers became known as 'Rational Religionists'. The utopia they advocated, like Thompson's, was still largely arcadian. It was also millenarian.

Minter Morgan's *The Revolt of The Bees* expressed the dream of all these movements with passionate and religious imagery:

At the fifth revolution [of a vast Globe] a far greater change had taken place than in any of the preceding. Wealth, which had before laid in

masses, was now beneficially diffused and greatly increased. And now pre-
vailed the invaluable riches of the mind, and all the virtues flourished – for
ignorance with its train of follies and vices had fled never more to return.
The lion dwelt in peace with the lamb, and eagle and the turtle dove took
their flight together. The waters gushed out in the dry places, and the
wilderness became converted into rich pastures. In the desert bloomed the
myrtle and the rose, while the clustering vine sprang up bearing its purple
fruit. The lowly hut was supplanted by the convenient and splendid
edifice; and the whole earth exhibited undescribable magnificence and
beauty.[38]

Such were the images that men were able to derive from the labour
theory of value.

Even Bray, an American established as a printer in Leeds and a
man much quoted by Marx, did not draw revolutionary socialist
solutions from the labour theory of value. Although he distinguished between the working classes and a working class in order to
point out the weaknesses of the working classes as a working class,
it was his view that political action would merely replace one
tyranny by another. His preferred solution to the problems of 1839
was a system of joint-stock producer co-operatives, comprising
1,000–1,500 persons in a system of mutual co-operation and one in
which the larger political community was meant to be conceptualized in a way reminiscent of Marx's Germanic community;
it was to be a coming together rather than a being together. He,
too, used religious imagery and in writing of the urgent need for the
working classes to develop their own leadership wrote: 'The
producers have but to make an effort – and by them must every
effort for their own redemption be made – and their chains will be
snapped asunder for ever.'[39] Thus, the working classes must be
their own redeemers. Accordingly a body of Leeds workers with
F. R. Lees as their most prominent theorist established themselves
as a society called The Redemptionists. Since they appear to have
followed Bray's advice they must have sought to achieve 'redemption' through voluntary co-operative labour and without the help of
a philosophy of revolution or political action.

All these writers – call them theoreticians if you wish: Ogilvie,
Spence, Hall, Gray, Morgan, Thompson, Owen, Bray as well as

[38] John Minter Morgan, *Revolt of the Bees*, 2nd edn. (London, 1825).
[39] J. F. Bray, *Labour's Wrongs and Labour's Remedy, or The Age of Might and the Age of Right* (London, 1839), p. 67.

others not discussed, such as Hodgskin and Ravenstone – worked with something close to a labour theory of value and all believed that the labourer had a right to the whole product of his labour. For most of them the chief source of oppression frustrating the enjoyment of that right was property in land and an aristocracy of wealthy landowners. Their writings were saturated with traditional physiocratic notions about the prime importance of the productiveness of labour in agriculture and strongly marked by primitive mercantilist and moralistic notions about the debilitating effects of too great a consumption of foreign luxuries. They also feared or were ambivalent about the effects of technology under competition and were hostile to the separation of agriculture from manufacture – a separation hailed by Marx as the first and most beneficial division of labour – and the urban society it had produced.

But they advocated many different utopias; peasant self-sufficiency, agrarian co-operative production, agrarian and manufacturing co-operative production, small-scale capitalist production, Tory welfareism. Almost all of these schemes were described within a mental milieu which favoured avoidance of direct confrontation with the established land-based centres of authority and advocated withdrawal from the growing urban and capitalist economic system. Running through all these schemes and utopias was a perception of an urban/rural antagonism as well as an antagonism between those with and those without property.

Further, all these writers appeared to favour solutions based on 'frame'-rather than 'class'-based perceptions of relationships. Thus, working men were to find life, purpose and redemption in small communities; the working family, the parish, the voluntary community, the joint-stock company, the small enterprise, but not in association with all other working men organized for collective political opposition to a class of capitalists.

It seems clear, therefore, that beliefs about labour's right to the whole of its product did not necessarily lead to collectivist and revolutionary socialism and did not produce Marxian proletarians among leading theoreticians. It would be surprising if it had. The real circumstances in which these men lived and wrote were far from being dominated by the large-scale industrial enterprises employing the unskilled detail workers of *Das Kapital*. For example, in the 1830s a quarter of the labour force still worked in agriculture and only a quarter of the population lived in urban areas with upwards of 25,000 people. In the textile industries there were many more handweavers than factory operatives and there were as many employed in the sub-professional occupations, such as national and local government, offices, banks, warehouses and so on, as in the textile industries. Furthermore, most of the population still lived in the southern counties where life in rural towns like Frome, Devizes, Colchester, Banbury, Lincoln and in Bristol was at least as 'typical' as life in industrial towns like Oldham, Sheffield, Manchester and Liverpool.

In short, even the existence and diffusion of notions about labour's right to the whole of its product can no more be taken as evidence of a working-class *class* consciousness (a proletarian consciousness) in Marx's sense than Francis Place's role in drafting the Charter can be taken as evidence of its absence. Therefore, even the identification of working-class radical leaders as Owenite socialists cannot establish the existence of *class*-conscious workers in a Marxian sense in Oldham or anywhere else. Moreover, such a *class* consciousness cannot be said to exist in the absence of consciousness of such ideas about labour's right to the whole of its product. Certainly, there were a series of awakenings of consciousness, and of that which I prefer to call class perception, among different sections of the 'working classes' but they arose out of the economic and political circumstances of their time and not those of a later more industrial epoch. In England in the first half of the nineteenth century those circumstances were not yet dominated by the economic organization and dynamic of industrial capitalism. On the other hand landed capital, small-scale manufacture and commerce still predominated. And Marx knew this to be so. He was also fully aware of the significance for political action of such a stage of economic development.[40]

The proposals of all except the Owenite socialists would have created a petit-bourgeois peasant class and a rural proletariat of indeterminate size. Even the proposals of the Owenite socialists

[40]Karl Marx, *Address of the Central Committee to the Communist League*, (March 1850) in *The Revolutions of 1848*, Pelican Marx Library, vol. I (Harmondsworth, 1973), p. 327.

were only fractionally closer to representing what Marx would have identified as *class* consciousness. Hence it is that E. P. Thompson's conclusion, referred to earlier, must stand. Only when diligent search of newspapers and bits and scraps of paper can show that the inarticulate and illiterate masses of the 'working classes' did hold some primitive notion of labour's right to the whole of its product, drew conclusions approximating to a revolutionary socialist nature from it that were not tinged with ideas of bourgeois right, and began to act in accordance with those conclusions, something which has yet to be demonstrated even for the Pentridge Rising, may it be possible to write of the beginnings of *class* consciousness in England.[41] Until that happens we must settle for class perception, a class perception which was frequently backward-looking and romantic and, more often than not, conservative and deferential. In short, while some notion about labour's right to the whole of its product is a necessary condition for the formation of *class* consciousness it is not itself sufficient. Further, the notions about labour's right which did exist must be placed in context. In the first half of the nineteenth century this context was still one in which wealth and power was seen to flow from the possession of land in an order-based society structured as Hall and Mill described it and as it is subsumed in the five-class model and as it was shaped in thought by the tradition of all the dead and rural generations.

The implications of this for an assessment of the significance for class consciousness of the Charter are clear. Although Chartism was to become a movement supported by many diverse groups of working men, some of whose leaders and spokesmen were working men, it had its origins in an older Radical tradition which was the

---

[41] John Dinwiddy in a recent survey of the issue concludes: 'Still, one may well doubt whether the revolutionary impulse that did occur was at all formidable . . . Nor was it very sustained . . . These years are . . . important, it may be suggested, as a stage in the process whereby working men came to regard democratic control of the state as an essential means to the improvement of their condition.' Luddism and politics in the northern counties, *Social History* **4** (1), 1979, pp. 33–63. However, see also, F. K. Donnelly and J. L. Baxter, Sheffield and the English revolutionary tradition, 1791–1820, *International Review of Social History* **XX**, 1975. 'We must assert that the revolutionary tradition was a significant factor . . . it constitutes a proto-working class response to the advance of early industrial capitalism.'

product of an order-based society and, in more recent times, in a class with a middling rather than a middle or proletarian class consciousness. But, in the hands of working men, the clarity of the political programme of middling-class Radicals such as J. A. Roebuck, J. S. Mill and William Napier was lost. Roebuck urged his artisan and Chartist supporters not to mix up social with political reform and to concentrate on the issue of a transfer of power, particularly through universal suffrage and the ballot. Working men, however, like Roebuck himself, found it impossible to make such a distinction and right from the start of Chartism the central political issue was surrounded and obscured with a variety of demands reflecting the immediately felt needs of sections of the working classes and their leaders. Thus there were anti-Poor Law Chartists, anti-Corn Law Chartists, teetotal Chartists, knowledge Chartists, Christian Chartists, Land Plan Chartists and, running through the history of Chartism, there were divisions on tactics and strategy. These factions and divisions simply revealed the fragmentation of the working classes resulting from uneven economic development and the immaturity of the capitalist mode of production in England, an immaturity which the development of Oldham does not contradict.

The consequential problem was that while working men had inherited a political/constitutional programme they were not a class with a sufficiently developed consciousness of its own able to generate a coherent programme of action in the industrial/social field and in the wider political sphere; the problem of the 'correct' position on the Crimean War and the inadequacy of conclusions derived by Radical and working-class spokesmen from the idea that labour had a right to the whole of its product have already been cited. Therefore, while it is undeniable that Chartism did much to raise the consciousness of working men and was a movement in which some of the working classes participated and may be thought of as a manifestation of the level to which working-class thought and perception had risen – a level still clearly marked by its origins in a Radical tradition and an order-based society – it may not be thought of as approximating closely to *class* consciousness. And that should not be thought surprising, at least by a Marxist historian.

In this chapter I set out to lay down some trails pointing to the truth about class and class consciousness in our period and to do so by reference to the products of minds. Before setting out on this task I expressed my doubts not only about the reliability of a behavioural approach in which the theoretical framework is not made plain but also questioned whether class consciousness could ever be explicated without knowledge of either individual or collective intent. Therefore, I argued, it is to products of minds we must look. Moreover, since *class* consciousness is an intellectual business it must be sought not merely in attitudes and beliefs but in the production of systematic thought and in the forms of utopian thought generated by response to perceptions about the distribution of power in a society characterized by private property. In looking at the products of minds I looked, all too briefly, at one of the *Catchpenny Prints*, William Hogarth, the Black Act, Adam Smith, Jane Austen, William Blake, Tom Paine, an anonymous writer, and William Hone's *The Political House that Jack Built*. I concluded that this survey suggested that some on both sides of the property divide saw their world as divided between those with and those without property and saw clearly that property determined the relations of authority and subordination in that society. I then turned again to the question of *class* consciousness.

At this point I focused upon a notion crucial for the development of *class* consciousness. This was the idea that the labourer had a right to the whole product of his labour. In order to evaluate what historians have said and still say about this notion in the context of *class* consciousness, I looked at the writings of that group of thinkers identified by H. S. Foxwell as Ricardian Socialists. I found that most of them were neither Ricardian nor socialist. Instead, I argued that their views were rooted in older perceptions about rights to property in agricultural society. I based an important segment of the analysis on Charles Hall's *The Effects of Civilization* and his order-based view of late eighteenth-century England. My general conclusion was that writers who developed their accounts and their utopias around the notion of labour's right and around primitive ideas about the labour theory of value generally recommended as alternatives either a reconstruction of peasant society, or some form of agrarian co-operative production. They did so because the context in which they wrote was still one in which wealth and power flowed, and was seen to flow, from the possession of land in an order-based society structured as Hall and Mill described it and as it is subsumed in the five-class model and as it was shaped in thought by the tradition of all the dead and rural generations.

In the 1830s in the minds of those who might otherwise have been thought of as leaders of the working classes, including Chartists, *class* consciousness was scarce anywhere in sight. The tradition of all the dead generations weighed like a nightmare on the brain of the living.

7
Women and Class Consciousness

With these there develops the division of labour, which was originally nothing but the division of labour in the sexual act, then that division of labour which develops spontaneously or 'naturally' by virtue of natural predisposition (e.g., physical strength) needs, accidents, etc. Division of labour only becomes truly such from the moment when a division of material and mental labour appears. From this moment onwards consciousness *can* really flatter itself that it is something other than consciousness of existing practice . . . and to proceed to the formation of 'pure' theory, theology, philosophy, ethics etc.

> Karl Marx and Frederick Engels,
> *The German Ideology* (Moscow, 1964), pp. 42–3

To abolish religion as the *illusory* happiness of the people is to demand their *real* happiness. The demand to give up illusions about the existing state of affairs is the *demand to give up a state of affairs which needs illusion*. The criticism of religion is therefore *in embryo the criticism of the vale of tears*, the *halo* of which is religion.

The *task of history*, therefore, once *the world beyond the truth* has disappeared, is to establish the *truth of this world*. The immediate task of philosophy, which is at the service of history, once the *holy form* of human self-estrangement has been unmasked, is to unmask self-estrangement in the *unholy* forms. Thus the criticism of heaven turns into the criticism of the earth, the *criticism of religion* into the *criticism of law* and the *criticism of theology* into the *criticism of politics*.

> Karl Marx, *Contribution to The Critique of Hegel's Philosophy of Right* (1884), in Karl Marx, Frederick Engels, *Collected Works* (London, 1975), vol. III, pp. 175–6.

Women and their perceptions or consciousness are plainly absent from this study of class and class consciousness. It was only to be expected that they would be. Except for the five-class model, which admits them as a sub-group in each of the five social classes, women are generally subsumed within the more or less homogeneous classes, with the aid of which historians think about the past, according to the positions allocated to their fathers and husbands. With the exception of E. P. Thompson, this is the practice of the historians mentioned in this book. It is so whether they employ a class-less, one-class, two-class, three-class or 'contemporary' class analysis – the indices to their books are revealing. Among them Morris's book, a short survey of the field. It includes but one comment on a woman, a servant girl, but only in the context of discussing the experience of her higher class husband, and omits any reference to the fact that the source referred to provides a remarkable instance of the class relationship in the sexual relationship. A. J. Munby, the man referred to, ordered Hannah, his servant lover, to climb and sweep chimneys and on at least one occasion arranged for her to blacken herself from head to foot like a chimney sweep and almost nude to be photographed in various poses: '. . . she was taken in the same black and forlorn condition, crouching on the ground at my feet – I doing my best to look down upon her like a tyrant! That was for "the contrast": contrast indeed – but which the nobler?'[1] The class relationship in this situation is particularly striking since there seemed to be no sexual exploitation in it. As the edition of Munby's diaries records, Hannah is the most thoroughly documented housemaid in Victorian history. However, in general texts on economic and social history as well as in those on class it is a rare event to see the world through the eyes of women in different classes and rarer still to find sexual attitudes and sexual relations referred to as manifestations of class relations and of class domination. The work of Steven Marcus has yet to enter the mainstream of historical reporting. Even my own reference to Hogarth's perception of sexual exploitation in a class context was a reference to a male perception of the sub-

---

[1] R. J. Morris, *Class and Class Consciousness in the Industrial Revolution, 1780–1850,* p. 29. Derek Hudson, *Munby, Man of Two Worlds* (London, 1972), pp. 132–4 and passim. For other perceptions, see, Walter, *My Secret Life,* Panther Edn. (London, 1972) and Steven Marcus, *The Other Victorians* (London, 1966). Also see, Leonore Davidoff, Class and gender in Victorian England: the diaries of Arthur J. Munby and Hannah Cullwick, *Feminist Studies* **5** (1), Spring 1979, pp. 87–141.

ordinate position of women. Yet, during the eighteenth century and
early nineteenth century, some women expressed their own perceptions of their position and some tried to break the grip that society
had on them. And if historians are mainly interested in the class
consciousness of a people and not only or even interested in the
problem of *class* consciousness, then the perceptions of women and
the position of women have at least an equal claim on their attention. Certainly the five-class model points historians in that direction.

In 1736 a little book of poems was published called *The Cupid, A
Collection of Love Songs*.[2] About a sixth of the book was given over to
songs and poems sung or written by a female lover. There is little
joy in them. The first began

> Since we, poor slavish women, know
> Our men we cannot pick and chuse,

and finished by recommending,

> For she whom Jointure can obtain,
> To let a Fop her bed enjoy,
> Is but a Lawful Wench for Gain.

Which would have been a suitable caption for *Marriage à La Mode*
as well as for other forms of prostitution.

Another poem read,

> How hard is the Fortune of all Womankind,
> For ever subjected, for ever confined;
> The Parent controuls us, until we are Wives,
> The Husband enslaves us the rest of our lives.

In these circumstances, and allowing for the curbs on as well as the
nuance of language, the brutal bawdiness of the struggle for power
contained in the next poem is plain.

> In vain poor *Damon* prostrate lies,
> And humbly trembles at my Feet,
> While pleading Looks, and begging Sighs,
> With moving Eloquence entreat,
> Pity persuades my trembling Breast,
> That Pains so great should be redress'd.

---

[2] *The Cupid: A Collection of Love Songs* (London, 1736).

Hannah as a Slave, photographed by A. J. Munby. By permission of the Master and Fellows, Trinity College, Cambridge.

But some strange Whisper interceeds,
And tells me I must let him wait,
And make him seal restrictive Deeds,
E'en I admit him to my State.
Women should triumph whilst they can,
Since Marriage makes 'em Slaves to Man.

And so it goes on through forty-three songs and poems. Married women were slaves to man. Therefore, they were slaves to property. Unmarried they were for sale to the highest bidder. Unmarried and with property they were, like Hogarth's patron Mary Edwards, prey to fortune hunters.

Of course there were compensations. Married women could not be imprisoned for debt nor be required to pay any monetary fine for a crime. Husbands were responsible in both instances. Should a wife commit a felony in her husband's company she could not be punished – the law assumed she acted under his compulsion – and she could not be punished for receiving and selling stolen goods. Should she be attacked by her servants when pregnant the law would protect her, and if guilty of a capital offence while pregnant, the law decreed she could not be executed. On the other hand she and her property could always be defended with impunity by her husband, and should she be deserted, her husband was bound in law to support her. Should he die she was guaranteed a reasonable dower out of his estate. William Alexander wrote:

We exercise nearly a perpetual guardianship over them, both in their virgin and married state; and she who, having laid a husband in the grave, enjoys an independent fortune, is almost the only woman among us who can be called free. Thus excluded almost from everything which can give them consequence, they derive the greater part of the power which they enjoy, from their charms; and these, when joined to sensibility, often fully compensate, in this respect, for all the disadvantages they are laid under by law and custom.[3]

This, of course, was a conventional gloss on the subordinate position of women in all social classes. That it was not regarded as an adequate statement of the compensation received even by upper-class women is shown in the defection of Lady Eleanor Butler and Miss Sarah Ponsonby and their 'elopement' to Llangollen in

[3] William Alexander, *The History of Women*, 1st edn (Dublin, 1779), vol. II, p. 439.

Wales and by the counter claims for adultery by Lady Grosvenor against her husband, who in his claim was awarded £10,000 for his wife's adultery with the Duke of Cumberland. Lady Grosvenor's claim was settled out of court.[4]

But women were not merely subordinate. They were completely alienated, or almost so; especially if they were associated in any way with landed property. And that brings us back to theory once more.

Marx's views about objectification, alienation and reification in relation to the production and domination of capital are probably generally well known. I touched upon them in chapter 1. Fewer people, I think, know that, in his discussion of Hegel's views about landed property, expressed in his *Philosophy of Right*, Marx also stood Hegel right way up with his feet firmly on the ground and simply demonstrated the unfreedom, that is, the alienation of property. Marx's comments arose from considering the facts of the entailed estate, that form of landholding which came to prevail in England in the eighteenth century, which effectively overrode common law preference for primogeniture and the barring of perpetuities. Marx wrote:

It is also consistent to say that where private property, landed property, is inalienable, universal freedom of will (to which also belongs free disposition of something inalienable, like landed property) and ethical life (to which also belongs love as the actual spirit of the family, the spirit which is also identified with the actual law of the family) are alienable. In general then, the inalienability of private property is the alienability of universal freedom of will and ethical life. Here it is no longer the case that property is in so far as I put my will into it, but rather my will is in so far as it is in property. Here my will does not own but is owned.[5]

In short, landed property in the eighteenth century – like capital in the nineteenth – was a non-human force derived from human activity, i.e. labour, which stood outside and above men and was as hostile as it was necessary to them. Thus the relation of landowners

---

[4] *Copies of the Depositions of the Witnesses in the Cause of the Divorce between the Right Honourable Richard Lord Grosvenor and the Right Honourable Henrietta Lady Grosvenor, his Wife* (London, 1771) and *D.N.B.*, vol. VIII.
[5] Karl Marx, *Critique of Hegel's Philosophy of Right*, ed. Joseph O'Malley (Cambridge, 1970), p. 101.

and their families to landed property was one of alienation. Property determined consciousness.

In general this was certainly the case in England. In the entailed estate the nominal occupier was merely tenant for life. As such he was subject to the will of trustees, prohibited from action damaging to the estate, bound to meet the claims of other family members from the proceeds of the estate, obliged to meet interest payments on mortgages as a first charge on the estate, and prevented from exploiting the estate for the maximising of its revenues. In these circumstances marriage was a business arrangement and family law, love and moral relationships were all determined by and subject to the needs of property.

What was true of the relationship of men to property was even more true for women, for while men might have the illusion of freedom, women never could. In short all family relationships, marriage, love and morality were determined by, and the servants of, property; they were facets of total alienation. There can, I think, be no gloss on this for the eighteenth century. It was there in Hogarth, in the poems in *The Cupid*, in *The Spectator*,[6] in Defoe's letters in *Mist's Weekly Journal* in which sexual relations were described in a legal terminology relating to property relations,[7] and in pornographic works like *A New Description of Merryland* printed at Bath in 1740 by James Leake, Bath's leading bookseller. This book, supposed to be written by, 'Roger Phfuquewell, with the addition of Esq.', described Merryland as a 'Paradise of Pleasure, and Garden of Delight'. It was a woman's body described in the manner of a topographical work describing new land ripe for settlement, wherein 'are exhibited all the Ports, Harbours, Creeks, Bays, Rocks, Settings, Bearings, Gulphs, Promontories, Limits, Boundaries, etc.'[8] Property *was* the material basis of civil society and its alienating consequences constituted the network of its social relationships.

In this world of property the value stance expected of women may be encapsulated in the word propriety – one might say that

---

[6] Richard Steele, *The Spectator*, 27th August 1711.
[7] *A Collection of Miscellany Letters Selected out of Mist's Weekly Journal* (London, 1722), vol. 1, pp. 288–93.
[8] Thomas Stretzer, *A New Description of Merryland* (Bath, 1741), p. 26. See also, David Foxon, *Libertine Literature in England 1660–1745* (New York, 1965), pp. 15–17.

among the landed classes propriety was to women as property was to men. And while Paley, who preached the gospel of property in seventeen English editions between 1785 and 1809 and eleven American editions before 1825,[9] seems not to have used the word, Hannah More gave it currency in eleven editions of her *Strictures on the Modern System of Female Education* between 1799 and 1811. She wrote:

Propriety is to a woman what the great Roman critic says action is to an orator; it is the first, the second, the third requisite. A woman may be knowing, active, witty, and amusing; but without propriety she cannot be amiable. Propriety is the centre in which all the lines of duty and of agreeableness meet. It is to character, what proportion is to figure, and grace to attitude. It does not depend on any one perfection, but it is the result of general excellence. It shows itself by a regular, orderly, undeviating course; and never starts from its sober orbit into any splendid eccentricities; for it would be ashamed of such praise as it might extort by any deviations from its proper path.[10]

According to Hannah More, propriety in women was to be the chief defence against subversion from inside and threat of revolution from outside the boundaries of civil society in England; only propriety could protect property.

It was Jane Austen's genius in *Mansfield Park* and in her creation of the character of Fanny Price to suggest that Fanny's moral stance on the performance of *The Lover's Vows*, apparently fundamentally concerned with sexual propriety, was actually an unrecognized defence of property and existing political conditions. And then to show her as a sort of existential heroine refusing to sell herself to property. To suggest, that is, the impropriety of conventional propriety yet all the while, through Fanny's and our own knowledge of the fact that the estate at Mansfield Park was propped up by the exploitation of slave labour in Antigua, to confront us with our own and Fanny's alienation.[11]

---

[9]William Paley, *The Principles of Moral and Political Philosophy*, new edn (London, 1829), especially pp. 191–2.
[10]Hannah More, *Strictures on the Modern System of Female Education*, 13th edn (London, 1826), vol. 1, p. 6.
[11]R. S. Neale, Property and alienation in *Mansfield Park*, unpublished paper. See also, Avrom Fleishman, *Mansfield Park* in its time, *Nineteenth Century Fiction*, **22**, 1967, p. 11.

But it is not through the exploration of a rare mind such as Jane Austen's that I wish to make my main points about the position and response of women in our period. I wish to do this by looking briefly at the products of the minds of two women whose lives were separated by some seventy years, by differences in class position, and by the emergence of those expressions of class perception referred to in the last chapter. The first is Sarah Scott who, in 1763, published *Millenium Hall* which has been hailed as a feminine utopia 200 years ahead of its time.[12] The second is Elizabeth Sharples who, in 1832, became the first woman in public to declare herself a non-Christian and to speak in support of radical politics.

Sarah Scott, who was born Sarah Robinson, came from a prosperous but non-aristocratic family. Her sister, Elizabeth, who by marriage became Elizabeth Montague, was a woman of great wit and considerable wealth. Also, she was perhaps the leading 'blue stocking' of the day. From the time they were young girls in the late 1730s through to the 1750s they wrote to each other interminably about headaches and stomach pains, the merits of Quinn and Garrick, the fate of the Patriots, Gothic architecture, Greek gods and goddesses, and the best time to wean Elizabeth's first baby.[13] They also wrote about their visits during the season to Bath and Tunbridge Wells and about the sexual experience of those places. Even as young girls they took a cynical view of their lives and the life of their class. When Elizabeth was twenty she wrote to the Duchess of Portland:

I wish your Grace would consider Bath water is no Helicar and affords no inspiration and that there is no place where one stands in greater need of something to enliven the brain and inspire the imagination. I hear every day of people pumping their arms or legs for the rheumatism, but the pumping for wit is one of the hardest and most fruitless labours in the World. As my own invention is like to fall short of a sheet of paper I would be glad to send you some news, but all the news of the place would be like the bills of Mortality; Palsey four, Gout six, Fever one . . . Indeed, the only thing one can do one day one did not do the day before is to dye.[14]

A few years later Sarah wrote to Elizabeth from Bath:

[12] Elizabeth Mavor, *The Ladies of Llangollen* (Harmondsworth, 1971), pp. 84 and 85.
[13] Correspondence of Sarah Scott and Elizabeth Montague, series M. O. Huntington Library, California.
[14] Elizabeth Montague to the Duchess of Portland, 4–1–1740, M. O. 293.

I can't bring you a great list of conquests nor will my admirers make a good figure in description. When they are about me I look like the best beloved nurse at an hospital and they all seem to be sueing for my care and attendance. They on their crutches come and may almost all be comprized under the three heads of the song; the halt, the blind, the lame. The wofull picture of the young woman giving an old man with a long beard suck through a grate is not half as good an image of the respect due to old age as I am almost every night.[15]

Yet, in spite of the cynicism, the image of a young woman giving suck to an old man and her perception of herself as a nurse in a hospital stayed with Sarah for most of her life. It was to be the very basis of her utopia.

By the early 1750s Sarah and her friend Lady Barbara Montague were fairly settled at Batheaston, a few miles on the London side of Bath, where they ran a charitable school for poor children. Since Sarah's utopia was built around a similar school one might suppose that *Millenium Hall* was a fictionalized account of her work with poor people in the neighbourhood and of her aspirations for them.[16] Inasmuch as it was it is also a window into her mind and her consciousness.

The nucleus of the community at Millenium Hall was a group of some thirty gentlewomen and their children. Their leaders all had unhappy experiences in marriage and society and had renounced the kind of social life epitomized by the season at Bath. Like the Ladies of Llangollen who had read *Millenium Hall*, they had gone into retirement. One of them asked:

Do you mistake a crowd for society? I know not two things more opposite. How little society is there to be found in what you call the world? It might more properly be compared to that state of war, which Hobbes supposes the first condition of mankind. The same vanities, the same passions, the same ambition, reign in almost every breast; a constant desire to supplant, and a continual fear of views at all in a state of unremitted tumult and envy.[17]

Whereas a true society was 'a state of mutual confidence, reciprocal services, and correspondent affections'.[18] This world, however, torn

---

[15] Sarah Scott to Elizabeth Montague, 28–8–1743, M. O. 5181.

[16] *A Description of Millenium Hall*, By a Gentleman on His Travels (Dublin, 1763). Oliver Goldsmith appears as the nominal author.

[17] *Ibid.*, p. 83.

[18] *Ibid.*, p. 83.

as it was by Hobbesian conflict, was a world of trials; the poverty of the lower orders tested their industry and patience, the riches of those with property tested their temperance, humility and humanity. Theirs was the more difficult lot. But, if they acquitted themselves well, their rewards would be greater. In the next world there would be no inequality.

The community, having renounced society, declared there were to be no card parties, no assemblies, no plays and no masquerades: 'We wish not for large assemblies, because we do not desire to drown conversation in noise . . . and we have no occasion to conceal our persons in order to obtain either liberty of speech or action.[19] Instead the community devoted its resources and energies to the care of the poor, the sick, the old, the orphaned and the outcasts of society. They ran a school for girls and boys, a carpet factory employing several hundred people from six to eighty years of age, and almshouses for the old. The community was a good employer, it paid good wages and paid the very young and the old more than the value of the product of their labour 'as a proper encouragement and reward for industry in those seasons of life in which it is so uncommon'. The community also paid those who were off work through sickness at rates equal to their weekly wages and provided them with a free nursing service. They also provided marriage benefits in the shape of a house for every couple marrying plus a dowry of £20 to £100 for every bride. In addition they stocked her dairy and supplied her with poultry. As children were born to these families, beyond four in number, they were helped by some of the old women who cared for them up to the age of four or five, after which they went to school. The community also took special care of the physically deformed, such as giants and dwarfs, and employed about the house, a housekeeper with a claw hand, a kitchen maid with one eye, a cook with crutches, a deaf dairy maid, a housemaid with one hand, one musician with asthma and another with 'a violent fit of the stones'.

Above all these 'retired' gentlewomen ran their school for girls with the purpose of turning them into good housekeepers, children's nurses or governesses. They measured their achievement by drawing attention to the fact that they had succeeded in

---

[19] *Ibid.*, p. 83.

apprenticing thirty girls to good trades and had placed sixty in excellent domestic situations. Another thirty had married. Their girls were so well trained, socially as well as vocationally, that they were in high demand in the neighbourhood. As one of their spokeswomen said:

Lest their being always in our company should make them think their situation above a menial state they attend us while we are dressing, and we endeavour that the time they are thus employed shall not pass without improvement. They are clad sparse and plain for the same reason, as nothing has a stronger influence on vanity than dress.[20]

Millenium Hall, for all that it was humane, was benevolent still and deferential, shaped in the image of an ordered society based on property. Its consciousness for women was withdrawal or retirement from society for gentlewomen, and passive docility for the servant class. Said one of their leaders:

We do not set up for reformers, we wish to regulate ourselves by the laws laid down to us, and as far as our influence can extend, endeavour to enforce them; beyond that small circle all is foreign to us; we have sufficient employment in improving ourselves; to mend the world requires much abler hands.[21]

So, Sarah Scott's object was not to create conditions for the development of *self*-help and *self*-improvement for all women but to stimulate upper-class women to 'Sentiments of Humanity', to lead their minds to a love of Virtue,[22] and to stamp more firmly into woman's consciousness Sarah's own perception of herself as a nurse in a hospital and her image of woman's role; a young woman giving an old man suck through a grate. With 'progressive' values such as these it is little to be wondered at that a hundred years later a servant maid like Munby's Hannah could cheerfully accept, even welcome, her menial position even within a love relationship.

It is not surprising, therefore, that unlike some other utopias *Millenium Hall* did not mark the beginning of any kind of social movement for women other than the fad for 'retirement', nor that the book has no place in the history of utopias as told in the last

[20] *Ibid.*, p. 152.
[21] *Ibid.*, p. 160.
[22] *Ibid.* The full title of the book is, *A Description of Millenium Hall as may Excite in the Readers proper Sentiments of Humanity, and Lead the Mind to the Love of Vurtue.*

chapter. The fundamental reason for this was the framework of religious belief within which it was written and Sarah's consequent failure to challenge any of the institutions of property. As its title suggests, *Millenium Hall* was an illusion. Yet, as Marx wrote,

To abolish religion as the *illusory* happiness of the people is to demand their *real* happiness. The demand to give up illusions about the existing state of affairs is the *demand to give up a state of affairs which needs illusion*. The criticism of religion is therefore *in embryo the criticism of the vale of tears*, the *halo* of which is religion.[23]

And it seems to be the case that until the halo of the 'secular' religion of the eighteenth and nineteenth centuries, which emphasized paternalism and property, forbearance and salvation, could be dislodged from its place in the minds of men and women the lot of women would be in the vale of tears and illusion their only relief. Accordingly, inspired by Hannah More, they would continue to bring up their daughters to sew samplers effectively combining the housewifely craft of needlework with the salvationist morality of fatalism:

> This little sampler is my last:
> It teaches me how moments fly:
> My infant days are quickly past:
> Eternity is drawing nigh.

> Elizabeth Brand   1838   Cornwell

> As for me I will call upon God
> and the Lord shall save me

> Mariann Crack   Aged 8.[24]

So we come to Elizabeth Sharples.[25] Elizabeth was born in Bolton in 1804. Her father, an orthodox and regular churchman, was a manufacturer of quilts and counterpanes. Her other relatives were all of the Wesleyan connection. Until she was twenty years old she was kept rather than educated in a college for young ladies, kept for marriage and family. Yet, it seems, there was not enough

---

[23]Karl Marx, *Contribution to the Critique of Hegel's Philosophy of Right*, (1884) in Marx/Engels, *Collected Works* (London, 1975), vol. III, p. 176.
[24]Samplers in my possession.
[25]The biographical detail on Elizabeth Sharples is in; *The Isis* (London, 1832); Guy Aldred, *Richard Carlile: Agitator* (London, 1923); Hypatia Bradlaugh Bonner, *Charles Bradlaugh* (London, 1895).

propriety in her upbringing. In some unexplained way Elizabeth has become acquainted with a local, freethinking bookseller, a Mr Hardie who sold 'infidel' literature. Then, in 1827, Richard Carlile visited Bolton as a freethinking or 'infidel' missionary. In the eyes of people like Hannah More, Carlile was little better than Tom Paine whose works he published and sold and whose ideas he touted from one end of the country to the other – by the time he visited Bolton he had already served eight years in gaol for various publication offences charged against him by the Vice Society. In spite of this he continued to publish Paine's writings and two years earlier, in 1825, had published his own *Every Woman's Book*. In this book he asserted that the sexual drive was natural and proper to both women and men. In order to increase the pleasures of sexual intercourse he aimed to remove the one great natural barrier to it – conception and fear of conception – by recommending to women that they use a small sponge inserted into the mouth of the uterus as a contraceptive device. Consequently: 'When Mr. Carlile first visited our town in 1827', wrote Elizabeth Sharples, 'his name excited the same horror in my bosom as it did in many others. He was then my devil.' And what a devil he was; atheist and anarchist, opponent of priests and aristocrats and kings, and of all the dark forces of power and unreason, and he was widely read – by 1828 *Every Woman's Book* had sold 10,000 copies.

In 1829 Carlile again visited Liverpool with another infidel missionary, Robert Taylor. This time Elizabeth was attracted by what they had to say. She attended their meetings and on one occasion asked a friend if he would allow her to stay in a room with him in order to listen to the conversation between Carlile and Taylor. The friend dealt with her in very summary fashion. 'To my surprise', she said 'he objected that it would be improper, and positively requested, that I should leave the room.' Like Hannah More and Fanny Price she meekly submitted and knew no more of Carlile until after the death of her father whom she had loved and valued. Then, one day, seeing Elizabeth at a loss, her cousin recommended her to read Carlile's newspaper the *Republican*. From this first reading she 'conceived an immediate passion for reading some of his writings!' And she did so avidly and secretly, unknown to her mother and sister. Then, said Elizabeth, 'I felt a new birth. I trust into righteousness.' The infidels had gained a convert.

In 1831 Carlile and Taylor were in prison again. Elizabeth wished to help. She persuaded Mr Hardie, her freethinking bookseller friend, to write to Carlile seeking his opinion on the help she could be. Carlile replied,

I, a bachelor locked up in prison am requested to write to a young lady to whom I have had no other introduction than that of being informed that she is young, amiable, beautiful, and has a mind to become a messiah. I will believe in this case without seeing having more faith than St. Thomas. The Devil tempts me to doubt the good tidings; but I am so much interested in the first English lady who will publicly advocate the truths which are a light needed to remove the present cimmerian darkness, that I swear eternal fealty to her before I see her.[26]

Elizabeth did not hesitate. She was twenty-eight. She knew her own mind. Determined to continue Carlile's work she set out immediately for London and the Rotunda.

The Rotunda was a great meeting place and lecture hall in Blackfriars Road, Southwark. It was frequented by all kinds of radicals and freethinkers and in 1830 for a period of three months after the revolution in France, it had been feared as the focal point of some outbreak of violence in London. Every night it had been surrounded by a small army of soldiers. Subsequently, in 1831, it had been the home of the National Union of the Working Classes from which sprang the London Working Men's Association which, in turn, produced the Charter. During all this time Carlile and Taylor had used the Rotunda as a platform from which to expound their extreme form of radical free thought.

Elizabeth arrived in London on 12th January 1832. On 29th January she gave her first public lecture at the Rotunda and became The Lady of The Rotunda and the talk of the town. She said:

The task which I purpose to perform I am told has no precedent in this country . . .
A woman stands before you, who has been educated and practised in all the severity of religious discipline, awakened to the principles of reason but as yesterday, seeking on these boards a moral and sweet revenge, for the outrage that has been committed on the Majesty of that Reason and on the Dignity of Truth . . . [the imprisonment of Carlile and Taylor] I have left a home, in a distant county, where comfort and even affluence

[26]Quoted in Guy Aldred, *Richard Carlile*, p. 152.

surrounded me, a happy home, and the bosom of an affectionate and a happy family. I have left such a home, under the excitement which religious persecution has roused, to make this first and singular appearance before you, for a purpose, I trust, that is second to none . . .

I purpose to speak . . . of superstition and of reason, of tyranny and of liberty, of morals and of politics. Of politics! politics from a woman! some will exclaim. YES, I will set before my sex the example of asserting an equality for them with their present lords and masters, and strive to teach all, yes, ALL, that the undue submission, which constitutes slavery is honourable to none; while the mutual submission, which leads to mutual good, is to all alike dignified and honourable.[27]

Elizabeth's claim that what she did was without precedent is true. Women had preached, founded churches and cults, and challenged marriage and the dual standard, but no woman in England, witches apart, had publicly declared herself a non-Christian, and none had spoken on politically radical matters. Only in America had Frances Wright anticipated Elizabeth Sharples in the late 1820s. And Frances was a Scot.

Certainly public opinion was shocked. The *Christian Advocate* declared: 'We fear . . . the change of performers will only occasion a re-iteration of those scenes of blasphemy and immorality which have so long been a disgrace to the metropolis, and which so loudly call for the interference of a Christian Legislature.' And *The Times*, unable, like so many, to see beyond the world of ranks and orders declaimed:

As to *'a lady of distinction'* holding forth at the Rotunda, the fact we need hardly say, is not so. It appears, however, that a certain female has been regularly installed as the responsible Pythoness of the temple. The reason of this is evident enough. The lady made her first appearance last night. She had got up her part pretty well; but we do not think this 'newline' will suit her. Would not the place of housemaid, or servant of all work, in some decent family, serve her purpose better? She is strong enough for either, and neither of them are so laborious as the treadmill.[28]

[27] *The Isis*, A London Weekly, edited by the Lady of the Rotunda, No. 1, Vol. 1, 11th February 1832. Elizabeth Sharples originally lectured twice on Sundays and repeated the Sunday lecture at the Theatre in Burton Street on Wednesday evenings. Entrance fees were 1s. or 6d. *The Isis* also cost 6d. In April she moved to a 150-seat lecture theatre in Bouverie Street, where she lectured on four evenings each week. Once the lecture had been delivered Elizabeth retired and discussion was led by old style radicals like John Gale Jones.
[28] Quoted in *ibid.*, p. 12.

It was this world of ranks and orders which structured the thought of *The Times* that Elizabeth Sharples opposed. And she used the language of ranks and orders rather than the language of class to oppose it. In her lectures she attacked the priesthood, religious superstition and all established authority. She declared herself a theist and pleaded above all else for rational discourse upon religious matters. On the nature of God she was adamant:

I can safely say God is Love, God is Light, God is Life, God is spirit, God is a word, God is the word in which we live and move and have our being.[29]

But such a God was not the God of conventional Christianity. Her God was without doubt incomprehensible and No-thing and only manifest in Man on earth. Therefore, she argued, Man, his language, thought and manners were perfectible on earth, and the only sin was an absence or denial of knowledge and free discussion. The chief offender against knowledge and free discussion was Christianity. 'Superstition, or religion or by whatever other name error may be called', she said, 'has found man a savage and left him still a savage.'[30]

Elizabeth's underlying argument was that all secular tyranny originated in Christian belief and that the priesthood as the agents of Christianity denied liberty to men and, therefore, denied them knowledge. She argued that this Christian belief fastened upon man a religious doctrine of necessity at the centre of which lay the belief that man is predisposed by nature and circumstance to do that which he does. According to her fundamentally Calvinistic view of Christianity, this God determined all. Thus; God endowed man with original sin, determined that he should fall, then placed the blame on woman (Eve). God also allocated worldly places to all men, including only subordinate positions to all women. Only God's grace granted by God could rescue men from their animal nature and these conditions. This doctrine of necessity was also a doctrine of religious tyranny and the basis and bulwark of all secular tyranny.

In opposition to the doctrine of necessity Elizabeth placed her own doctrine of liberty. She postulated that men and women

[29] *Ibid.*, p. 177.
[30] *Ibid.*, p. 20.

possessed a natural free will that enabled them to act freely and to accept responsibility for their actions. According to this doctrine Man was God. All that prevented living men from realizing this fact was their own ignorance. The key to self-realization was knowledge. But men could not achieve knowledge without women. Thus, while she dubbed the doctrine of necessity a bachelor's religion she identified Eve as the symbol of knowledge and self-realization. She wrote:

The forbidden fruit-tree story is a pretty picture of the allegory of liberty and necessity. The tyrant God, *Necessity*, said to the subject man: 'Of the tree of the knowledge of good and evil thou shalt not eat.' Sweet and fair Liberty stepped in, took counsel of the best counsellor then existing, 'saw that the tree was good for food, and that it was pleasant to the eyes, and a tree to be desired to make one wise;' she spurned the order or command of the tyrant Necessity, 'she took of the fruit thereof, and *did eat*, and gave also unto her husband with her, and he did eat.' Do you not, with one voice exclaim, *well done woman! LIBERTY FOR EVER!*

If that were a fall, sirs, it was a glorious fall, and such a fall as is now wanted. The tree of knowledge is still monopolized: its fruit is so taxed as to be forbidden to the poor, and who will quarrel with another Eve, or fair picture of liberty, who shall break the bounds and barriers that surround it, hold up her shield of virtue to the tyrant's frown and shaft, and plucking the tree bare, throw down its golden fruits, as a prize of moral contention to the whole human race. I will be such an Eve, so bright a picture of liberty![31]

It was from this standpoint of liberty that Elizabeth Sharples made her attack on Owenite Socialism. Socialism or Co-operation was all the rage in the late 1820s and early 1830s and, as we have seen, was one of the most advanced manifestations of working-class class consciousness based on the notion of labour's right to the whole of its product. The principle she attacked, however, was not socialism – this was a word she did not use – but 'co-operation' or, more accurately, co-operation as appropriated by Owenites whom, she said, did not face up to the problem of the centralization of power in society:

The word [co-operation] has not yet been applied, as it should be applied, to the union and action necessary to the pulling down of those evil institutions which minister only to the happiness of the few, while they inflict an

[31] *Ibid.*, pp. 131–2.

injury on the many; for while tyranny is established by law, and makes the law for the general community, affecting every man's property and every man's labour, union and co-operation for an evasion of that tyranny, will avail but little, or only for a time, and is not a competent struggle for general reformation. There is then, a larger view to be taken, a stronger and more useful sense, in which the word co-operation may be used and acted upon, even to the extent of a moral warfare; or a physical warfare if necessary, with all the evil institutions that afflict mankind?[32]

Elizabeth claimed that the way in which the central power worked was an issue which had to be settled before economic co-operation could be called upon to relieve the economic needs of the poor. She argued that in addition to controlling land and taxation, the ruling power, through the priesthood, controlled thought, and through the army it controlled life itself. The ruling power could also declare war and suppress civil war, and in peace as well as in war, it would quarter regiments of soldiers anywhere it chose. Thus, she said, 'your co-operative communities can only be successful, when you are not surrounded with an army of soldiers, or priests, and of an usurping aristocracy.'[33]

But it was not only the problem of power in the larger political society which co-operation ignored, it also ignored the problem of power within the co-operative communities themselves and the power-seeking doctrinaire nature of the co-operative (socialist) solution. According to Elizabeth Owenism seemed to offer a rigid final blueprint for utopia contrary to the doctrine of liberty and human nature:

It is the nature of all human speculations to lead to nothing permanent; for permanency would imply perfection. Improvement should be always sought in experiment and discussion; and, for improvement, change should be always tolerated. He would be a presumptuous man who should propose to bring anything to a *final* arrangement in human society. True liberty will ever consist of thought, discussion, experiment, and change leading to improvement.[34]

Elizabeth also spoke on the Reform Bill, and welcomed it until she realized, in September 1832, that it was really a bill of general disfranchisement. At that point she changed her mind and believed

[32] *Ibid.*, p. 467.
[33] *Ibid.*, p. 467.
[34] *Ibid.*, p. 465.

that it marked but the beginning of the political struggle in England, a struggle that should be fought by Paineites. Consequently, her test for radical candidates at the election would be, Have you read and do you approve the political works of Thomas Paine? If the candidate could truly answer Yes, he could be accepted. What such a candidate might be expected to do once returned is shown by Carlile's own election programme put out when he stood for Ashton-under-Lyme. It shows that Carlile's perception, like Paine's was still rooted in the eighteenth century. Carlile would: disestablish the Church, abolish excise, customs and stamp duties, abolish tithes, abolish the standing army, settle the national debt and abolish the new police system in favour of a local police. And he believed that the citizen householder made the best soldier and the best constable. The state would be left to do very little.

Elizabeth Sharples endorsed this political programme. That endorsement and all that she spoke and wrote show clearly that she perceived the barrier to women's improvement to lie in Christianity and the Church and in the legal powers of a tyrant state. At the centre of this tyranny lay the ignorance and oppression of men as well as of women. This stemmed from the doctrine of necessity as preached by the organized Christian Church as she experienced it. Her attack on the Church was sustained and bitter. It became the nub of her developing consciousness as she passed from orthodox Anglicanism to Theism, from being Miss Elizabeth Sharples to becoming The Lady of the Rotunda. As she did so she claimed that Jesus was Reason. She said, do not repeat 'Repent ye, for the kingdom of heaven is at hand', but 'think, for the age of reason is at hand'. She also urged that the Lord's Prayer be changed into a prayer of reason that would read:

O Knowledge! that liftest man above the animals of the earth, hallowed be thy name, thy kingdom come, thy will be done, Give us each day our daily bread, and teach us to do as we would be done unto. Lead us not into temptation, but deliver us from evil, for thine is the kingdom, and the *power*, and the glory, for ever. Amen.[35]

This rationalistic religion was similar to that rejected by Methodism at its birth a hundred years earlier and rejected again

[35] *Ibid.*, p. 180.

by the Primitive Methodists only a few years before the Lady of the Rotunda made her appearance. Since many a 'working-class' woman played an active and leading role in Primitive Methodism such a rationalistic religion would have had little appeal to them. It also had no appeal for women of the middle classes from whom she sprang. In fact Elizabeth Sharples's middling-class message, redolent with ideas that might be thought of as borrowed from 'The Enlightenment', went unheard except by her audiences three or four times a week and passed unread except by the readers of the weekly *Isis* which, under her own editorship, reported her lectures verbatim. It has also largely passed unnoticed by historians. For that very reason, her words of hope and exhortation are worth reproducing in full for the level of consciousness they reveal:

And to you, ladies, sisters, with your leave, I would say, I appeal, and ask in what way are you prepared to assist me? Will you gather round me, and give me that countenance in virtuous society which we all seek and need, and without which life to us is wretchedness? Are you prepared to advance, as you see I have already advanced? Breathes the spirit of liberty in you, or are you content to be slaves, because your lords may wish it? What say you, sisters? Will you advance, and seek that equality in human society which nature has qualified us for, but which tyranny, the tyranny of our lords and masters, hath suppressed? I have need of your assistance, as, I am sure, you have need of mine. I think we have souls, which no scripture has yet granted; that we are worthy of salvation, which no religion has yet promised us; that we are as men in mind and purpose; that we may make ourselves 'helps meet for them', on the conditions that they shall not seek our degradation, that they shall not be our tyrants, but that we shall be free to all the advantages, all the privileges, all the pleasures of human life.

Will you let your children gather round me, and learn from me a love of truth; not to learn to lisp the language of superstition with their first sweet prattlings, but that we may *teach the young idea how to shoot* in matters of reason, preserving the purity of the infant mind from those overwhelming corruptions which now pervade the general society.

Let your sons and your daughters come, and, as the Pagans of old personified and deified the virtues and the graces in their temples, and made a pursuit of them a matter of worship and religion, so here will I aspire to be, in example, an Isis Omnia. Here, in this temple, shall every virtue and every grace be taught; not in the sculptured marble or teinted painting alone, but in life and all its practices. So, come, let us reason together; let us pursue that alone which will bear to be publicly reasoned upon; let us leave that of which we are publicly ashamed. Let us lead a new life, after being born again, to nobler purposes than those in which we have been educated. Let us be free! but let that freedom consist of wisdom, of honour, and of virtue.[36]

I leave it to other quantitative historians to dispute over the extent of response to Elizabeth's appeal. All I claim for it is that it points to a level of consciousness alive in the mind of this one young woman and probably stirring into life in the minds of some of the women and men who listened to her lectures and bought her journal, which is rarely if ever noted as existing among women in the 1830s. This consciousness arose out of deeply felt and resented subordination to all forms of religious, political, economic and sexual power, what J. S. Mill called the 'Toryism of Sex'.

For all that the immediate response was almost certainly slight, Elizabeth's ideas as they smouldered throughout the nineteenth century posed a far greater threat to the existing form of society than any of those of the Primitive Methodists, the Owenite Co-operators, the Land Nationalisers or even the Ricardian Socialists – a threat which only now, with some perfection of Carlile's contraceptive device, shows signs of becoming real.

Elizabeth Sharples suffered for flouting conventional and religious society. When Richard Carlile, whom she converted to Deism, came out of prison Elizabeth lived with him as his *de facto* wife and bore three children, Hypatia, Julian and Theophilia. Their home at Enfield was comfortable enough while Carlile lived but he died in 1843 leaving Elizabeth in poverty. For the next eighteen years she struggled to survive and to educate her three children. In 1849 she added to her family by taking in Charles Bradlaugh who, at sixteen, had been driven from his home for holding freethought ideas which he had picked up at the Warren Street Temperance Hall run by Elizabeth Sharples. Her kindness and influence upon him were considerable. But while Charles Bradlaugh became a significant figure in nineteenth century history, Elizabeth Sharples died, poor and unknown, in 1861. Thereafter, her children migrated to America: Hypatia to work as a milliner and die in poverty sometime in the 1870s, Julian to die in the Civil War, Theophilia to live in Chicago and die in old age in the early years of this century, the forgotten daughter of the forgotten Elizabeth Sharples who had once been generously

[36] *Ibid.*, pp. 3–4.

described by Charles Bradlaugh as one 'to whom the English free thought party in great measure owe the free press and free platforms we use today'. This might be praise and epitaph enough. But we know that she did more. She was the first woman to give public lectures on politics in England and she was the first woman to publish and edit a weekly newspaper, the *Isis*, which, according to Hypatia Bradlaugh, she dedicated to 'The young women of England for generations to come or until superstition is extinct.'[37]

Elizabeth and Marx never met. They probably had no inkling of the other's existence. Yet, when Marx, drawing upon Feuerbach's criticism of religion, wrote: 'the criticism of heaven turns into the criticism of the earth, the *criticism of religion* into the *criticism of law*, and the *criticism of theology* into the *criticism of politics*'[38] he described Elizabeth's own intellectual development which so clearly arose out of her own experience and 'criticism of the vale of tears, the halo of which is religion'. Marx also identified religion as a continuing barrier to the generation of *class* consciousness, and that, too, has become a subject much written about by historians concerned with class and class consciousness. Their difficulties with it, for example, whether Methodism did more to engender than inhibit the rise of class or *class* consciousness, also highlights some of the problems of the approach I have adopted in these last two chapters, problems of the meaning and interpretation of the products of minds within the *Verstehen* method similar to those connected with interpretations of actions within the behavioural method. Problems which may only be settled by reference to theory and to the epistemological status of theories. And so, in the final chapter, I turn again to consider the question of the status of the Materialist Conception of History which I raised but did not settle in the Introduction. I do so because everything in this book, including the subjects I have selected for special consideration in these last two chapters, is structured by that view of history; remove it and the whole would collapse like a house of cards. On the other hand without it the house of cards could never have been built in the first place – the cards *are* the structure and the structure the cards.

---

[37] Hypatia Bradlaugh Bonner, *Charles Bradlaugh*, vol. 1 p. 10.
[38] Karl Marx, *Contribution to the Critique of Hegel's Philosophy of Right*, p. 175–6.

8
Theory and the Poverty of Theory

Whilst the writer pictures what he takes to be actually my method, in this striking and (as far as concerns my own application of it) generous way, what else is he picturing but the dialectic method?

Of course the method of presentation must differ in form from that of inquiry. The latter has to appropriate the material in detail, to analyse its different forms of development, to trace out their inner connection. Only after this work is done, can the actual movement be adequately described. If this is done successfully, if the life of the subject-matter is ideally reflected as in a mirror, then it may appear as if we had before us a mere a priori construction.

Karl Marx, From the Preface to the Second German Edition of *Capital*, in Marx/Engels, *Selected Works* (Moscow, 1950), vol. 1

In the English-speaking world historians, sociologists and political philosophers barely acknowledge the existence let alone the intellectual worth of each other's discipline. With few exceptions it is only in Marx studies that they ever meet in a situation of mutual tolerance if not mutual understanding. That is until recently. For now, with the publication of E. P. Thompson's *The Poverty of Theory*, the lines of difference between Marxist philosophy and sociology on the one hand and Marxist historiography on the other have been sharply drawn. So much so that Marxist historiography is in crisis. And this should not please non-Marxist historians either for what has been said recently within Marx studies about Marxist historiography is as relevant to all atheoretical history, which is most of historiography, as it is to theoretically based Marxist historiography. Further, the influence of this break in Marx studies on the historical analysis of *class*, indeed, on the historical analysis of any of the questions highlighted by Hobsbawm and referred to in the Introduction, could be profound. The explicit use of theory other than positivist theory could disappear altogether from history and the real experience of class could continue to be mystified either by mere empirical relativism or that form of it which always flows from the practice of Historical Idealism lacking an *a priori* element. This is because relativism, in whatever guise it appears, is at bottom anti-intellectual; it substitutes opinion for thought and contributes to the hegemony of those who wield power whoever they may be. Of course, the same result may also be expected from any reified theory, whatever that theory, except that in its structures it identifies the origins of power and warns us against its dangers. Therefore it is worthwhile to identify the causes of and review the lines of conflict within contemporary Marxism. To do this we must begin with epistemology because the central issue arises from the epistemological status of Marxist historiography as seen from the critical standpoint of positivist science and out of attempts to respond to that criticism. As will become apparent the discussion has a great deal to do with the 'current situation'.

English Marxist historians like their European colleagues have always prided themselves on possessing in the corpus of Marx's theoretical writings a body of theory and concepts which they believed gave them a certain intellectual edge over their non-Marxist colleagues. Some of them may even have regarded themselves as practising history as a science and categorized all other history as ideology. These self-perceptions plus the fact that many English Marxist historians were outstanding in their field; Christopher Hill, Eric Hobsbawm, Rodney Hilton, V. G. Kiernan, Maurice Dobb, Ralph Miliband and Edward Thompson among them, have given a certain status or cachet to the more modest practitioners of Marxist history and have helped to sustain them as a minority group in a generally alien and hostile world. This growing strength among the practitioners of Marxist history was especially important in the early post-war years because Marxism in general and Marxist historiography in particular was severely challenged at what it claimed was its point of greatest strength, its basis in theory.

This attack began in 1936 when Karl Popper delivered a paper at a private session in Brussels. The paper was called 'The poverty of historicism'. Shortly afterwards he read a similar paper at Professor Hayek's seminar at the London School of Economics. Although it was published in *Economica* in 1944 and 1945, 'The poverty of historicism' was not published in English in book form until 1957. Since then, with support from *The Open Society and its Enemies* (1945), it has become the main text of those who wish to show that Marxist historiography and, by implication, almost everything in this book, is 'sheer superstition', 'misconceived' and 'suffering from an inherent and improbable weakness'. This latter claim was particularly damaging. The alleged weakness was held to be in that area of historical inquiry regarded by Marxist historians as their special strength – the theoretical nature of the Materialist Conception of History. According to Popper this theoretical structure, which claims to be able to determine the laws of development of whole societies with the object of predicting the future, is not history but Historicism. He argued that the fatal weakness of Historicism is that the future it predicts incorporates new knowledge but that new knowledge cannot be predicted. (If it could be predicted we would know it now and it would cease to be future knowledge.) Therefore the future, which incorporates new knowledge cannot be predicted. Hence the *Poverty of Historicism*: the Materialist Conception of History is not knowledge. Therefore *class* consciousness as described in chapter 1 cannot be regarded as true knowledge.

The conceptual framework for Popper's argument and conclusion was his belief that physics is the paradigm of science coupled with his belief in the unity of scientific method. This meant nominalism, observation, experimentation and prediction as it did to positivists. But, above all, it gave priority to the formulation of theories or hypotheses in ways that endowed them with great content and rendered them subject to falsification rather than to experimental proof. According to Popper's paradigm the object of science is the pursuit of truth via the principle of falsifiability. Therefore only nominalist propositions or hypotheses so stated as to be in principle falsifiable by the method of repeatable experiments, on the basis of which the theory may be expanded and predictions made, can lay claim to produce knowledge. Since

Historicism as described by Popper is concerned with the essence of things and, therefore, not nominalist and since it is concerned with social wholes and social change its propositions cannot be formulated in ways to make them amenable to falsification. Hence Historicism cannot lay claim to produce knowledge.

Furthermore, according to Popper, the search for laws of change should give way to a search for laws of structures and true history should concern itself only with particular facts. Popper wrote:

The thesis of the unity of scientific method, whose application to theoretical sciences I have just been defending, can be extended, with certain limitations, even to the field of the historical sciences. And this can be done without giving up the fundamental distinction between theoretical and historical sciences – for example, between sociology or economic theory or political theory on the one hand, and social, economic, and political history on the other – a distinction which has been so often and emphatically reaffirmed by the best historians. It is the distinction between the interest in universal laws and the interest in particular facts. I wish to defend the view, so often attacked as old-fashioned by historicists, that *history is characterized by its interest in actual, singular, or specific events, rather than in laws or generalizations.*[1]

According to this view Marxist historiography is no different from other forms of historiography. It is not truly theoretical and cannot generate theories – only interpretations which may be set alongside other *equally* tenable points of view. According to this view all the interpretations of class discussed in this book are equally tenable. All Historicist interpretations, said Popper,

are more or less interesting points of view, and *as such* perfectly unobjectionable. But historicists do not present them as such; they do not see that there is necessarily a plurality of interpretations which are fundamentally on the same level of both, suggestiveness and arbitrariness (even though some of them may be distinguished by their *fertility* – a point of some importance). Instead, they present them as doctrines or theories, asserting that 'all history is the history of class struggle', etc. And if they actually find that their point of view is fertile, and that many facts can be ordered and interpreted in its light, then they mistake this for a confirmation, or even for a proof, of their doctrine.[2]

Clearly, in spite of Popper's protests to the contrary, his line of reasoning placed him in the mainstream of positivist thinking. It

[1] Karl Popper, *The Poverty of Historicism* (London, 1961), p. 143.
[2] *Ibid.*, p. 151.

certainly led him to the same conclusion arrived at some 250 years
ago by David Hume who then expressed it far more elegantly and
comprehensively than Popper. Writing of the causes of belief about
the connections between phenomena Hume wrote: 'Thus all probable reasoning is nothing but a species of sensation. 'Tis not solely
in poetry and music, we must follow our taste and sentiment, but
likewise in philosophy.'[3] But so it is with Popper's scientific
method, positivism, and the unity of scientific method, because
claims about the superiority of the path to knowledge whether laid
down by the principles of experimental proof or falsifiability are not
subject to their own principles. The question, how can we know
whether positivist or Popperian epistemology are not themselves a
matter of taste? has to be answered.

However, in a generally positivist world it goes without saying
that this question is rarely posed, let alone answered. Consequently
in the late 1940s, when for ideological reasons it was expedient to
attack Marxist historiography, there were many positivist critics of
Marxist historians. Apparently theoretically strengthened by the
Popperian argument these critics turned their minds to the production of empirical falsifications of particular aspects of the
Materialist Conception of History. In this attack in England on
English Marxist historiography the London School of Economics
and Professor Hayek were again prominent. The scene was set
by Hayek's *Road to Serfdom* and the initiative was taken by
Professors Hayek and Ashton and others of the Mont Pélèrin
persuasion. They resolved that almost every aspect of economic and
social history, which was contaminated by Marxism, was false
history. Since it was false it either intentionally or unintentionally
undermined the notion that absolute economic freedom was the
handmaiden to 'democracy'. Thereby it prepared the ground for
some kind of national socialist takeover of the state and society in
England. And in *Capitalism and the Historians* these historians
launched their crusade to rectify this false history. They did so in
the guise of mere concrete or empiricist historians to whom facts
could speak for themselves unadulterated by preconceived notions
or theories.

In these early years the main trust of their attack focused upon

---

[3]David Hume, *A Treatise on Human Nature* (Oxford, 1973), p. 103.

the question of the standard of living in England during the Industrial Revolution. It seemed that they believed that as they showed, to their own satisfaction, that material standards rose on average for the mass of the working population in England that they could undermine Marx's notion of immiseration. They believed, thereby, that they were falsifying Marx and could 'prove' that he was wrong. The men of Mont Pélèrin were joined in this enterprise by Max Hartwell. Over the next twenty years he became the chief musketeer in this cause. Hartwell's argument, apparently based on hard facts, was in fact based on guesses about the size of the national income at ten-yearly intervals between 1800 and 1850 and on assertions about the unchanging share of that income accruing to wage earners. In more recent years he has also argued that the economic and cultural benefits of industrialization to subsequent generations greatly outweighed the negligible economic and cultural costs to the first generations of industrial workers. The greatest benefit of all, he argued, was the emergence of a class of working-class women and the stimulus they gave to the emancipation of women. The thrust of all his argument was that economic growth was ever and always in the best interests of wage earners and that they were foolish and misguided in their negative and hostile reactions to it. More recently Hartwell has also argued, contrary to Marx, that the coercive power of the state did not play a part in generating economic growth in England in the first instance. Rather, the achievement and benefits of economic growth in the eighteenth century were consequences of the deliberate liberalization of both statute and common law in that period. According to these views generations of workers in England from the early eighteenth century were not only economically and culturally better off they were also freer and uncoerced. There were, one might say, no objective conditions either of position in the production process or of power relations for the development of *class* or of *class* consciousness.

It was fortunate for Marxist historians that they had the fetishism of commodities and the recently rediscovered concept of alienation to fall back upon. Although these theoretical and philosophic concepts were never employed in the debate on the standard of living in England, Marxists could still employ them in general and show that for all the empirical work that had gone into proving Marx wrong, the debate on the standard of living in England, stemming as it did from economist perceptions about *class* formation, had little bearing on the Materialist Conception of History, or on the question of *class* formation. At the same time merely positivist historians could believe the case against Marx to be proven. Thus, according to positivist epistemology as instanced by Popper, both these views or opinions could live comfortably side by side in the historiographical supermarket. If you paid your money you could take your choice.

Even as the debate on the standard of living got under way another anti-Marxist stand was taken by J. D. Chambers. Chambers attributed to Marx an extremely naive view about the effects of enclosure on labour supply during the Industrial Revolution and in a simplistic and internally contradictory paper attempted to refute Marx's notion of 'so-called' primitive accumulation, a notion which has an honourable place in this book. Although *Our History* put out an effective refutation of Chambers's article, there was never any prolonged debate on the issue. Consequently, in positivist history, Chambers's views have held the field for more than twenty-five years. That they do not bear upon any crucial aspect of the Materialist Conception of History is scarcely noticed because to become aware of their deficiencies in this respect requires a greater knowledge and understanding of the Materialist Conception of History than is common among positivist historians. Further, the fact that much of Chambers's evidence affords good empirical evidence of Marx's 'so-called' primitive accumulation is never appreciated within positivist historiography because the concept is not part of the corpus of positivist historiography. Consequently the conventional view about the labour side of the capital/labour relation in the eighteenth century obscures the fact that it was the outcome of a property relationship between people and emphasizes the overriding importance of an autonomous population growth.

In the early seventies Chambers's attack on the labour side of Marx's 'so-called' primitive accumulation was complemented by François Crouzet's critique of the second aspect of the concept; the accumulation of a stock of monetary wealth that is not yet capital but which becomes available for use as capital setting labour to produce for purposes of exchange. Crouzet's argument was that capital in the eighteenth century had its own unique origins in the industriousness and thriftiness of small producers – a fact, he said, 'so obvious as to be almost a cliché and the point is not worth labouring'.[4] Thereby he emphasized a significant discontinuity between the sources of loanable funds and financial institutions in pre-industrial capitalism and those characteristic of and produced by the industrial capitalist mode of production in the second half of the eighteenth century. Hence he acclaimed the novelty and thriftiness of industrial capital and appeared as an advocate of the heroic model of capital accumulation during the eighteenth century.

On the other hand the Marxian notion of 'so-called' primitive accumulation emphasized significant continuity and evolution between these two phases in the development of the capitalist mode of production and emphasized thereby the unsavoury and exploitative origins of capital. Thus, said Marx, 'capital comes into the world soiled with mire from top to toe and oozing blood from every pore'. Crouzet's comment upon this Marxian notion was that it lacked empirical evidence of direct conversion of either agricultural or bourgeois commercial wealth into industrial capital. There was, he said, a 'missing link' in Marx's analysis. Needless to say there was much more that was missing from Crouzet's positivist understanding of Marx, notably Marx's treatment and understanding of money and credit and his critique of the general fetishism of appearance in classical political economy. Therefore, Crouzet's criticism of primitive accumulation, like Chambers's was wide of the mark. Nevertheless and although there has been a good deal of empirical writing which undermined Crouzet's analysis of capital formation during the eighteenth century, even within positivist historiography, he has only recently been challenged within the context of his critique of Marx; his views are probably characteristic of positivist historians. These views are also in direct line of descent from *Capitalism and the Historians* and Ashton's perennially popular *Industrial Revolution*. They help to refute the notion of *class* consciousness by denying any inherently exploitative component in a system based on private property.

In 1959 a more general attack was launched on Marxist historiography by W. W. Rostow. His *The Stages of Economic Growth*

[4]François Crouzet, *Capital Formation in the Industrial Revolution* (London, 1972), p. 188.

was a polemical non-Communist manifesto presented in the guise of theoretical empiricism and directed in true Popperian fashion to social engineering. The central concept of the book, 'take-off', was defined as a period of about twenty years during which a nation's investment proportion, concentrated in a few 'leading sectors', would double from a mere 5 per cent or less to 10 per cent or more. The significance of this was that the rate of growth of output would outstrip the rate of population growth and begin to generate increases in national income per head. According to Rostow this concept could be demonstrated empirically in history and was therefore applicable in the present as a strategy for economic growth now. 'The lesson of all this', he wrote, is that 'the tricks of growth are not all that difficult.'[5] The critique of Marx contained within this work was that 'take-off' showed – indeed, was designed to show – that the standard of living in underdeveloped countries could begin to double in a man's lifetime without the sort of social class conflict predicated in the Materialist Conception of History as a prerequisite for social revolution. In relation to English history the idea of 'take-off' also helped to undermine the notion that there were any objective conditions for the growth of *class* consciousness. It was no wonder that Rostow's book was hailed by the *Economist* as, 'the most stimulating contribution to political and economic discussion by any academic economist since the war'.[6] Accordingly the *Economist* devoted sixteen pages to a summary of the argument, wrote two editorials on it and published Rostow's lengthy reply to *Pravda*'s criticism of the 'theory'.

In the face of such an open-armed welcome from the academic establishment and the persuasiveness of Rostow's writings it is perhaps excusable that at least one knowledgeable and experienced Marxist historian was won over by them, at least for the time being.

Altogether the twenty years or so after the Second World War were bad years for Marxist historiography as students of history were offered grotesque empiricist formulations of fragments of the Materialist Conception of History and simplistic empirical refutations of them. But there it was; primitive accumulation in respect to both labour and capital was falsified, the coercive role of the state at the point of the transition from Feudalism to Capitalism and within

---

[5] *Economist*, 22nd August 1959, p. 531.
[6] *Ibid.*, 15th August 1959, editor's preamble.

the Capitalist Mode of Production was falsified, immiseration was falsified, social conflict and revolution were falsified. At the same time the notion that the English Civil War was a bourgeois revolution was falsified and the notions of Feudalism and Capitalism were also falsified. And we have already seen that it was also claimed that England on the eve of industrialization was either a 'one-class' or a 'class-less' society. At the end of it all there was not much left of the Materialist Conception of History, at least within the mainstream of positivist historiography, and nothing much was left of the general theory within which the analysis of *class* in this book has been carried out.

Even when the Materialist Conception of History was presented in a strong form for purposes of positivist historical inquiry it finished up being damned with faint praise. The latest author to appraise it in this manner was William H. Shaw in *Marx's Theory of History*, published in 1978. Shaw's purpose in this book was to state the Materialist Conception of History as a positivist theory subject to the scientific criterion of empirical falsifiability. He did not set out to revise or defend that theory nor did he attempt to test it empirically. The theory as stated by Shaw turned it back into the vulgar Marxist model, consisting of base/superstructure with linear causal relations running from the one to the other, which was popular at the turn of the century. Shaw took as his starting point what he thought was the fundamental technological determinist proposition in Marx, particularly the relationships between productive forces and relations of production. He defined the former as the means of production, labour power, and science and co-operation and the latter as work and ownership relations. He claimed that these two concepts corresponded to distinct and separate things, the contradictions between which constituted the dialectical centrepiece of Marx's thought. Indeed, he believed that Marx regarded the development of productive forces as independent of the social form of production and as some kind of autonomous natural occurrence which pushes society towards new relations of production. Marx, he said, was a technological determinist although of a humanist kind – after all, productive forces were defined by Shaw to include labour power which is an exclusively human attribute.

Using these concepts as the core of his analysis Shaw offered a conventional description of Marx's capitalistic dynamic and the development of socialism. He also found, according to this definition of the model, that there is no general theory of the transition from Feudalism to Capitalism. Marx's system is deficient in this respect and cannot, therefore, be regarded as amenable to empirical falsification. It is fortunate for Marx, said Shaw, that there is no rival theory of history, for although his theory still offers a plausible vehicle for social and historical research it is a deteriorating paradigm scarcely qualifying as a progressive and energetic research programme. Presumably, therefore, there can be little substance in the main body of this book.

In spite of the apparently devastating theoretical attack of Popper and the empiricist onslaught, the new generation of Marxist historians, previously referred to, produced some outstanding work as if they were oblivious of the scurry going on around them. It was as if the strength of their theory with its emphases on practice and the role of knowledge in generating *class* consciousness gave them an intellectual conviction untroubled by attacks launched outside their own conceptual framework. It is significant that one of the most lively and continuous debates among Marxist historians about the Materialist Conception of History was over the *nature* of the transition from Feudalism to Capitalism and that they did not enter into discussion with non-Marxist historians about the concepts themselves. These English Marxist historians were also protected in part by the wholly empirical nature of English historiography and the merely empiricist persuasion of most historians. Hence purely theoretical criticism such as Popper's carried little weight with positivist historians themselves and many varieties of empirical history were allowed to exist. In this way many historians and students of history came to regard Marxist historiography as another empirical history. Where the Materialist Conception of History was not clearly formulated in an empirically falsifiable manner and then empirically falsified it frequently passed unnoticed as Marxist historiography. It was in this fashion that a good deal of Marx slipped into the writing of English history where it lodges still.[7]

---

[7]See, for example, the survey of Marxist historiography in Jon S. Cohen, The achievement of economic history: the Marxist school, in *The Journal of Economic History* **XXXVIII** (1), 1978.

Perhaps the most outstanding example of this development, referred to in the Introduction, was the re-emergence of social history as an alternative to a more clearly theoretical development within traditional positivist economic history. This latter development, the 'New Economic History', arose out of attempts to use neo-classical economic theory or aspects of it to formulate nominalist hypotheses in such ways as to render them falsifiable by recourse to strict quantification and mathematical techniques. In place of experimentation as used in the physical sciences many of the New Economic Historians used the device of the counterfactual. In regard to causal explanations in economic history, they asked of all alleged causal explanations, what would have been the outcome if the stated causal agent were to be removed from the equation. These procedures enabled econometricians to pursue rigorous, quantitative analysis of the short-run behaviour of economic variables and to claim that they pursued history as a science in the strict Popperian fashion. The New Economic Historians also castigated and denigrated traditional history for not conforming 'to what a modern empiricist might demand of it'.[8] They claimed that traditional history was atheoretical, descriptive, terminologically imprecise, based on common-sense judgements and tolerated the co-existence of 'explanations'. Accordingly the New Economic Historians sought to impose their 'correct' shortrun linear procedures on all other historians with the result that economic history became increasingly specialized and more narrowly circumscribed in its application.

A reaction to these positivist procedures; the narrowing of economic history and attacks on the epistemological status of all non-econometric history, was a flight from economic history and the revival of social history as total history. While this was happening, Harold Perkin (in 1962) put forward holistic claims about social history. He wrote that the task of the social historian should be to:

present the natural history of the body politic, exposing and explaining its ecology, anatomy, physiology, pathology, and, since the body politic may be presumed to exist on more than the physical plane its psychology too; its awareness of itself, its conscious aims, criteria and ideals.[9]

[8]G. S. Murphy, The 'new' history, in R. L. Andreano (ed.), *The New Economic History* (New York, 1970), p. 1.
[9]Harold Perkin, Social history, in H. P. R. Finberg (ed.), *Approaches to History* (London, 1962), p. 61.

Since this was a prescription for doing anything in any way it was no defence against the attacks by positivist theoreticians and New Economic Historians against unscientific history. In fact, as I have already suggested in this book, social history existed throughout the 1960s in so many guises that one might have thought of it as a confusion of subjects looking for a discipline.

It was probably not fortuitous that out of this search emerged a weak version of the Materialist Conception of History as the recommended and apparent backbone of social history. As I emphasized in the Introduction, this development came to a head with Hobsbawm's *Daedalus* paper in 1971. The central thrust of his paper was that social history was virtually the Materialist Conception of History, albeit in a theoretically weak and loosely-articulated form. And it was in this form that it was re-published in 1974 by two non-Marxist historians, M. W. Flinn and T. C. Smout. They were so attracted by it that they used it as an introduction to their miscellany of papers on social history. In doing so they waived their right as editors to write their own introduction, apparently regarding it as the latest if not the last word in defining and systematizing social history as a discipline. It was in ways such as this that the Materialist Conception of History lodged in the mainstream of empirical historiography.[10] Unfortunately, even as it found its place in empirical historiography, it did so in weakened form. Consequently the Materialist Conception of History has tended to become fragmented, heavily empirical and culturally and ideologically determined. Even in the hands of Marxist historians it has become increasingly divorced from Dialectical Materialism and from practice. The result is there are now many variants of the Materialist Conception of History whose advocates vie with each other about such matters as the development of *class* and *class* consciousness and in whose hands the Materialist Conception of History has become domesticated. Thus, as it wins it loses.

It was at this point but in the world of practice that there developed a reaction against the liberalization of contemporary European Marxism which had followed the Twentieth Congress of

---

[10]See the symposium on social history in *The Journal of Social History* **10**, 1976/7 where the ghost of Marx haunts all the contributors.

the Communist Party in the USSR. The theoretical mirror of this reaction had profound significance for the epistemological status of Marxist historiography, particularly for the attenuated form of the Materialist Conception of History in which it successfully entered the mainstream of old-style positivist historiography. The attack on Marxist historiography set in train by these events was launched by philosophers working within the Marxian tradition. It was, therefore, more damaging to Marxist historians than Popper's critique and less easily rejected as ideologically motivated and, therefore, theoretically untenable. The attack was led by Louis Althusser, a philosopher at the École Normale Supérieure and a member of the Communist Party since 1948. Throughout the early 1960s he published a series of papers critical of developments in Marxist thought since the denunciation of Stalin. These papers were subsequently collected and published under the title *For Marx* in 1965. They became available in English in 1969. The theoretical underpinning for these essays was further elaborated in *Reading Capital*, also published in 1965 and available in English in 1970. Since then Althusser has also published, *Essays – Essays in Self Criticism*, 1976 and *Politics and History*, 1977. Althusser was not alone in his criticism of Marxist historiography and was joined by Nicos Poulantzas writing on political power and social classes. In its turn Althusser's proposal for a science of history was also criticized by Hindess and Hirst in *Pre-Capitalist Modes of Production*, 1975 and more recently in *Marx's Capital and Capitalism Today*, 1977.

The importance of the political context and of political practice for the severity of Althusser's philosophic attack on the epistemological status of Marxist historiography is not a matter of opinion. Althusser has set his own political scene for his philosophy which is anti 'Marxist Humanism' and hostile to liberal/humanist interpretations of Marx's early works. These works, he said:

have been a war-horse for petty bourgeois intellectuals in their struggle against Marxism; but little by little, and then massively, they have been set to work in the interests of a new 'interpretation' of Marxism which is today being openly developed by many Communist intellectuals. The 'humanist' interpretations of Marxist theory which have developed under these definite circumstances represent a *new* phenomenon as compared with the period just past (the period between 1930 and 1956). However, they have many historical *precedents* in the history of the worker's movement. Marx, Engels and Lenin, to refer only to them, ceaselessly struggled against ideological interpretations of an idealist, humanist type that threatened Marxist theory. Here it will suffice to recall Marx's rupture with Feuerbach's humanism, Engels's struggle against Dühring, Lenin's long battle with the Russian populists, and so on. This whole past, this whole heritage, is obviously part of the present theoretical and ideological conjuncture of the international Communist movement.[11]

To combat these humanist threats to Marxist theory Althusser argued for a 'strong' theory of history. He claimed that when Marx wrote *Capital*, and only then, he founded a new science: the science of history. This science of history opened up a whole new continent of knowledge comparable to the Greeks' invention of mathematics and Galileo's invention of physics. However, because it revealed the exploitative nature of capitalist society, this science could not be like other sciences, a science for 'everyone'. It is easily comprehended by the proletariat whose class instinct enables them to see themselves in the science of history and they only need to be educated in it. But intellectuals, who at bottom are all petit bourgeois, need to be revolutionized. They must read *Capital*, preferably in the sequence indicated by Althusser, and to read it as philosophers posing the question of its *relation to its object* and applying to it the same kind of reading that Marx gave to classical political economy. That is to say that Marx produced answers to questions he had not really asked and could not ask because of the paucity of concepts available to him. We, however, can see that Marx was really producing structuralist answers without adequately or clearly posing structuralist questions. This meant that Marx, like Althusser, had broken epistemologically with historicism, humanism and empiricism. Thus Marx's science of history is a study of structures at the level of theory. In this respect, in the priority he gives to theory, Althusser has much in common with Popper.

Althusser's first move was to raise the question of historical time and to attack the view which holds that historical time is mere chronology or sequence of events. He argued that since different aspects of the past have different time sequences, 'It is only possible to give a context to the concept of historical time by defining historical time as the specific form of existence of the social totality

[11] Louis Althusser, *For Marx* (Harmondsworth, 1969), pp. 10–11.

under consideration'.[12] There is, he said, 'no history in general, but only specific structures of historicity'.[13] I take this to mean that historians should not concern themselves with merely linear time since there are an infinite number of linear times but should define their object in terms of whole social structures in which lateral and reciprocally-structured relationships take precedence. For Althusser the central concept defining such social structures was the Marxian notion, mode of production.[14] These whole social structures or eternities have no necessary succession, they are not even an historical progression. Indeed, each level of a whole social structure, economic, political, ideological and so on has a different temporality and the whole is constituted by 'the articulation of dislocations between these temporalities'. These dislocations are time lags or fractures between different components in the whole social structure such as that between ideology and other practices. It is the existence of dislocations which means that one cannot discover the articulation of a whole social structure by taking a section of the society studied at any point in time. Thus its articulation cannot be understood using the linear time of general historiography nor the lateral time of indepth studies. Whole social structures, including, presumably, their classes, can only be understood conceptually. And they are only a logical series. In this way Althusser dispensed with both linear and lateral time. He wrote:

This definition of historical time by its *theoretical* concept is aimed directly at historians and their practice. For it should draw their attention to the empiricist ideology which, with a few exceptions, overwhelmingly dominates every variety of history (whether it be history in the wide sense or specialized economic, social or political history, the history of art,

---

[12] Louis Althusser, *Reading Capital* (London, 1970), p. 108.
[13] *Ibid.*, p. 108.
[14] The following is a table of the elements of any mode of production, a table of the invariants in the analysis of forms:

1   Labourer;
2   Means of production;
   (i) object of labour;
   (ii) means of labour;
3   Non-labourer;
   (a) property connection;
   (b) real or material appropriation connection.

literature, philosophy, the sciences, etc.). To put it crudely, history lives in the illusion that it can do without *theory* in the strong sense, without a theory of its object and therefore without a definition of its theoretical object. What acts as its theory, what it sees as taking the place of this theory is its *methodology*, i.e., the rules that govern its effective practices, practices centred around the scrutiny of documents and the establishment of facts. What it sees as taking place of its theoretical object is its 'concrete' object. History therefore takes its methodology for the theory it lacks, and it takes the 'concrete' of the concrete obviousness of ideological time for its theoretical object. This dual confusion is typical of an empiricist ideology. What history lacks is a conscious and courageous confrontation of one of the essential problems of any science whatsoever: the problem of the nature and constitution of its *theory*, by which I mean the theory within the science itself, the system of theoretical concepts on which is based every method, and every practice, even the experimental method and practice, and which simultaneously defines its theoretical object. But with a few exceptions historians have not posed history's vital and urgent problem, the problem of its *theory*. And, as inevitably happens, the place left empty by scientific theory has been occupied by an ideological theory whose harmful influence can be shown in detail precisely at the level of the historian's methodology.[15]

There is, I think, a great measure of truth in this criticism of history which is relevant for the practice of all historians, especially for those interested in class and class consciousness. And in this book I have attempted to come to grips with some of the issues raised by Althusser.

In the place of historical methodology posing as theory Althusser brought forward the notion of *'the theory of history in the strong sense'*. He meant by this that the theory of political economy, as in *Capital*, and the theory of history as a science are one and the same except that political economy considers only one relatively autonomous element in the social totality whereas history embraces the complex totality. With the exception of this difference, he said, 'there can be no distinction between the science of political economy and the science of history, from a theoretical point of view'.[16] Accordingly, history is the 'application' of a theory of history which is the theory of political economy conceptually clarified, re-written and expanded to embrace the social totality. In fact, 'the theory of economics is a subordinate region in the theory of history,

[15] *Ibid.*, p. 109.
[16] *Ibid.*, p. 109.

understood of course in the non historicist, non empirical sense in which we have outlined the theory of history'.[17] In this theory of history, 'knowledge of a real object is not reached by immediate contact with the "concrete" but by the production of the *concept* of that object as the absolute condition of its *theoretical* possibility'.[18] Causal relations in this theory are neither linear nor teleological but structural and the structure determining economic objects is the unity of the forces of production and the relations of production within a mode of production, but only in the last instance. Such a structure cannot be defined as a concept without resort to another concept, that of the global structure of the mode of production, which, as I have said, lies at the very heart of Althusser's theory of the Marxian system. The complexity of this system of structural causation which Althusser identified in Marx's *Capital* is, perhaps, expressed most clearly in Althusser's explanation of Marx's use of the term '*Darstellung*' (representation, *mise en scène*) to describe it:

> Now we can recall that highly symptomatic term 'Darstellung', compare it with this 'machinery' [of political economy] and take it literally, as the very existence of the stage direction (*mise en scène*) of the theatre which is simultaneously its own stage, its own script, its own actors, the theatre whose spectators can, on occasion, be spectators only because they are first of all forced to be its actors, caught by the constraints of a script and parts whose authors they cannot be, since it is in essence an *authorless* theatre.[19]

Except that in the hands of Althusser the actors, who in Marx's system are members of classes fighting their own way towards *class consciousness*, must move according to an invisible Althusserian script in the tradition of an idealist theatre of the absurd in which Althusserian concepts *are* the rhinoceros of the mind, and, therefore, structure the actions of those classes.

On the other hand Althusser claimed that Marx produced no theory of the transition from one mode of production to another or, using Althusser's use of Marx's analogy, gave no suggestions as to how the play might be transferred from one theatre to another. Thus modes of production and the whole social structures, including their component classes, to which they give rise are locked in

[17] *Ibid.*, p. 183.
[18] *Ibid.*, p. 184.
[19] *Ibid.*, p. 193.

separate theatres. Clearly, therefore, the strong theory of history may only examine structures and cannot encompass change, except it employs the notion of over-determination. Moreover, because we cannot take what goes on on the stage at its face value, empiricism as well as historicism is also suspect. Consequently, history is debarred from examining structures other than through the concepts handed to them by Althusser. History it seems is not only political economy but philosophy as well. Its object and its product is knowledge of itself and it knows itself to be 'true'. It is ahistorical history. One vital implication of Althusser's view of the Materialist Conception of History is that an historical investigation of *class* and *class* consciousness, such as that attempted in this book, can have no bearing upon or significance for a Marxist's understanding of the concept of *class* in Marx.

As Hindess and Hirst rightly observed,

why should this general theory of Althusser's be called a theory of history? What is historical about it? . . . What is called a 'history' is something quite different, a general theory of modes of production . . . The radical conclusion to Althusser's argument would be that the supposed real object, 'history', which the thought object is not, is not a real object. There is no real object 'history', the notion that there is a *real* history is the product of empiricism. The word 'history' should be confined to designating the ideological non-object constituted by philosophies of history and the practice of the writing of history.[20]

And that was their general position. Marxist theory, said Hindess and Hirst, is concerned only to analyse the 'current situation'. By a 'current situation' they meant not, 'a specific unitary element of being', not an entity but any aspect of current practice requiring resolution. Just in case this smacked of pragmatism they emphasized that the relation between theory and political practice is the essence of Marxism. But they made the strong claim that, in exploring relationships between theory and practice, history has no place:

Marxism as a theoretical and political practice gains nothing from its association with historical writing and historical research. The study of history is not only scientifically but also politically valueless. The object of

[20]Barry Hindess and Paul Q. Hirst, *Pre-Capitalist Modes of Production* (London, 1975).

history, the past, no matter how it is conceived, cannot affect present conditions.[21]

Clearly, whereas Althusser's science of history was ahistorical and only potentially anti-historical, Hindess and Hirst's Marxist political theory was explicitly anti-historical. They propounded the grounds of their objection to history, reminiscent of Oakeshott or Collingwood, as if they were some new discovery. And as they revealed to the world that the past is accessible only through its representation in surviving artefacts, records and documents, they claimed that the real object of history, the past, is inaccessible to knowledge. Therefore, they said, the object of history is whatever is *represented* as having existed and history is a present activity (a notion which Gardiner says historians find bewildering). As Hindess and Hirst put it with their penchant for Marxian paradox, 'It is present as its opposite and absent as itself'.[22] They also repeated certain positivist propositions in support of their views that history is not accessible to knowledge: it is not subject to experimentation, historical explanations are *post hoc* rationalizations and historical phenomena, being finite and unrepeatable, cannot give rise to general laws.

In respect to the Althusserian notion that there can be a general theory of modes of production, they rejected that, too. They claimed that the concepts of specific modes of production, such as the concept of pre-capitalist modes of production, for example, feudalism, do not require that they exist prior to capitalism or that they are necessarily succeeded by capitalism. These concepts are abstractions within theory not history. Therefore they have no need of recourse to anything outside themselves, such as history, to verify or falsify them. According to Hindess and Hirst: 'They cannot be refuted by any empiricist recourse to the supposed "facts" of history . . . concrete conditions are not "given" to theory in order to validate or refute its general concepts. On the contrary, it is the general concepts that make possible the analysis of the concrete.'[23] Like Popper they rejected the inductive method and claimed that: 'Concepts are formed and have their existence within knowledge.

[21] *Ibid.*, p. 312.
[22] *Ibid.*, p. 309.
[23] *Ibid.*, p. 4.

They are not reducible to or derivable from any set of "given", "real" conditions.'[24] Consequently, and no doubt supported by social theorists of all kinds, they rejected 'the notion of history as a coherent and worthwhile object of study'.

With that determination they consigned to the ideological dustbin all the work of that generation of English Marxist historians who had kept at bay Popper, the men of Mont Pélèrin, and the New Economic Historians and who were about to storm the heights of positivist historiography. Also, they consigned this book, in advance as it were, to that same dustbin where, I have no doubt, they would like it to stay.

And with that they sacrificed the best of the radical troops and retired into Fortress Theory (apparently unaware of creating conditions for the existence of an infinite number of Fortress Theories) and set about defending Marxism by attacking Fortress Theory A, postal address 'Science of History'.

In the meantime the best of the radical troops, consigned to the wasteland 'history' did not lie down and die. Instead through the inspiration of the creator of the English working class and inspired by his banner 'The Poverty of Theory' they have been invited to declare war against all Fortress Theories. They, too, can marshal their scattered troops within the crumbling ramparts of castle Marx to decide whether to sally forth from its shattered gates or to retire to grow their own flowers in the wasteland. If there is to be a sustained guerrilla war they will undoubtedly need the support of all those petty craftsmen who also inhabit the wasteland 'History' because it will be a global conflict. A conflict it is true, scripted by Althusserian actors bent on compelling the audience to sit through a repeat of Marx's own confrontation with all idealist builders of philosophic systems not rooted in material life, human practice and the growth of consciousness. But a conflict, too, in which all positivist and structuralist philosophers and social theorists have a committed interest against the interest of all who inhabit the wasteland 'History', some of whom, in seeking refuge in Historical Idealism, put the rest of us at risk.

It is as well then to see what alternative programme appears in the script under the banner, 'Poverty of Theory'.

---

[24] *Ibid.*, p. 1.

E. P. Thompson's criticism of Althusser and all neo- and post-Althusserians such as Hindess and Hirst had two parts. One, a polemical philosophic attack. Two, a core statement or defence of historical practice. Under one, Thompson argued that Althusser's system was contrary to reason and could not encompass the notion of social being determining consciousness and the changing of experience. It was a system in stasis. Next he distinguished what he called an empirical idiom from empiricism and accused Althusser of confusing the two. He also accused Althusser of idealism and intellectual imperialism. His imagery was attractively vivid:

> Arrayed in this scarlet and furred gown of Theory, Althusser may now storm into every adjacent lecture theatre, and, in the name of philosophy, denounce the incumbents and expropriate them of their poor defective disciplines which pretend to be knowledges. Before these disciplines may proceed at all, they must first sit before his rostrum and master his lessons.[25]

Under his defence of what he calls historical logic Thompson put forward his case for history as a knowledge. It is unlikely that this case will persuade Althusser of the error of his ways and almost certain that it will have no effect on Hindess and Hirst. Yet for us, as historians, particularly as historians of class, the question must be, is it a banner under which we will join each other at the intellectual barricades to defend our practice even though E. P. Thompson, having written a call to arms and summoned us to action, intends to return to his own garden to watch things grow?

In introducing his notion of 'historical logic' Thompson told the following story:

> Not very long ago, when I was in Cambridge as a guest at a seminar of distinguished anthropologists, when I was asked to justify a proposition, I replied that it was validated by 'historical logic.' My courteous hosts dissolved into undisguised laughter. I shared in the amusement, of course; but I was also led to reflect upon the 'anthropological' significance of the exchange. For it is customary within the rituals of the academy for the practitioners of different disciplines to profess respect, not so much for the findings of each other's discipline, as for the authentic credentials of that discipline itself. And if a seminar of historians were to laugh at a philosopher's or anthropologist's very *credentials*, (that is, the logic or discipline

[25] E. P. Thompson, *The Poverty of Theory* (London, 1978), p. 215.

central to their practice) this would be regarded as an occasion for offence. And the significance of this exchange was that it was very generally supposed that 'history' was an exception to this rule; that the discipline central to its practice was an occasion for laughter; and that, so far from taking offence, I, as a practitioner, would join in the laughter myself.

It is not difficult to see how this comes about. The modes of historical writing are so diverse; the techniques employed by historians are so various; the themes of historical enquiry are so disparate; and, above all, the conclusions are so controversial and so sharply contested within the profession, that it is difficult to adduce any disciplinary coherence. And I can well see that there are things within the Cambridge School of History which might occasion anthropological, or other, laughter. Nevertheless, the study of history is a very ancient pursuit, and it would be surprising if, alone among the sciences and humanities, it had failed to develop its own discipline over several thousand years: that is, its own proper discourse of the proof. And I cannot see what this proper discourse is unless it takes the form of historical logic.[26]

By 'historical logic' Thompson meant:

a logical method of enquiry appropriate to historical materials, designed as far as possible to test hypotheses as to structure, causation, etc. and to eliminate self confirming procedures ("instances", "illustrations".)[27]

There were, he said, eight propositions underpinning this logic the first six of which might get general assent from historians. They were:

1   'Facts' have a real existence knowable according to vigilant historical procedures.
2   Historical knowledge is provisional, incomplete, selective, limited but not therefore untrue.
3   False historical knowledge is capable of disproof.
4   The relationship between historical knowledge and its object is one of *dialogue*.
5   A 'present' does not change its ontological status by becoming a 'past'.
6   There is an interaction between concept and evidence such that a notion endorsed by the evidence 'does exist, "out there", in the real history'.
7   Historical Materialism differs from other interpretive orderings

[26] *Ibid.*, pp. 229–30.
[27] *Ibid.*, p. 231.

of evidence not in any epistemological premises but in its categories, its characteristic hypotheses and attendant procedures.

8   Certain categories and concepts in Historial Materialism are *historical categories*, i.e., they necessarily change over time. There is a necessary fluidity in them alien to philosophy and sociology.

Historical 'logic' so based, said Thompson, can generate historical knowledge, the court of appeal for which 'lies within the discipline of history and nowhere else'.[28]

I have no doubt that to historians this looks like a strong hand. Equally I have no doubt that to Althusserians and positivists alike it will appear as a hand playing into their hands. For my part I would like to try to sort out its strengths and weaknesses and to use both to effect a greater humility on both sides.

First, the conclusion that history is its own court of appeal in matters of the epistemological status of its own product. If this is to be accepted then Althusserian structuralism, Popperian indeterminism, Positivism, Husserlian phenomenology, Historical Idealism and all other self-enclosing systems must be allowed to be their own courts of appeal. Which is all right if we are content to be back in the eighteenth century with David Hume or if we wish to see Fortress History join Fortress Theory, Fortress Science of History, and all the other Fortresses, as moated islands of mutual incomprehension. In which case the intellectual world will become a madhouse, and I fear that, in the face of attacks from better organized madmen, history will further lose its credibility. I fear this because historical courts of appeal, in spite of Thompson, have no agreed procedures. Moreover their membership changes over time. Consequently history itself comfortably accommodates a variety of moated islands of mutual incomprehension. It is because the historians' court of appeal changes in ways mentioned earlier in this chapter that one set of procedures becomes more favoured than another, which is to say that history, too, has a history. Hitherto in this history of history, the court of appeal has not favoured Marxist historiography for the very reason that non-Marxist historians do not assent to Thompson's points seven and eight nor, it seems, to

[28] *Ibid.*, p. 236.

the central propositions underpinning the analysis in this book. The question arises, therefore, whether judgements in the court of appeal should continue to depend on ideology or whether we should admit that there is an epistemological problem and try to reveal the conceptual and theoretical deficiencies of historical explanation by reference to some criteria outside historiography but different from those of conventional (positivist) epistemology such as those of a restructured sociology of knowledge, a meta-theory, practice in a Marxian sense, or of that most recent dialectical product of Marxism, Critical Theory.

Of course this problem of the court of appeal would be much less important if it could be agreed that *all* historical 'facts' do have a real existence and that the real past they represent and the notions about it to which they lead could be objectively observed, or endorsed to show that they do exist 'out there' in the real history. Unfortunately, Thompson's assertion about these matters is not convincing. It is true that some facts may be thought of as there, in evidence before us. But it is also true that many other 'facts' come to light only when questions are asked of the evidence and that other 'facts', unasked, remain hidden. Since the questions we ask, for example, about class and class consciousness, must always be asked within some conceptual framework it is difficult to see how these 'facts' can be regarded as other than 'produced' by the questions asked – Althusserian Marxism is a case in point. Further, other facts are actually manufactured, for example, statistical series, indices, averages, random samples, tables of social stratification and class composition and so on. And I would like to remind readers of the conclusion reached by Collingwood, possibly the doyen of English-speaking philosophers of history and the discoverer of the historical imagination. After a long struggle with himself Collingwood wrote:

I am now driven to confess that there are for historical thought no fixed points thus given: in other words, that in history, just as there are properly speaking no authorities, so there are properly speaking no data.[29]

But these problems of 'facts' are not peculiar to history – they arise in politics, economics, sociology, psychology, indeed in all the

[29] R. G. Collingwood, *The Idea of History* (Oxford, 1961), p. 243.

social sciences. Therein lies the significance of Thompson's proposition that a 'present' does not change its ontological status by becoming a 'past'. A point which he states but does not elaborate even though the notion that such a change does take place seems to be the keystone of Hindess and Hirst's relegation of history to an intellectual wasteland.

The significance of this point in relation to an analysis of the 'current situation' which, according to Hindess and Hirst, cannot be done historically, is that it, too, can only be studied through its representations – that is, by the written, numerical, oral and pictorial record of its reality – and that the opportunity for directly testing the correspondence between the 'real' and its representation is so severely restricted as to be without significance. Except that we set up something like a court of law, the historian's practice, it cannot even be attempted. To the extent that we do set up a court of law we necessarily become more dependent upon representations of the 'real' and faced with the problem of distinguishing which representation *is* 'real' and faced with the problem of the status of the *a priori* perception through which alone we can grasp the 'real'. Further, to the extent that we are more dependent upon the representation of the 'real' for our study of the 'current situation' in all its complexity, the more we become dependent upon representations separated by time from the 'real' they represent. That is to say, the representations enter the field of history. In fact, if the analysis of the 'current situation' is to be anything more than the pragmatism of the moment that Hindess and Hirst wish to protect themselves against by recourse to theory, it can *only* be analysed through its aging representations including representations of theory, i.e., through its history.

The problem of the place of theory in analysing the 'current situation' as posed by Hindess and Hirst, should they ever wish to subject their theory to Popper's test of falsifiability, can be taken to illustrate this point of view. In order to enter into dialogue with them about the possibility of an historical analysis of the 'current situation' I must have recourse to their writing. I take their writings to be a representation of their views about it. They are a record of what they said in the past not what they are saying now. Thus they have the same representational status for me as any other aspect of 'reality' I might study as an historian. Furthermore I study the representation of their views in a context made up of other views and epistemological positions and within a knowledge about that context all of which I have derived from representations. In which case, since most of the representations I have used are in the form of words, which are themselves representations of their objects, I am as it were twice removed from the real object of the 'current situation'.

It is in this context that I must seek (and in this chapter am seeking) to test the truth of their observations by reference to criteria outside their own system. (They offer no scientific reason why I should enter their system.) These criteria I also learned in the past from other representations of some other 'real'. In fact I must confess that I have no way of 'knowing' Hindess and Hirst other than through their representations and that I take their 'real' existence on trust having looked them up in the *Commonwealth Universities Yearbook*. Since that information – like all my information about them – is historical, they may even be dead and therefore not 'real'. In which case my position as historian in relation to Hindess and Hirst writing on the 'current situation' is exactly the same as my relation to David Hume, Adam Smith and Karl Marx writing on their 'current situations' – except that these three heads are much better than the other two. It is true that I could travel to the Universities of Liverpool and London to match their representations against their reality, but the game would not be worth the candle, for unless I remained with them all the while their current views on the historical analysis of the 'current situation' would always slip away from me, and if I remained with them I would lose the views of others on the 'current situation' such as those at the seminar at which a first version of this chapter was delivered, views which are now also in the past but lost to history.

Because all I know in the 'current situation' about Hindess and Hirst and their concern about the 'current situation' was necessarily derived from representations of their contribution to it, I deliberately spoke about them at that seminar, as about Althusser and all the rest, in the past tense, and that is how I have written about them in this chapter. I intend by this to show that for me they are already as 'past', therefore, as 'historical' as they will ever be and that they have been so, if I may be allowed to think dialectically about them, from the moment they wrote in reality. And no amount of linear time can affect either that reality or the pastness of their views about it. Even as you read this chapter and turn one page after another it, too, takes on the quality of pastness. Consequently the problem of the correspondence of this chapter as a representation of one aspect of the reality of the 'current situation' to its reality will not be different tomorrow from what it is today. All that will vary with time will be the opportunity to authenticate the document itself and the number of people with experential knowledge of that situation to which it refers. Thus it is that a 'present' does not change its ontological status by becoming a 'past'. Therefore, my truth claims about the nature and significance of Hindess and Hirst's epistemology will be no stronger because they are made now rather than when I first made them in the past nor later, i.e., in the future when Hindess and Hirst will have slipped even further into the past and into the wasteland history. In short the problem of the correspondence of the representation of the real to its reality is not confined to history. It also arises in the 'current situation' in those areas of inquiry deemed relevant to it by Hindess and Hirst.

An additional problem for Hindess and Hirst is that as their work slips into the wasteland history – where it is already – study of it can contribute nothing to the 'current situation'. At least according to Hindess and Hirst. One begins to wonder why they wrote the book at all!

However, if we recognize that the past itself, including my version of it, does enter the present and if we choose to regard Hindess and Hirst's historical contribution to the discussion of history as relevant to the 'current situation' it is possible to employ other of Thompson's components in historical logic to test the correspondence of my critical, historical, 'representational' account of their contribution to its reality. Thus, Hindess and Hirst's book, *Pre-Capitalist Modes of Production*, has real existence as a representation of reality drawn from the wasteland of history. Although my knowledge about it may be incomplete, selective, limited and provisional it is not therefore necessarily untrue. If I have reported on it falsely or so inadequately as to distort its meaning anything I have said is subject to disproof. As a result of 'dialogue' between the conceptual framework I am using, which is structured by the Materialist Conception of History and the power of negative thinking which is its dialectical core, and in which everything that is is in process of becoming and therefore of ceasing to be, and the representation of Hindess and Hirst's views in their book, I may change my views about their contribution to the 'current situation'. And, if, when all this has been done, and what I say about them is endorsed by the evidence of the book (the representation of their thought) then I am entitled to say that my notion of their position on the 'current situation' is real, that it is true, that it is a knowledge which is part of a wider historical knowledge generated by the Materialist Conception of History. This knowledge is no more true today, because it is part of the 'current situation', than it will be in twenty years time. In fact in twenty years time its current truth may well be seen to be less true.

The point of this is, while the epistemological status of the Materialist Conception of History may be weak and that of history weaker, it is inherently no weaker *because* it is history than the epistemological status of sociology, politics, political philosophy, economics or any other subset of the social sciences you may choose to identify. They share the same problems and must subject themselves to the same tests. In fact inasmuch as Marxists acknowledge the epistemological problems of their theory and methodology and work to remedy them, a small part of which task I have attempted in this book, it will have a stronger epistemological base than those social sciences whose practitioners, including historians, hold their truths to be self-evidently based on the facts; Hindess and Hirst's notion that Marxist historiography is lacking in epistemological rigour is an illusion of those remnants of positivist epistemology which straggle through everything they write. And about positivist epistemology I will say only this: except for the argument of utility buried deep in its formal procedures, it, too, is neither stronger nor weaker than any other theoretically coherent epistemology except that the argument from utility is a powerful one. But one has to remember (chapter 2) that utilitarian arguments are also subjective and that Marxist historiography may also be 'useful'.

I would like to conclude by using an Althusserian 'reading' of Hindess and Hirst and even of Althusser himself in order to isolate their problem and to show that they pose not a 'real' epistemological threat to the Materialist Conception of History only an ideological one and, therefore, that they pose no insuperable epistemological problem for those who believe that the historical analysis of *class* and *class* consciousness is a meaningful activity which also has real significance in the 'current situation'.

In their original 'problematic', Althusser and Hindess and Hirst were rightly concerned to defend the Materialist Conception of History against charges that it was mere humanistic historicism and to protect it against positivist formulations and consequential empirical refutation or falsification – the kind of attacks identified at the beginning of this chapter. But, having rejected empiricism they were left only with theory. Since, through their rejection of historicism, they were also led to reject the dialectic and the notion of an ongoing relationship between the material base and human consciousness, they were left with a merely idealist theory, which seeks to shape the world in its own image. That is they found themselves back in heaven where Marx first found German ideology. Thus they finished up by propounding idealist and non-dialectical answers to questions they were unaware of asking. Instead of producing the 'immense theoretical revolution', attributed by Althusser to Marx, they turned Marxism full circle. Their position was idealist because it was concerned with constructing eternal categories (Althusser even called them 'eternities') in thought which were then allowed to circulate in the mind in self-confirming fashion and according to which the world was to be shaped. Their position was non-dialectical because it was found that 'eternities' or 'structures' could not incorporate the development of consciousness and the determination – social being, social consciousness, that is, notions of process and change, difficult to conceptualize and specify – without falling back upon teleological models and essentialist notions, faded from their purview. As well as being idealist and non-dialectical – perhaps *because* of being so – they were also authoritarian. In the hands of Hindess and Hirst even positivism reasserted itself. Further, in isolating Marxist historiography for special critical attention they seemed to take the outward form of knowledge – Marxist historiography as history – as it appears fragmented in the various disciplines and quasi-disciplines, history, politics, economics, sociology, political philosophy, for the reality of knowledge. Then, mistaking this appearance for reality they set out to produce explanations of the special futility of history which were also intentionally harmful to the Materialist

Conception of History and therefore damaging to much of the work in this book.

But in all these ways the Althusserian 'revolution', which claimed to be the mainstream of Marxist thought, actually placed itself outside it.

Therefore, practitioners of the Materialist Conception of History which is grounded in *dialectical* materialism and rooted in practice and the development of consciousness need give no special attention to Althusserian and post-Althusserian criticism of Marxist historiography. That is not to say that they should take no cognizance of the strictures about theory and history with which Althusser began. They should. They should plunge into the conceptual crystal waters of Althusserianism but come out ready for a good rub down with the rough towel of praxis followed by a dusting with the empirical idiom. This should heighten their consciousness as historians, sharpen their perception of the epistemological strengths and weaknesses of the Materialist Conception of History, give a further intellectual edge to their ongoing analyses of *class* and *class* consciousness and strengthen their confidence that in so doing they also contribute significantly to an analysis of the 'current situation'.

Index

Adorno, Theodore, 143
Alexander, William, 197
alienation, 28, 31–2, 198–9, 221
Althusser, Louis, 11, 16, 98, 143, 229–46 *passim*
analytical cubism, 51–2, 56
Antal, F., 162
Antigua, 200
architecture, 12
Aron, R., 81
art, 12, 52
  Baroque, 159
  Hogarth's, 158–63
  Magritte's, 134
  method of history of, 54, 56, 60
Ashley, Lord, 42

Ashton, T. S., 220, 223
associations, imperatively coordinated, 124, 131
Austen, Jane, 164, 167, 191, 200–1
authority relations, 124–8, 157, *see also* power; property
ballot, secret, 136, 150
Banbury, 188
Bath, 10, 42, 84, 117, 143, 151, 156, 159, 199, 201–2
Batheaston, 202
Bebel, M., 34
Beer, Max, 178–9
Benbow, William, 102
Benthamism, 8

Berkhofer, R. F., 104
Best, Geoffrey, 61, 102–5
Bill of Rights, 165, 167
Birmingham, 151
Black Act, 163, 191
blacking, 163
Blake, William, 164, 191
Blaug, Mark, 3
Bolton, 205
Bolwell, Thomas, 42
bourgeois/bourgeoisie, 19, 21–2, 29, 33, 35, 37–8, 42, 52, 69, 72–3, 77, 80, 115, 121, 161
  landowners as surrogate bourgeoisie, 77
Bradlaugh, Charles, 214–15
Bradlaugh, Hypatia, 215

Braque, Georges, 51
Bray, Charles, 171, 182, 186
Briggs, Asa, 3, 8, 61, 96,
    101–2, 179
Bristol, 74, 143, 188
    riots in, 157
Brougham, Henry, 102
Brussels, 218
Butler, Lady Eleanor, 197
Cadogan, William, 75
Canning, George, 167
capital, 22, 28–33, 72, 79,
    110, 152, 222–3
capitalism/capitalist
    society, 8, 22, 26–33,
    36, 44, 65, 69–70,
    77–81, 94, 99, 114, 188,
    224, *see also* labour
    theory of value;
    primitive accumulation
capitalist, 8, 18, 21, 187
Carlile, Richard, 184,
    206–7, 212, 214
Carlyle, Thomas, 138, 143,
    155
Cartwright, Major John,
    136
caste, 94, 95
Castlereagh, Lord, 167
Cendrar, Blaise, 52
Chambers, J. D., 123, 222
Chapman, H. S., 144
Charter, the, 22, 136, 148,
    189–90, 207
Chartists/Chartism, 42,
    151, 173, 183, 189–90
civil society, 9, 23–6, 30, 94,
    96, 161, 200
Civil War, English, 72, 77,
    225
class, 3, 5, 8, 13, 14, 16,
    17–49, 66, 71–119
    passim
    moral component in,
    128–30, 137, 142
    class consciousness, 5, 8,
    14, 16, 17–46, 71–3,
    94, 109–19, 210
    class and *class consciousness*
    (in Marx), 13, 17–49,
    66, 72–3, 77, 82,
    97–8, 110–14, 118,
    120–3, 127, 132, 150,
    152, 154–92 *passim*,
    215, 217, 218, 221,
    222, 225, 226, 228,
    233, 234, 245, 246

false consciousness, 32, 33
    43, 45, 112, 125, 127
class(es):
    agrarian capitalists, 75
    disqualified, 145–51
    forgotten middle, 107, 118
    intermediate, 21
    lower middle, 38
    middle, 66, 101–19 *passim*,
    133–6, 145–9
    middling, 118, 133–53
    passim, 155, 190–213
    peasantry, 74, 78, 87, 184
    privileged, 145–51
    social cranks, 107–8
    socially unattached
    intelligentsia, 58–60,
    66, 129–30
    uneasy, 151
    universal, 24, 26, 27, 59
    upper, 133
    urban free peasantry, 115,
    118
    viable, 3, 106, 113
    working, 43, 44, 66,
    101–19 *passim*, 133–4,
    148–50, 184, 186, 210
class and class society,
    definitions and
    descriptions of:
    Best, 102–5
    Briggs, 101–2
    Dahrendorf, 123–7
    Foster, 41–4, 111–15
    Hall, 177–82
    Kitson Clark. 105
    Laslett, 68–73
    Marshall, T. H., 107
    Marx, 17–46 *passim*,
    121–3
    Mill, 145–51
    Mousnier, 94–6
    Nakane, 84–6
    Neale, 131–77
    Perkin, 81–4, 106–9
    Thompson, 96–8, 109–10
    Vincent, 115–17
class conflict, 72, 73, 102,
    122, 126, *see also* class
    struggle
class, language of, 3, 96,
    101, 102, 179, *see also*
    order(s) in society
class, models of:
    one-class, 70–3, 80, 81,
    98, 100, 163, 194, 225
    two-class, 21, 22, 26, 72,

    77, 110, 114–16, 131,
    179, 194
    three-class, 18, 28, 105–8,
    118, 128, 137, 194
    four-class, 108
    five-class, 119, 128,
    130–53 *passim*, 192,
    194
class-less, 73, 81, 96, 100,
    101, 163, 225
class perception, 45, 98, 110,
    132, 155–92 *passim*
class struggle, 96–8, 114,
    123
class and women, 134,
    159–61, 193–215 *passim*,
    221, *see also* sex; women
Clubmen, 77
Coats, A. W., 3, 8
Colchester, 188
Collingwood, R. G., 104,
    141–2, 235, 240
Colquhon, Patrick, 175
communism/communist
    society, 35, 36, 65
Communist League, 39
Communist Party, USSR,
    229
Comte, Auguste, 1
conflict groups,
    determinants of, 124
conservative thought, 52, 53,
    see also ideology
contraception, 177, 182
cooperation, 184–7, 191,
    210, 214, *see also* Owen;
    socialism
copyholders, 74, 75
Coram, Thomas, 10
corresponding societies, 136
    London, 166
cottagers, 75
credit, 30, 31, 223
Crimean War, 22, 38, 43,
    44, 155, 190
Croce, B., 141
Cullick, Hannah, 194, 196
Cumberland, Duke of, 198
Dahrendorf, Ralf, 12, 18,
    71, 115, 119, 120,
    123–7, 131, 152
Danto, Arthur C., 141
Defoe, Daniel, 26, 199
Delaunay, Sonia, 52
demography, 3, 5, 12
Devizes, 188
dialectic, 25, 27, 32, 33, 72,

80, 81, 96, 225, 242–5
Diggers, 157
Dilthey, Wilhelm, 51, 141
Disraeli, Benjamin, 143, 155
Dobb, Maurice, 217
Durham, Lord, 145
Durkheim, Émile, 12
econometric history, 1, 6,
    227, 236
economics, 227, 240, 245, *see
    also* political economy
Edwards, Mary, 197
enclosure, 84, 222
Engels, Friedrick, 39
Enlightenment, the, 162,
    213
entail, 92, 198, 199
family, 7, 12, 198–200, 205
    Japanese *ie*, 85–91
fetishism of commodities,
    221
feudal society/feudalism,
    26, 37, 38, 44, 52, 66,
    69, 80, 81, 99
    contractual relationship
    in, 83, 91
    transition from, 226, 235
Feuerbach, Ludwig, 59, 215
Flinn, M. W., 3, 6, 228
Foster, John, 3, 7, 18, 41–3,
    101, 106, 111–15, 155,
    156, 170, 171
Foxwell, H. S., 171–4, 178,
    191
frame, 84–91
freeholders, 74
friendship, 82, 83, 93
Frome, 188
Gattungswesen, 25, 28, 32, 33
German emancipation, 23
German Social Democrats,
    43
Germanic Military
    Constitution, 19
Germanic society, 19, 26,
    29, 186
Germany, 15, 37
Godwin, William, 171, 175
Gotha Unity Congress,
    34–8, 43, 44
Gray, John, 108, 151, 175,
    177, 182, 186
Gris, Juan, 51
Grosvenor, Lady, 198
Grote, George, 144
Habakkuk, John, 82, 93
habeas corpus, 167

Hackabout, Moll, 159–61
Hall, Charles, 143, 170, 171,
    177–82, 184–6, 189, 191
Hampden Clubs, 136
Harrison, Brian, 103
Harrison, J. F. C., 152
Hart, Jenifer, 4, 8
Hartwell, Max, 221
Hayek, F. A. von, 218, 220
Hegel/Hegelian, 23–8, 32,
    51, 59, 198
Hill, Christopher, 217
Hilton, Rodney, 217
Himmelfarb, Gertrude, 128,
    130, 137–44, 155
Hindess, 11, 234–45 *passim*
Hirst, 11, 234–5 *passim*
historical idealism/ideal-
    ists, 141–4, 153, 184,
    217
historical imagination, 141,
    142, 155
historical logic, 237–9
historicism, 10, 218, 219,
    233, 245
history, theoretical, 16, 216,
    230–5, *see also* social
    history
Hobsbawm, E. J., 2–6, 8,
    106, 116, 217, 228
Hodgskin, Thomas, 104,
    108, 143, 171, 187
Hogarth, William, 10, 84,
    97, 158–63, 167, 191,
    194, 197, 199
Holcroft, Thomas, 185
Hollis, Patricia, 102
Hone, William, 143, 166,
    167, 183, 191
Hume, David, 60, 220, 242
Hungary, 15, 41
Hunt, Henry, 136
Husserl, Edmund, 51
ideological thought, 49,
    52–5, 57–60, 66
ideology, 11, 12, 33, 48, 53,
    59, 60, 94, 217, 240, 245
ie, 85, 86
immiseration, 221, *see also*
    standard of living
imperialism, 43, 66, 113,
    114
industrial/pre-industrial
    epochs, 70–2, 80
Industrial Revolution, 6, 7,
    66, 79, 115, 221, 222
infidels, 206

Japan, 15, 84–93 *passim*, 96, 99
Jeffreys, Judge John, 136
Jones, David, 173
Jones, Ernest, 43, 44
Jones, Gareth Stedman, 5,
    15, 130
Kahnweiler, Henry, 10, 11,
    52
Kantian aesthetics, 51
Kiernan, V. G., 217
Kings of England:
    George I, 159
    Prince Regent, 167
    William I, 165
    William and Mary, 159
Kitson Clark, G., 18, 105
knowledge:
    history as a, 237, 244–6
    objective, 50–67, 130, 139
    relative, 54, 55, 60
    sociology of, 9–13, 15,
    50–67, 105, 240
labour, 28–33, 36, 72, 110,
    152, 171
    division of, 187
    labour power, 28–33, 36,
    225
    necessary labour, 30
    supply of, 222
    surplus labour, 30
    theory of value, 171–88
    whole produce of and
    labour right to, 34,
    170–92 *passim*, 210
Lady of the Rotunda (*see*
    Elizabeth Sharples)
land, birthright in, 176
Lask, Emil, 51
Laslett, Peter, 68–84 *passim*,
    98, 99, 104, 106, 119,
    122, 123
law, 12, 24, 124, 163
    Germanic Military
    Constitution, 19
    Iron law of wages, 36, 37
    legal decisions, 161
    Poor Law, 3
    primogeniture, 198
    wage contract, 20, 32
    women and law, 197–200,
    see also property
Leake, James, 199
Leeds, 186
Lees, F. R., 186
Leninism, 114
Levellers, 157
liberal thought, 52

Liberalism, 66
liberty, 157, 165, 210, 211
Lichtheim, George, 172
Liebknecht, Karl, 34
Lincoln, 188
Liverpool, 188
Llangollen, Ladies of, 197,
    202
Locke, John, 9, 163, 165,
    167, 170
Lockwood, W. W., 129
London, 74, 84, 160, 162,
    164, 207
  Cooperative Society, 178,
    182
  Corresponding Society,
    166
  Working Men's
    Association, 148, 207
Lovett, William, 178
Lukács, Georg, 12, 23, 40,
    41, 51
Macfarlane, Alan, 83
McKeown, T., 4
Magna Charta, 167
Malthus, Thomas, 108
Manchester, 188
Mandelbaum, Maurice,
    61–7, 103, 143
Mannheim, Karl, 1, 12, 13,
    15, 49–67 *passim*, 69,
    129, 143
Marcus, Steven, 194
marriage, 197–200
Marshall, T. H., 107–10
Marx, Karl, 6, 12–14, 17–50
    passim, 77–81, 103–28
    passim, 133, 215–46
    passim
  Capital, 18, 100, 210, 230,
    233
  Communist Manifesto, 73,
    78, 79, 121, 154
  *Critique of the Gotha
    Programme*, 34–8, 45
  *Critique of Hegel's Philo-
    sophy of Right*, 23,
    24, 193, 198
  Paris Manuscripts, 25
  Preface to *The Critique of
    Political Economy*, 25
  The German Ideology, 47,
    68, 193
  The Holy Family, 17, 22, 39
  Theses on Feuerbach, 59
Marxists/Marxism, 12, 44,
    106, 108, 217

Materialist Conception of
    History, 5, 6, 16, 44, 45,
    80, 216–46 *passim*
Menger, Anton, 171–5
Methodism:
  Primitive, 105, 213, 214
  Wesleyan, 205, 212, 215
Miliband, Ralph, 217
Mill, James, 108
Mill, John Stuart, 14, 104,
    143–53 *passim*, 180, 183,
    189, 190, 214
Millenium Hall, 201–5
mode of production, 231,
    235
Molesworth, Sir William,
    144
monied interest, 75, 78, 79
Monmouth Rebellion, 136
Montagu, Elizabeth, 201–5
Montague, Lady Barbara,
    202
Moore, Barrington Jnr., 12
moral economy, 77
moral imagination, 137–44
    passim, 155
More, Hannah, 200, 205,
    206
Morris, R. J., 128, 156, 194
Mousnier, Roland, 94–9,
    104, 122, 123, 152
Nakane, Chie, 12, 84, 85, 99
Napier, William, 190
National Union of the
    Working Classes, 207
Neale, R. S., 106, 118
Neisser, Hans, 11
Newgate, 163
Norwich, 74
Oakeshott, Michael, 235
O'Brien, Bronterre, 43
O'Connor, Feargus, 151,
    154, 182
Ogilvie, William, 170–7,
    185, 186
Oldham, 7, 41–3, 112–14,
    170, 171, 188
order(s) in society, 94–9
    passim, 122, 127, 151,
    179, 180, 189, 190, 209
Owen, Robert, 108, 171,
    175, 185–9, 210–11
Paine, Thomas, 9, 136, 165,
    191, 206, 212
Parliamentary Reform, 136,
    144–5, 173, 211, *see also*
    Reform Bill

patronage, 81, 83, 106
Paulson, Ronald, 162
peasants/peasantry, 74, 78,
    182–9
  in Japan, 87–91
Pentridge Rising, 189
Perkin, Harold, 2, 3, 18,
    81–4, 93, 98, 99, 101,
    104, 106–10, 118, 123,
    172, 173
Peterloo, 167
Philosophic Radicalism,
    136, 150
Picasso, Pablo, 10, 15, 51
Place, Francis, 178, 188
political economy, 24, 25,
    28, 29, 232
political unions:
  Bath, 143
  Bristol, 143
poll books, 115
Ponsonby, Sarah, 197
Popper, Karl, 7, 10, 15,
    218–20, 226, 229, 230,
    236, 241
population growth, 222
pornography, 199
Portland, Duchess of, 201
positivism, positivist,
    positivistic, 9, 19, 48,
    50, 61, 138, 217–28
    passim, 239, 245
Poulantzas, Nicos, 229
power, 20, 21, 36, 37, 45, 70,
    94, 109, 120–53 *passim*,
    180, 211, 212
Price, Fanny, 200, 206
primitive accumulation, 19,
    29, 79, 94, 162, 222, 223
productive forces and rela-
    tions of production, 225
profit, falling rate of, 30
proletarian(s), 22–41 *passim*,
    47, 52, 77, 187
proletariat, 22–41 *passim*, 43,
    45, 115
property, 9, 21–37 *passim*,
    45, 74–77, 81, 106, 112,
    123, 124, 128, 132, 152,
    157, 159, 161–92 *passim*
property and women,
    159, 197–200
propriety, 199, 200, 206
prostitution, 159, 195
Pulteney, William, Earl of
    Bath, 75, 76
radicalism, 136, 144–51, 190

Movement Radicalism, 144, 150
Ravenstone, P., 187
Reading, 163
Record, R. G., 4
Reform Bill, 144, 145, 211
regional loyalties, 76, 82
relational thought, 55–61 *passim*
relativism, 55–61 *passim*, 140, 217
religion, 205, 208–12, *see also* Methodism
reserve army, 31
revolution, 22, 33, 39, 40, 44, 77, 111, 114, 170, 172, 200, 207, 224
of 1688, 163, 165
in Cologne, 39
Ricardo, David, 171, 174, 175
Ricardian Socialists, 172, 174, 191, 214
Rickert, Heinrich, 51
riots:
Bristol, 157
Gordon, 97, 157
Pentridge Rising, 189
Roebuck, J. A., 42, 144, 151, 190
Rostow, W. W., 80, 223, 224
Rowse, A. L., 2
Rudé, George, 116
Runciman, W. G., 70, 81
Russia, 44
Samplers, 205
Saville, J., 4
Saxon Myth, 136
scientific method, 220
Scott, Sarah, 16, 201–5
sex:
dual standard, 161
exploitation, 159–62, 194–200
Toryism of, 214
Shaftesbury, Anthony Ashley, Third Earl, 9
Sharples, Elizabeth, 16, 201, 205–15
Shaw, William H., 225, 226
Sheffield, 188
Sidmouth, Lord, 167
slavery, 37, 196, 200
Smelser, Neil J., 3, 6, 7, 12
Smith, Adam, 9, 163, 164, 175, 178, 179, 191, 242

Smout, T. C., 3, 6, 228
social being, 26, 27, 33, 45
social class, 132–5
social history, 1–16, 50, 137–44, 227–8
behavioural approach to, 139, 140, 155–7
as history of society, 5, 6, 7, 9, 227–8
social structural history, 69, 70
and theory, 6, 9, 12, 16, 50–61, 63–7, 104–19 *passim*, 128–31, 137–44, 216–46 *passim*
social stratum / stratification, 19, 75, 94–6, 105, 114, 131–9 *passim*
social structure:
in Japan, 85–93
in seventeenth century England, 73–81
vertical relationship in, 81–4
socialism, 154, 171, 172, 210–12
socialist(s), 171–92 *passim*
national socialist, 220, *see also* Ricardian Socialists
socialistic thought, 52–5, 172
socially unattached intelligentsia, 58–60, 66, 129, 130
sociological historians, 138, 139
sociology, 216, 240, 245
sociology of knowledge, 11–13, 15, 50, 52, 54, 55, 65, 66, 69, 240
Spence, Thomas, 170, 175–7, 182, 184, 186
Stalin, Joseph, 229
standard of living, 221, 222, 224
state/state power, 20, 25, 26, 37, 75, 78, 79, 114, 122, 221, 224
status, 71, 75, 82, 94
St John, Henry, Lord Bolingbroke, 76
strikes, 155
Oldham 1841, 41, 113
Shoemakers' 1802/3, 157
Wiltshire Shearmen's 1802, 157

structuralist/structuralism, 229–46 *passim*
Sturgeite Conference, 151
Systematic Colonization, 136, 150

Taylor, Robert, 206
Ten Hour Movement, 42, 113
Thompson, E. P., 3, 8, 77, 83, 96–8, 106, 109, 110, 117, 163, 172, 173, 189, 194, 216, 217, 236–41
Thompson, William, 151, 171, 175, 182, 184, 185, 186
Thornhill, Sir James, 159
Titmus, M., 4
Trilling, Lionel, 140
truth:
correspondence theory of, 61–3
tests of, 50–60 *passim*, 66–7, 228–46 *passim*
Tunbridge Wells, 201

urban environment, 12
urban studies, 3, 5
utopia, 12, 53, 59, 94, 176–92 *passim*, 201–4
utopian thought, 50–60 *passim*, 66–7, 157

Vice Society, 206
Victorian Ballot, 136
Vincent, J. R., 106, 115–17, 119

Wadsworth, A. P., 3
wage contract, 20, 32, 36
Wages, Iron Law of, 36, 37
Wallerstein, Emmanuel, 12
Walpole's Administration, 76
war (*see* Crimean War; Civil War)
Weber, Alfred, 58
Weber, Max, 6, 12, 51, 59, 70, 71, 81, 94, 129, 130
Winstanley, Gerrard, 157
Wollstonecraft, Mary, 9
women in history, 4, 134, 159–62, 193–215 *passim*, *see also* sex
workers:
Hungarian, 41
industrial, 18, 22
Wright, Frances, 208
York, 74